Getting
what you deserve

Getting
what you deserve

A handbook for the assertive consumer

Stephen A. Newman
Professor of Law, New York Law School

and Nancy Kramer
Senior Attorney, New York Public Interest Research Group, Inc.

Art research by Melissa Gordon Newman

A Dolphin Book

Doubleday & Company, Inc., Garden City, New York   1979

Library of Congress Cataloging in Publication Data

Newman, Stephen A
    Getting what you deserve, a handbook for the assertive consumer.

    (A Dolphin book)
    Includes bibliographies.
    1. Consumer protection—United States. I. Kramer, Nancy, joint author. II. Title.
HC110.C63N48   381'.3
ISBN: 0-385-13688-9
Library of Congress Catalog Card Number 78–22642

To our parents, Oscar and Sophie Newman
and Edith and Stanley Kramer,
who taught us how to write.

ACKNOWLEDGMENTS

During the course of writing this book, there were some people who came through in the best of times and in the worst of times. First and foremost is Melissa Gordon Newman, who researched, found, and selected the graphics in the book—we don't know what we would have done without her.

Very special thanks go also to Richard Weiss, who saw Nancy through all phases of this book, and contributed to every stage.

We received excellent research assistance from Diana Lee Bixler, who found the unfindable with alarming regularity. Janel Radtke and Edith Kramer also tenaciously tracked down information.

The motley yet witty crew that contributed generously with ideas, titles, captions, and editing includes: Arthur Best, James Brook, Paul Cooper, Gail Davidson, Bill Eskridge, Jane Freeman, Alvin and Elaine Gordon, Todd Gordon, Stanley Kramer, Barbara Kronman, Ellen Novack, Jane Rosenberg, and Allen Thurgood.

Typing of the final manuscript was done with tireless effort, great skill, and amazing cheer by Janel Radtke. She was ably assisted by Mildred Dicker and Sheila Green.

Our photographer friend whose speedy shutter enhanced this book is Cliff Ratner (an ophthalmologist in real life). Ron Hollander (a journalist-photographer) and Robert Davidson and Richard W. Golden (both lawyers) also looked through their lenses for our benefit. Caroline Howard, Donald Bowden (of Wide World Photos), and Esther Brumberg (of the Museum of the City of New York), in helping us to locate the photos of others, were themselves the picture of helpfulness.

Both of us worked full time while writing this book. It would not have been possible to do so without the support of two people in particular. Nancy appreciates the help and friendship of Donald K. Ross, who taught her much of what she knows about advocacy, and of the New York Public Interest Research Group, Inc. staff, from whom she is constantly learning. New York Law School provided outstanding institutional support, thanks to the exuberance, warmth, and encouragement of its dean, E. Donald Shapiro.

A final word of thanks is reserved for our understanding editor, Joseph Gonzalez.

Contents

Introduction

Americans are consumed with consuming. We have bought the idea that goods will do more than they are intended to. So we look to them to give us social status, to fill up our leisure time, to win attention and approval, and to add variety to our increasingly routinized lives. We place a premium on newness, which leads people to buy things not because they are better, more useful, or longer lasting, but solely because of novelty.

And we like to buy big. Annual consumer spending in this country has passed the trillion-dollar mark. The huge quantity of goods and services available grows day by day. Over $40 billion is spent on advertising every year to persuade us to increase and indulge our appetite for consuming. Unfortunately, a dramatic decline in the quality of products and in the responsibility and accountability of sellers has accompanied the explosion in consumer spending. This is the heyday of junk. Junk food is gobbled up for breakfast, lunch, and dinner, junk appliances are spewed out daily, and planned obsolescence is taken for granted.

Against this backdrop, what's the ideal consumer like? At the very least, the perfect purchaser would be trained in chemistry, mechanical engineering, food science, pharmacology, medicine, law, finance, and home economics. He or she would be aggressive, discriminating, impervious to psychological manipulation, able to retain a multitude of uninteresting facts, possessed of a photographic memory, articulate and assertive, with unlimited time to spend in product investigation and comparative shopping. Such a person would always make excellent buying choices (although would be impossible to live with).

Where does this leave the rest of us? The much-vaunted consumer revolution has made people more aware of problems that have been around a long time. Yet its accomplishments have in truth been modest. The marketplace is still a minefield for the unwary consumer. Consumer rip-offs continue on a large scale across the country and the legal remedies are generally inadequate.

Typically, consumers get far less than their money's worth. Very often, they accept bad treatment as one of the inevitable frustrations of modern life. But, in our careers as consumer advocates and lawyers, we discovered that you can do better than you think. You can become an expert at self-defense in the marketplace by knowing your legal rights and how to assert them. Consumer self-defense also means protecting yourself by avoiding transactions that lead to trouble.

Three techniques can help you: taking time to think, maintaining a healthy skepticism, and learning all you can. This book shows you how these techniques work in a myriad of buying environments.

If you deal with a fox, think of his tricks.

— JEAN DE LA FONTAINE

Getting
what you deserve

Part I

Into
the fray

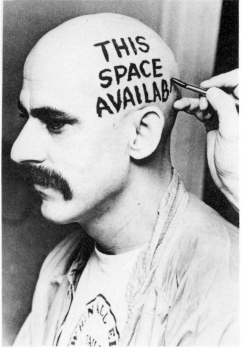

place is safe from advertising. (Wide World Photos)

1

Green giants and white knights: advertising

> We have seen too many patterns of deception: in political life, impossible dreams; in advertising, extravagant claims; in business, shady deals.
> — RICHARD NIXON (address at General Beadle State College)

> . . . advertising is really a science and it is mostly a science of human motivation and behavior. When we get ready to pitch a new soap at you, we know more about what you do in your bathroom than your own wife or husband. Not only that, we know why you do it, how you do it, and what makes you do it. — CARL WRIGHTER, *I Can Sell You Anything*

> Advertising may be described as the science of arresting the human intelligence long enough to get money from it. — STEPHEN LEACOCK

What would you think of a society which allocated billions of dollars every year for the purpose of giving "personalities" to inanimate objects? Where some of its brightest, most talented members spent their time making up songs and slogans about diapers, bathroom odors, loose dentures, dirty dishes, and floor wax? Where the population was exposed to hundreds of these silly messages every day? Would you willingly choose to live in such a society?

Whether we like it or not, that society is ours, and the raucous clamor of advertising intrudes, uninvited, upon all of our daily lives. The volume and variety of advertising is staggering: it is crowded into magazines and newspapers, radio and television shows, billboards, packages, handbills, matchbooks, T-shirts, sandwich boards, and almost every other available public space.

How did we get ourselves into such a state? Thousands of years ago, advertising was relatively straightforward. A baker would put up a sign in front of the bakery, with a simple picture portraying the goods available inside. The more enterprising merchants put signs on walls to attract public attention. A wall sign in ancient Pompeii, for example, announced:

THE TROOP OF GLADIATORS OF THE AEDIL WILL FIGHT ON THE 31ST OF MAY. THERE WILL BE FIGHTS WITH WILD ANIMALS AND AN AWNING TO KEEP OFF THE SUN.

In the Middle Ages, merchants hired criers to walk in the streets and cry out their messages (perhaps the first singing commercials). It was not until the widespread use of the printing press, however, that advertising began to grow to prodigious dimensions. By 1759, Samuel Johnson was moved to remark:

> Advertisements are now so numerous that they are very negligently perused, and it is therefore necessary to gain attention by magnificence of promises, and by eloquence sometimes sublime and sometimes pathetic. Promise, large promise, is the soul of an advertisement.

Dr. Johnson was spared the assaults of radio and television advertising, which by volume and intensity dwarfed all prior efforts, and made advertising the dominant occupier of the public space.

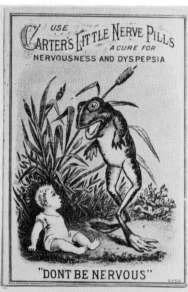

Trade cards used by early advertisers. (Museum of the City of New York)

DECEPTION IN ADVERTISING

Bogus claims and pretense have long found refuge in advertising. Ferreting out deceptive advertising is the job of the Federal Trade Commission. Unfortunately, the FTC's budget for this task is between $2 and $4 million a *year,* while total advertising in the nation exceeds $3 billion a *month*. The nation's single largest advertiser, Procter & Gamble, spends approximately one hundred times more each year on its own advertising than the FTC does in monitoring all advertising of all companies. Investigations by the Commission are costly and notoriously slow.

Because the legal machinery to prevent misleading advertising is too weak and cumbersome to do the job, and because the monetary incentive to shade the truth is so great, few Americans believe all they read in advertising. Still, there are many tricks which elude public awareness and unfairly induce people to buy. The kinds of deception range from outright misrepresentation to optical illusions made possible by modern photographic and film techniques. A sampler of deceptive practices follows.

OUTRIGHT FALSITY

One of the most outrageous examples of pure deception in advertising was the case of Listerine mouthwash. The product first went, on the market in 1879. For the next hundred years, its makers represented that it helped prevent and relieve colds and sore throats. Advertising campaigns boasted that Listerine "kills germs by millions on contact." Unfortunately, as the Federal Trade Commission demonstrated, mouth bacteria (the "germs" referred to) don't cause colds or cold symptoms. As for Listerine's effect on sore throats, the same result would be achieved by gargling with warm water. The Commission ordered the Warner-Lambert Company, maker of Listerine, to state in its future ads that "Listerine will not help prevent colds or sore throats or lessen their severity." This "corrective advertising" order is a new remedy for false claims in ads. We can only hope that it is a better cure for deceit than Listerine was for colds.

ILLUSIONS

Pictorial illusions abound in advertising. A friendly camera eye can enhance the size, shape, and physical attractiveness of any person or any thing. On television, cars look longer and roomier. With the proper camera angle, the interior of a Buick can be made to resemble the flight deck of an aircraft carrier. Prepared foods are invariably more appetizing on the screen than on the table; even dog food looks like the king's dinner. Toys and games are bigger and more impressive than they are in real life, an illusion reinforced by grossly oversized packaging. The list could go on and on. In the world of pictorial advertising, what you see is not even close to what you get.

CLAIMS OF UNIQUENESS

A great number of goods competing in the marketplace are so similar to each other that they are, for all practical purposes, indistinguishable. Some products are literally identical. As an advertising copy writer (interviewed by Studs Terkel in *Division Street: America*) stated: "One of our clients puts out a product in three different boxes. It's the same stuff, comes out of the same tube. It goes into different boxes with different labels. One advertising agency has one name to sell, another agency has another name to sell, and we have the third."

Advertisers of goods which are virtually identical to their competitors' depict their products as better than the rest nonetheless. Some do this by using statements that sound comparative but really are not. For example, one pharmaceutical firm claimed that its brand had "twice as much" of the pain reliever doctors recommend most. It never said twice as much as what. In fact, its competitors used equal amounts of the pain reliever.

Another common trick is to select a common characteristic of the product and pretend that it is unique to one brand. Thus, an airline advertises a "super-saver" fare which sounds like a unique bargain—until you discover all airlines are charging the same price. Or a bank says it's offering the "highest rates" on savings accounts, but the apparently fabulous rates are duplicated by every bank on the block. Phony exclusivity claims like these have been used to sell bleach, household cleaners, toothpaste, aspirin, and a host of other functionally identical products.

CLAIMS OF NEWNESS

In response to the most commonly asked question in our society ("What's new?"), and in order to arouse our curiosity, advertisers regularly claim that their products are "new." The oldest product on the market is called "new" if the maker changes its color, alters its formula in some trivial way, redesigns the package, or makes any other superficial change in its appearance. Other synonyms for "new" which are equally enticing but often meaningless include: "introducing," "for the first time," "now, it's here," "announcing," "a revolutionary development," "improved." The misleading use of these terms is rampant, but law enforcement agencies do not have the time or staff necessary to prove the claims are false.

HERMAN

©1977 Universal Press Syndicate

"What exactly is 'new, improved lettuce?'"

RIGGED DEMONSTRATIONS

In a television commercial a few years ago, a man applied a well-known shaving cream to a piece of rough, gritty sandpaper. With a single stroke of the razor, the sandpaper immediately became smooth. A convincing demonstration of the softening power of the lather? Yes. True? No. The "sandpaper" was really Plexiglas, with sand on top. The demonstration which viewers saw with their own eyes *never happened,* nor could it, unless the sandpaper was first soaked in water for an hour and twenty minutes. The entire exercise, shown on television to millions of Americans, was a fraud.

The perpetrator of this hoax was not a fly-by-night huckster looking to make a quick buck. It was the Colgate-Palmolive Company, one of the nation's largest makers of consumer products.

Many other ads feature the results of scientific "tests" which prove the superiority of a product. Too often, the tests are not properly performed, using invalid testing procedures, no control groups, and biased "testers" who are seeking a "favorable" outcome. Results obtained are scientifically unreliable. Yet they have been used to support numerous claims, ranging from the safety of automobile tires to the efficacy of medicinal drugs.

DISTORTED LOGIC

A familiar drugstore product advertised itself as the preferred pain relief for headache. Its support? A test at a major medical center which showed it was very effective for "pain other than headache." The illogical connection didn't faze the confident announcer, and many casual listeners, not paying close attention to every word, may have assumed the test was for headache pain.

Other ads ask the consumer to draw imprecise or irrelevant analogies. Even if a shaving cream works on sandpaper, what guarantee is there that it works on a man's beard? Sandpaper and whiskers are not very much alike, but the advertiser relies on our susceptibility to logical fallacies.

HALF-TRUTHS

The maker of a hair restorer advertised that the product was effective against "the second most common form of baldness." What the ad didn't say was that the first most common cause, heredity, is responsible for nearly *all* baldness in American men. Thus, only a minuscule percentage of men can be helped by the advertised product. This slippery claim, telling only part of the truth, deliberately left a false impression about the usefulness of the product.

A similar claim by the makers of Geritol precipitated a fourteen-year battle with the Federal Trade Commission. The ads proclaimed that Geritol was the perfect remedy for "tired blood." According to them, if you felt tired, it might be due to iron deficiency anemia, and Geritol was for you. "You'll *feel stronger fast* . . . in just seven days." The ad didn't mention that of the many causes of fatigue, iron deficiency anemia ranked near the bottom of the list. If one felt tired, the odds were overwhelming that it was *not* caused by lack of iron, and therefore not curable by Geritol. The government finally ordered the company to stop making the claim without disclosing the full facts about the causes of tiredness. But the claim apparently was too profitable to give up. The company continued to produce similar commercials, and in 1976 it was forced to pay $280,000 in civil penalties to the government, at that time the largest such penalty ever obtained for deceptive advertising.

EMOTIONAL ADVERTISING

Resisting the effect of advertising is extremely difficult, because modern advertising appeals more to emotion than to reason. Advertisers have learned that buying behavior depends upon irrational states of mind. Thus there has been a dramatic increase in the number of "informationless" ads. Data or facts have been replaced by psychological appeals and the creation of product "images."

Advertisers hope to generate a series of favorable associations with their goods. They concentrate on selling the *image* instead of the more mundane *product*. Cars, for example, are often named after wild animals, which are then featured in ads. Jaguars, cougars, and wildcats evoke all sorts of associations: they are free, confident, strong, virile, unafraid, wild, daring, and dangerous. The prospective car buyer, assumed to be a male, identifies, if only in his fantasies, with this image and irrationally transfers it to the inanimate chrome-and-steel beast which sits placidly on the showroom floor. The animal analogy works in the consumer's mind, not in reality. After all, how many real cougars are recalled for structural defects?

The reliance on imagery instead of fact extends to all sorts of products. A beer commercial shows a group of sportsmen hauling in a swordfish. Ac-

The authors shamelessly promoting their book. (Photo by Cliff Ratner)

cording to the ad, the brand of beer they drink is somehow related to the kind of people they are (i.e., active, manly, gutsy). The emotional message: If you are, or wish you were, this kind of guy, then drink this beer. A soft-drink ad urges you to join "the Pepsi generation." If you're young, modern, carefree, sexy, and glad to be alive—or would like to be—then you can find your identity in a can of soda. Similar nonsensical messages sell toothpaste, mouthwash, hair spray, and dozens of other items, without the slightest mention of any relevant facts about the product. In these ads, the image is the message.

Image advertising is often resorted to when there is little or no difference between the advertiser's product and the competition. As ad executive David Ogilvy wrote: "The greater the similarity between brands, the less part reason plays in brand selection. There isn't any significant difference between the various brands of whiskey, or cigarettes, or beer. They are all about the same. And so are the cake mixes and the detergents, and the margarines. The manufacturer who dedicates his advertising to building the most sharply defined *personality* for his brand will get the largest share of the market at the highest profit."*

Thus we have whiskey, cigarettes, and beer with personality. The "Marlboro man" image, rugged virility in the great outdoors, lends animation and excitement to a piece of paper wrapped around some dried-out leaves. Another brand of cigarette attempts to link itself to the women's movement, with the theme "You've come a long way, baby." The ads feature slim, feminine, sexy, modern-woman types smoking a slender cigarette. Undoubtedly all of these qualities, as artificial and unrelated to the cigarette as they are, make a much deeper impression than the other message in the ad: that smoking cigarettes (even "feminist" cigarettes) causes cancer. The latter message, required by law, appears in a stilted written text without pictures, and unfortunately doesn't satisfy any psychic needs.

Psychological appeals have made the greatest inroads in television commercials, where our own immature fantasies and deep-seated desires are paraded in front of us daily. Housewives tired of their drudgery watch a fantasy of rescue and adventure in the form of a white knight on a magnificent charger stampeding into the kitchen. The thrill is not really from the Ajax detergent he brings, but the subconscious will finish the fantasy and thank Ajax by buying it. This ridiculous commercial was the subject of many jokes and ribaldry at the time, but no matter how many people consciously dismissed it as ridiculous, one fact is undeniable—the commercial worked. Whatever the sophisticated modern housewife *thought* about the pitch, something less sophisticated and more emotional in her responded, and she bought. Before long, commercials presented all manner of bizarre events in the kitchen: doves flying in windows, white tornadoes sweeping everything clean, even a coronation in which the bedraggled housewife is crowned a queen. Clearly these ads are not appealing to our reasoning power; emotion, fantasy, and wish fulfillment are the new tools of the advertiser's trade.

* David Ogilvy, *Confessions of an Advertising Man* (New York: Ballantine Books, 1971), p. 89.

100 LEADING NATIONAL ADVERTISERS (ad dollars in millions: 1977)

1	Procter & Gamble	$460.0	51	Loews Corp.	$ 66.1
2	General Motors Corp.	312.0	52	H. J. Heinz Co.	65.8
3	General Foods Corp.	300.0	53	Esmark Inc.	65.0
4	Sears, Roebuck & Co.	290.0	54	Schering-Plough	63.0
5	K mart	210.0	55	Quaker Oats Co.	60.8
6	Bristol-Myers Co.	203.0	56	Hanes Corp.	60.3
7	Warner-Lambert Co.	201.0	57	Campbell Soup Co.	60.0
8	Ford Motor Co.	184.0	58	Borden Inc.	59.3
8	Philip Morris Inc.	184.0	59	Jos. Schlitz Brewing Co.	59.1
10	American Home Products Corp.	171.0	60	SmithKline Corp.	57:6
11	R. J. Reynolds Industries	164.7	61	Nissan Motor Co.	57.0
12	General Mills	160.5	62	Avon Products	55.0
13	Richardson-Merrell	148.8	63	Volkswagen of America	52.7
14	Unilever	145.0	64	CPC International	51.0
15	Mobil Corp.	142.8	64	Mars Inc.	51.0
16	American Tel. & Tel. Co.	132.0	64	Standard Brands	51.0
17	Norton Simon Inc.	127.1	67	Greyhound Corp.	50.8
17	Chrysler Corp.	127.1	68	Toyota Motor Sales U.S.A.	49.2
19	PepsiCo Inc.	124.0	69	S. C. Johnson & Son	48.9
19	RCA Corp.	124.0	70	Clorox Co.	47.9
21	Beatrice Foods Co.	123.0	71	Miles Laboratories	46.5
22	McDonald's Corp.	122.2	72	Union Carbide Corp.	46.1
23	Colgate-Palmolive Co.	120.0	73	American Express Co.	46.0
24	U.S. Government	116.2	74	Time Inc.	45.9
25	General Electric Co.	112.2	75	North American Philips Co.	44.0
26	Heublein Inc.	106.5	76	Polaroid Corp.	38.9
27	Int'l. Tel. & Tel. Corp.	104.7	77	A. H. Robins Co.	38.8
28	Gulf & Western Industries	100.6	78	Mattel Inc.	38.5
29	J. C. Penney Co.	100.0	79	Pfizer Inc.	37.5
30	Kraft Inc.	99.0	80	Squibb Corp.	37.1
31	Nabisco Inc.	96.4	81	Morton-Norwich	36.1
32	CBS Inc.	96.3	82	Exxon Corp.	35.3
33	American Cyanamid	96.0	83	Noxell Corp.	33.3
34	Goodyear Tire & Rubber Co.	93.9	84	Eastern Airlines	32.5
35	Johnson & Johnson	91.8	85	Carnation Co.	31.9
36	B.A.T. Industries	91.3	86	American Motors Corp.	31.5
37	Gillette Co.	90.0	87	Kimberly-Clark Corp.	31.1
38	Coca-Cola Co.	89.0	88	Wm. Wrigley Jr. Co.	31.0
39	Pillsbury Co.	85.8	88	Block Drug Co.	31.0
40	Eastman Kodak Co.	85.5	90	Beecham Group	30.8
41	American Brands	84.0	91	UAL Inc.	30.3
42	Ralston Purina Co.	80.7	92	American Airlines	28.9
43	Revlon Inc.	80.0	93	ABC Inc.	26.8
44	Seagram Co.	78.0	93	Shell Oil Co.	26.8
45	Anheuser-Busch	75.4	95	Trans World Airlines	26.5
46	Sterling Drug	72.0	96	Consolidated Foods Corp.	25.9
47	Nestle Enterprises	71.3	97	Delta Air Lines	25.7
48	Kellogg Co.	69.8	98	Scott Paper Co.	25.5
49	Liggett Group	68.4	99	Honda Motor Co.	23.6
50	Chesebrough-Pond's	67.3	100	E. & J. Gallo Winery	22.0

(Reprinted with permission from the August 1978 issue of *Advertising Age.* Copyright © 1978 by Crain Communications)

INSTITUTIONAL ADVERTISING

Not all advertising tells you to go out and buy a particular product. Some of the more subtle ads aim at making you remember a name, favorably, so that you'll turn to the seller when the need arises. Thus there are funeral homes which promise "dignified, loving care for members of your family," banks which promise to "be your friend," and medical insurers who tell you how much they are doing to hold down hospital costs. Even public utility companies have gotten into the habit of buying magazine and newspaper space to tell their users what fine and public-spirited outfits they are—all at the users' expense!

Much corporate advertising relates to issues rather than to products. The oil companies, for example, have spent many advertising dollars trying to convince the public that their analysis of the national energy crisis is correct. Their ads, of course, carefully select some favorable facts and statistics, and screen out unfavorable ones (as do their product ads).

A campaign by several insurance companies not long ago illustrated the pitfalls of this kind of advertising. As part of a nationwide effort to change state laws so that victims of accidents would recover less, the companies took out ads explaining how their proposals would lower insurance rates for everyone. They so twisted the facts and misrepresented the actual situation that they were called to task by a congressional subcommittee for their misleading statements.

The fact is that profit motivates this kind of advertising just as much as it does any other kind—and just as much skepticism about its trustworthiness and reliability is in order.

ADVERTISING TO CHILDREN: SELLING CANDY TO BABIES

On Saturday morning at 7 A.M. you are probably in bed. But: do you know where the children are? If your slumber is undisturbed, they're probably watching television, where, away from your watchful eye, the snack-food manufacturers and the toy industry are barraging them with powerful messages. The average two- to eleven-year-old in this country watches over 1,300 hours of television annually. This includes a staggering *20,000* commercials. Teams of researchers, psychological testers, ad agency personnel, visual arts experts, and communications specialists orchestrate this massive selling effort which costs advertisers hundreds of millions of dollars annually. The sophisticated ad campaigns they produce are aimed at an audience which literally cannot think straight. The youngest listeners don't even understand the selling purpose of commercials. All they know is that the friendly fairies, elves, talking animals, and cartoon characters they love want them to eat candy.

A huge number of ads directed to kids are for sweets—breakfast cereals loaded with sugar, chocolate drinks, cookies, cakes, and snacks of all kinds. In a nine-month study of daytime weekend food commercials, the Council on Children, Media and Merchandising reported that the three networks aired *four* advertisements for meat, cheese, and vegetables, and 5,459 for sugared cereals, candy, and gum.

In 1978, the FTC initiated an investigation into the ethics and honesty of children's advertising. Preliminary staff findings support the need for severely restricting the huckstering that influences children to do the advertisers' bidding. The staff found evidence that TV ads

- promote non-nutritious junk foods and sometimes denigrate healthful ones (one ad for a cream-filled cookie showed a fruit peddler tasting the cookie, smiling, and throwing away his cartful of fresh fruit).
- exploit children's ignorance of the relation between sweets and tooth decay and of the value of good eating habits in general.
- undermine the parent-child relationship by creating conflicts over food and generate resentment against parents who deny their offspring advertised products.
- encourage the lifelong addiction to sugar characteristic of virtually all Americans (our sugar consumption is 126 pounds per person every year!).
- manipulate children into becoming little sales agents for the advertisers (one ad executive states: "When you sell a woman on a product and she goes into the store and finds your brand isn't in stock, she'll probably forget about it. But when you sell a kid on your product, if he can't get it he will throw himself on the floor, stamp his feet and cry. You can't get a reaction like that out of an adult." FTC report).

To remedy all of this, the FTC is considering a rule which would ban all televised advertising directed at children under eight; prohibit ads to children of any age for products posing a serious risk to dental health; and require advertisers of decay-causing foods to disclose this negative aspect of their products.

In the meantime, kids are on their own. Your best course of action may be to sit with them as they watch and ask what they think about the programs and commercials they see. If they're taken in by the sweet-faced panda selling chocolate-flavored garbage, tell them what's really going on. The littlest consumers need consumer education too.

BETTER WAYS OF CHOOSING PRODUCTS

Advertisements are designed to sell, not to convey information. Thus advertisers regularly play with statistics, tell half-truths, and, on occasion, lie. Other, more reliable sources of data on products exist, but you have to seek them out: they don't come after you, as commercials, billboards, and other advertisements do.

There's no way of buying wisely without doing a little homework. The larger the purchase, the more time you'll need to invest.

Here are several worthwhile sources of buying information:

1. Periodicals. The best-known and most reliable consumers' guide is *Consumer Reports,* a monthly magazine put out by Consumers Union, an organization which does objective research and product testing in its own laboratories. Some articles rate specific products, others deal with consumer issues generally. The magazine has 1.75 million subscribers who pay $11 a year for 11 issues plus a December *Buying Guide,* a paperback book synopsis of the year's findings. Buy it on newsstands or subscribe (write to Subscription Department, *Consumer Reports,* P.O. Box 1000, Orangeburg, N.Y. 10962).

An excellent overview is contained in an annual paperback publication called *HELP: The Useful Almanac,* published by Consumer News, Inc. (Washington, D.C. 20045).

2. Government and consumer group publications. Market surveys and buying guides are useful when available. State and local agencies are another source of objective information. And Uncle Sam has a good deal to offer—there are a plethora (256 at last count) of federal publications, available free or at low cost, dealing with such diverse topics as what to look for in buying tires, how to create playground equipment out of junk, and reading food labels. The quality varies as widely as the topics. To see what's available, send for a free brochure, *The Consumer Information Catalog* (write to Consumer Information Center, Pueblo, Colo. 81009).

3. Comparison shopping. By looking around, especially when you've decided not to purchase yet, you can often learn a lot. Whenever possible decide on a replacement item (even if you don't want to spend the money until absolutely necessary) before an old one wears out. Buying in a hurry is often a losing proposition, but you have no choice when your hair dryer disintegrates and it's choose quickly or go to work with soggy locks.

4. Asking friends. People whose judgment you trust and who have used a product can give you valuable information. The most dependable goods and the most reliable services often don't need any advertising other than word of mouth. So keep your ears open, and when you find something good, spread the word.

COMPLAINING ABOUT ADS

What can the individual consumer do when outraged by offensive, tasteless, or deceptive advertisements? The first line of defense is: *don't buy the product,* and tell the advertiser *why* you're not. If more people reacted this way, we might see fewer annoying and insulting advertisements. Second, if you find the product does not measure up to the promise made for it, complain to the advertiser, the medium in which you saw the ad, and your local consumer protection agency. If the ad is on national television, complain to the Federal Trade Commission, Bureau of Consumer Protection, Washington, D.C. 20580.

SELECTED BIBLIOGRAPHY

PACKARD, VANCE. *The Hidden Persuaders.* New York: Pocket Books, 1958.
WRIGHTER, CARL. *I Can Sell You Anything.* New York: Ballantine Books, 1972.

2

Contracts and warranties:

all you ever wanted to know about small print but were afraid to ask

[This contract] was printed in such small type, and in lines so long and so crowded, that the perusal of it was made physically difficult, painful, and injurious. Seldom has the art of typography been so successfully diverted from the diffusion of knowledge to the suppression of it.

— Opinion of the Court, *De Lancey v. Rockingham Insurance Co.,* 52 N.H. 581, 587 (1873)

[Lawyers have] a peculiar Cant and Jargon of their own, that no other mortal can understand.

— JONATHAN SWIFT,
Gulliver's Travels

A contract is a legally enforceable agreement between two (or more) people. Each one promises to do or pay something. It need not be labeled a "contract," and need not even be in writing. In less complicated times, consumer contracts were often unwritten agreements sealed by a handshake between buyer and seller. Today, they are finely printed, technical documents written in language that would make a Ph.D. run for cover. Some sport a dozen paragraphs cramped onto a single page; others, like leases and mortgages, go on interminably, approaching the size of a small bed sheet.

Virtually all consumer agreements made today are "standard forms"— contracts which the seller has preprinted for use with all customers. We deal with these contracts all the time. Theater tickets, railroad tickets, parking-lot stubs, and laundry receipts, for example, are typically standard-form contracts spelling out the terms of conditions of sale.

Form contracts are written for merchants and lenders by their lawyers and are offered to buyers on a "take it or leave it" basis. Blank spaces are left on the forms for the few matters on which the buyer will be consulted (size of down payment, number of monthly installments, etc.). All the remaining terms are dictated by the seller and frozen in print. Given the sole power to determine what goes into the contract, the seller can hardly be expected to draft a fair, well-balanced agreement that treats both parties equally. In fact, in most standard-form consumer contracts, every term favors the seller. Unfortunately, the law has been slow to respond to the problem of unfair, one-sided contracts, and courts usually (but not always, as explained later) give them full force and effect. For this reason, consumer advocates are constantly urging people to read every contract and to refuse to sign anything they don't understand. This advice, while theoretically sound, is utterly impractical when the contract is in legalese, no one present (least of all the salesperson) is qualified to explain it, and the buyer doesn't have three hours to spend poring over a maze of fine print.

This chapter will warn you about some of the common troublesome terms appearing in contracts and warranties, and will describe the legal doctrines which, to a limited extent, aid victims of unduly harsh contracts.

WHAT'S IN THE FINE PRINT

Standardized agreements contain a predictable series of clauses which whittle away the buyer's rights. Form contracts vary from industry to industry and sometimes from store to store, but the most insidious terms appear in all of them. In most consumer transactions the contract is never consulted after it is signed, because no problems arise which require the parties to know their rights. But once anything goes wrong, the fine print is there to give the seller every advantage. Here is a guide to the interpretation of the most common fine-print clauses:

WAIVER OF SELLER'S LIABILITY FOR NEGLIGENCE

Buyer hereby releases Seller from any and all liability for the negligent or wrongful acts or omissions of Seller and its employees.

This merciless provision relieves the seller of all responsibility for its own negligent acts which harm the buyer. A California man seeking admission to a hospital in Los Angeles signed a form containing this type of release. At the time of signing he was in great pain and under sedation. He later died, and his wife sued the hospital, claiming that it was negligent in caring for her husband. The hospital pointed to the release and asked the court to dismiss the case. The Supreme Court of California refused, saying that the release was against public policy because of the essential nature of the service offered and the decisive superiority of bargaining strength possessed by the hospital.

Another injured consumer was not so lucky. A woman joined a Vic Tanney gymnasium, and fell one day near the edge of the gym's swimming pool. She claimed the fall was caused by excessive slipperiness which should have been prevented by proper care by the gym employees. Her membership contract contained the waiver-of-responsibility-for-negligence clause, and the gym asked the court to throw her case out. This time the request was granted. The court found no reason to invalidate the clause, despite the obvious fact that the health and safety of members of the public were at stake.

WAIVER OF RIGHT TO JURY TRIAL

Buyer hereby waives the right to trial by jury in the event of litigation arising out of this agreement.

Sellers don't like jury trials. By this provision the buyer "waives," or forfeits, the right to have any dispute over the contract resolved by a jury. There are two possible reasons for the seller's reluctance to go before a jury. First, if a lawsuit occurs, it is cheaper and quicker to have the case tried by a judge instead of a jury. Second, the jury is made up of ordinary individuals, who are all consumers, and tend to be sympathetic to buyers. This, coupled with the inclination of juries to occasionally reject principles of law when they seem unfair, explains much of the widespread antagonism of sellers to the venerated tradition of "judgment by your peers."

PAYMENT OF SELLER'S ATTORNEY'S FEES

In the event of this Contract becoming due and payable and being referred to an attorney for collection, Buyer shall pay, in addition to the amount due, a further amount equal to twenty percent (20%) thereof where permitted by law.

This is a good example of imbalance in the form contract. The seller, by this term, imposes the costs of its attorney on the buyer. But if the buyer has to hire a lawyer to force the seller to live up to its obligations under the contract or warranty, no provision requires the seller to pay the buyer's attorney's fee.

This clause often results in an unfair windfall for the seller. Its attorney may have done no more than send a letter, yet the 20 percent added fee on a $1,000 loan or purchase, for example, is $200. Thus, the fee set by the contract is grossly disproportionate to the legal work performed. Several states absolutely prohibit the collection of seller's attorney's fees. California, for instance, says that a contract may require the buyer to pay seller attorney fees if the seller prevails, but the law will read into the contract a reciprocal provision, requiring the seller to pay buyer attorney fees if the buyer wins.

ACCELERATION CLAUSE

If Buyer should default in the payment of any sum payable under this Contract, or in the performance of any of the other terms and provisions hereof, any and all amounts then owing shall at the option of the Seller become immediately due and payable.

This "acceleration clause" speeds the day when you have to pay the full amount of a loan or installment contract. By its terms, the buyer (or borrower) who misses a single payment by even one day must, if the seller so chooses, pay the entire debt immediately. Debtors can rarely pay so quickly. Used-car sellers sometimes use this clause to declare a buyer in default, sue for the remaining installments, take back the car, and resell it to another purchaser. Other unethical dealers may use it to force debtors to part with valuable collateral, such as their homes, put up as security for their debts.

Reputable businesses usually are reluctant to invoke the acceleration clause, preferring to give the debtor a chance to maintain the original schedule of payments. The clause is used only when the debtor refuses to pay. Instead of having to sue for each separate installment as it falls due, the creditor accelerates payments and sues for the entire amount owing.

DELINQUENCY CLAUSE

Should Buyer default in payment of any installment and such default continue for a period of ten days, Buyer agrees to pay a delinquency charge of 5% of the amount of each installment in default, or the sum of $5, whichever is less.

This clause imposes a "late fee" when the buyer's installment payment is made more than ten days after it is due. While this is not so bad in itself, it is a typical one-sided term: there is never a corresponding penalty imposed on the seller for missing a delivery date or delaying in making promised repairs.

SELLER'S RIGHT TO ASSIGN

Seller may assign this contract at any time.

The seller may "assign," or transfer, its right to collect payments under the contract to another company, usually a finance company. Thus, if you owe $120 to a seller, which you are paying off the rate of $10 a month, the seller may sell its right to receive your monthly payments to the XYZ Finance Company. XYZ will pay the seller something less than $120, since it is getting not cash today, but only a right to receive $10 a month in the future. XYZ also takes the risk that you will skip town and avoid your payments. So it pays the seller $100 for the assignment of the contract, and informs you that you are to make your monthly payments to XYZ. In legal terms, the seller is the assignor, and the finance company is the assignee.

This simple transfer is not a bad thing in itself, but until 1976 a related legal doctrine made it a source of extreme consumer abuse. The doctrine, known as the "holder in due course" rule, stated that the consumer had to pay the assignee (the finance company) even if the seller did not live up to its obligations under the contract. A consumer who bought a defective television set, for example, and whose installment contract was assigned, would find that the law required that the set be paid for even if the seller refused to replace it with one that worked. Under this system, sellers lost the incentive to resolve consumer complaints once the consumer's contract was assigned to a finance company.

To remedy this problem, the Federal Trade Commission enacted a rule requiring sellers to include in their installment contracts the following clause:

Any holder of this consumer credit contract is subject to all claims and defenses which the Debtor could assert against the Seller of goods or services obtained pursuant hereto or with the proceeds hereof. Recovery hereunder by the Debtor shall not exceed amounts paid by the Debtor hereunder.

This FTC-created clause is not a model of clarity, but it means that the consumer (the "debtor") can assert against a finance company (or any other "holder" of the contract) any and all complaints about the seller's performance (or lack of it) under the contract. If the purchaser of a defective television set learns that a finance company holds the contract, that consumer can refuse to make the monthly installments, and demand a refund from either the seller or the finance company of any money paid so far.

MERGER CLAUSE

This writing is our entire agreement and cannot be changed orally.

OR

This agreement contains the entire understanding of the parties hereto. Buyer acknowledges that Seller shall not be bound by any representations, promises, or inducements of any agent or employee of Seller which is not set forth in this agreement.

By this term, the seller seeks to avoid responsibility for any promises made by sales personnel which are not contained in the contract. It is called a "merger clause," presumably because all previous discussions and understandings are merged into one document, the contract. This clause provides good reason to insist that sales agents point out precisely *where* in the contract their promises are written. If a promise is not in writing, it can't be trusted.

When a salesperson lies to the buyer, courts will usually ignore the merger clause. Proving this kind of fraud, however, is not easy.

SELLER'S RIGHT TO REPOSSESS GOODS

Title to the merchandise shall remain in the Seller as security for the performance of Buyer's obligations under this agreement.

Generally, retail installment contracts state that the item sold (and sometimes other items too) stands as "security" for the debt. This means that if the payments are not made, the security may be taken, sold, and the proceeds applied to pay off the amount still owing.

How does a seller retake the security? This is usually *not* spelled out in the contract. By law in most states, a seller or lender is permitted to

"repossess" any item named as security without giving any notice to the con-
sumer-debtor. So they can legally grab back property in order to satisfy a
debt. If you miss the payments on your car, for example, you may wake up
one day to find it has disappeared without a trace. Soon after, you'll hear
from your creditor, who will offer you the opportunity to get the car back, in
return for full payment of the balance due.

There are a few limits placed upon the way in which goods can be
repossessed, but one restriction, universally imposed, is very important. No
one is permitted to "breach the peace" in the course of repossessing goods.
This means that individuals hired to retake someone's property may not
break down doors, smash windows, bully people, or threaten violence in
order to complete their task. This may explain why household furniture, for
example, is rarely repossessed—there is no way, short of breaking and entering or intimidation, for sellers' agents to get at the goods. Cars, on the
other hand, are more frequently repossessed, because they are parked in
public streets and thus readily accessible.

If repossession doesn't work, the seller or creditor must go to court to get
an order requiring the debtor to pay or to surrender the property. This is a
much fairer procedure, because it allows the debtor to explain why payment
wasn't made.

LIQUIDATED DAMAGES CLAUSE

> *In the event of any breach of this contract by Purchaser, the Seller shall
> be entitled to recover a sum equal to 25% of the total agreed contract
> price as and for liquidated damages.*

If you breach an agreement to buy, the seller is entitled only to compensation for expenses incurred and for lost profit. Some contracts, however,
contain a clause like the above, which set a figure (in this case, 25 percent of
the contract price), known as "liquidated damages," which establishes what
the buyer must pay to the seller. The clause is valid only if this sum is a fair
and reasonable estimate of the seller's lost profit. If it is too high—as may
often be the case in a seller's form contract—it is unlawful. Contracts for
health club memberships and for vocational school courses frequently contain
unenforceable liquidated damages clauses, which allow the school to keep
excessive fees when the consumer cancels or drops out. Because consumers
do not challenge them, these merchants hold on to their unlawful fees.

ESCAPE HATCHES

Although a contract is viewed with great respect by the law, there are
times when signed agreements are not enforced. For consumers, there are
three important reasons permitting them to get out of contracts, described
below.

1. FRAUD

A court will not enforce a contract procured by fraud. Fraud is generally defined as an intentionally false statement by the seller which leads the buyer to sign a contract or make a purchase.

At times, this legal doctrine is restrictively interpreted against consumers. Thus, some untrue statements by sellers are considered harmless "puffing" by the seller, and not fraud. The attitudes of judges vary considerably from state to state, and even within a state it may be impossible to predict how a court will treat a claim of fraud. For example, if Joe Blowout, the friendly used-car dealer, tells you a snazzy '55 Chevy "runs like a dream" but two days later you feel like you're driving a Sherman tank, one court might call the statement fraudulent, while another might call it permissible puffery. A third court might refuse to consider the statement fraudulent because you had "no right to rely" on the salesman's word, that is, you could have found out for yourself, by test driving the car, just how smooth a ride it gave. And a fourth court might turn down your claim on the ground that Mr. Blowout was not stating a fact, but only his opinion, with which you might agree or disagree. (For a more extensive discussion of the law of fraud, see chapter 4.) If a court does find that you were induced to sign a contract because of fraudulent statements made to you, the contract will be declared void.

2. UNCONSCIONABILITY

An old legal concept which has been rediscovered and put to new use in the last decade is the doctrine of unconscionability. A judge may declare a contract "unconscionable" and therefore unenforceable if it is too harsh. In a common phrase, an unconscionable bargain is one which "shocks the conscience" of the court.

There is no limit to the types of contract terms to which this doctrine can be applied. A grossly excessive price, for example, may be considered oppressive. To be unconscionable, the price must be more than just "high," it must be unfair in the extreme. In one New Jersey case, a judge voided the sale of a food freezer to a couple paying more than twice the price normally charged by all reputable sellers in the community.

Where questionable sales tactics are used to take advantage of buyers, courts may also invoke the unconscionability doctrine. A New York judge permitted a student to cancel a contract for a data processing technician course. School sales agents had persuaded the student to enroll despite his poor educational background, extreme difficulty with spoken and written English, and complete lack of aptitude for technical training. Although the student failed all of the achievement tests given during the course and wanted to drop out, his instructor told him to continue with the course and not be "chicken." The judge condemned the school's sales practices and refused to allow the school to collect its full tuition under the contract.

Despite the flexibility and great potential of the unconscionability doctrine, it has not appreciably reduced the incidence of exploitative practices in the marketplace. Because unconscionability is so inexact a concept, even lawyers can't be sure if a one-sided contract term will be deemed so unfair as to "shock the conscience." Furthermore, some judges apply the doctrine only when the most pitiable consumer signs the harshest contract. Most important of all, perhaps, is the fact that consumers can not afford the expense of hiring a lawyer and going to court to get a determination that an unfair contract is unconscionable. Since relatively few cases come to the attention of judges, it is possible for unfair practices to flourish, safe from the prying eyes of the courts.

3. MINORITY

State laws protect children from the dangers of incurring contract obligations by permitting them to break their contracts without penalty. A seller contracting with a minor (variously defined as one under 18 or 21 years of age) will be bound by the agreement if the minor desires to go through with the transaction. But the minor is free to cancel it anytime.

Given this rule, it is not surprising that most sellers refuse to enter into contracts with minors. A common exception is made for the necessaries of life. Minors over a certain age may be held to contracts for goods falling in this category. Some states also permit minors over a specified age who are married to assume full contract responsibilities. This is done to encourage merchants to deal with these individuals as they would with adults.

THE PLAIN LANGUAGE MOVEMENT

In the words of George Santayana, "Nothing is so powerful as an idea whose time has come." The idea that all consumer contracts should be in plain English so that consumers can understand what they sign, may be one of those powerful ideas Santayana was talking about. A New York law requiring contracts to be "written in non-technical language . . . using words with common and everyday meanings" is the nation's first, but there are indications that its rippling effects will carry far beyond that state's borders. Similar laws have been introduced in several jurisdictions, and even the massive federal bureaucracy has been ordered to recast governmental regulations into language people can comprehend.

A number of private institutions have begun to simplify their contract forms. Prior to the passage of the New York law, Citibank, one of the largest commercial banks in the country, revised its consumer loan agreements using ordinary English, shorter phrases, and simple declaratory sentences. The bank's new form contains only one third as many words as the one it replaced. The extent of the change can best be appreciated by comparing one paragraph of the old and new loan agreements:

Old:	New:
In the event of default in the payment of this or any other Obligation or the performance or observance of any term or covenant contained herein or in any note or other contract or agreement evidencing or relating to any Obligation or any Collateral on the Borrower's part to be performed or observed; or the undersigned Borrower shall die; or any of the undersigned become insolvent or make an assignment for the benefit of creditors; or a petition shall be filed by or against any of the undersigned under any provision of the Bankruptcy Act; or any money, securities or property of the undersigned now or hereafter on deposit with or in the possession or under the control of the Bank shall be attached or become subject to distraint proceedings or any order or process of any court; or the Bank shall deem itself to be insecure, then in any such event, the Bank shall have the right (at its option), without demand or notice of any kind, to declare all or any part of the Obligations to be immediately due and payable, whereupon such Obligations shall become and be immediately due and payable, and the Bank shall have the right to exercise all the rights and remedies available to a secured party upon default under the Uniform Commercial Code (the "Code") in effect in New York at the time, and such other rights and remedies as may otherwise be provided by law.	I'll be in default: 1. If I don't pay an installment on time; or 2. If any other creditor tries by legal process to take any money of mine in your possession. You can then demand immediate payment of the balance of this note.

Opponents of "plain language" laws claim that they will tend to complicate matters, because the use of technical terms takes less space, saves time, and promotes certainty (by enabling contract writers to use terms with well-established legal meanings). While there is a bit of truth in this, it appears that the opposition—mainly lawyers—expends more energy bewailing these problems than finding solutions to them. Nevertheless, as long as public support for the idea of plain language continues, the time may yet come when "legalese," driven from the pages of consumer contracts, fades into its own obscurity.

Without plain language, contracts have always been difficult to understand. (Culver Pictures, Inc.)

ELEVEN PRACTICAL POINTS ABOUT CONTRACTS

While you can't be expected to scrutinize intelligently contracts not written in plain English, there are some things you can do to protect yourself from the danger of harsh contract terms. The following suggestions deal with important matters which the alert consumer can do something about.

1. Devote careful attention to the payment terms of the contract. Under the federal Truth-in-Lending law,* any "buy now/pay later" contract or any loan agreement must state the interest charges both as a percentage (the "Annual Percentage Rate") and as a dollar amount (the "Finance Charge"). If the interest seems too high, put off signing and see if you can get a lower rate elsewhere. (For a discussion of other sources of credit, see chapter 19.)

* 15 U.S.C. 1601.

2. Don't trust people who say their promises don't have to be in the contract. Insist that any verbal promises made be written in ink on both your copy and the store's copy of the contract. Both you and the store representative should sign your initials after any changes or additions to the contract.

3. Make sure you can afford the monthly payments in an installment contract. Failure to keep up payments later on may result in loss of prior payments and the goods too.

4. Beware of a "balloon payment" clause. This is a large final installment (the balloon) which is considerably greater than the other monthly payments, sometimes used as a device to trick the careless buyer.

5. If a down payment is required, make it as low as possible. This allows you to withhold a larger payment if the goods are delivered in unsatisfactory condition. Also, some contracts call for the forfeiture of the down payment if you wish to cancel the order. Thus, the smaller the down payment, the better.

6. See that the goods purchased are described adequately. The seller should write in size, model number, other identifying characteristics, and any quality assurances given, on the face of the contract. This will prevent the substitution of inferior merchandise at delivery time.

7. Don't co-sign a contract for a friend, unless you are prepared to pay the entire balance and to lose your friend. A co-signer is equally liable with the purchaser, and the merchant can go straight to the co-signer without trying to collect first from the purchaser.

8. Make sure all the blank spaces in the contract are filled in before you sign. Otherwise they can be filled in to your disadvantage later. The spaces are usually for monetary amounts, such as credit charges, which can be considerable.

9. Get a copy of every contract you sign and keep it.

10. Don't sign anything because of pressure or a desire to get rid of a persistent sales agent.

11. You can force the seller to change or delete unfair terms in a form contract by refusing to sign unless the desired change is made. Watch as salespeople frantically run to check with everyone they can find to see if it's O.K. (They always expect *you* to sign without consultation, but when the tables are turned they seek all the help they can get.)

WARRANTIES

A warranty is simply a promise or guarantee about a given product. It may be a promise contained in a contract or one appearing in a separate document. Warranties can even be created by advertisements.

In a remarkable California case, a sportsman intent on killing a Bengal tiger purchased a Winchester rifle advertised as suitable for hunting rhinoceros, Cape buffalo, and other big-game animals. The intrepid hunter traveled all the way to India, hired a safari, and set out for the jungle. The fourth day on safari he squeezed the trigger. Victory was his—almost. The rifle's faulty safety mechanism rendered it incapable of being fired. The tiger escaped, and the crushed hunter sued the gun manufacturer, alleging that its advertisements created a warranty which the company had to honor. A California court agreed with him.

Most consumer goods manufacturers embody their warranties in formal written statements accompanying their products. During a congressional investigation of these product warranties, Senator Warren Magnuson, sponsor of a bill to require clear disclosure of warranty terms and conditions, made this provocative observation:

> Warranties have for many years confused, misled, and frequently angered American consumers. . . . Consumer anger is expected when purchasers of consumer products discover that their warranty may cover a 25-cent part but not the $100 labor charge or that there is full coverage on a piano so long as it is shipped at the purchaser's expense to the factory.

The main problem with warranties is simply that they are not what they pretend to be. Dressed up in fancy script, and prettily enclosed in a scalloped border, they masquerade as promises of buyer protection. But, like contracts, they carry fine-print time bombs that go off whenever the buyer seeks protection. By way of illustration, here are the five most common fine-print warranty terms, along with explanations of what they really mean.

This warranty is in lieu of all other warranties, express or implied, including any implied warranty of merchantability or fitness for a particular purpose.

Through this provision, known as a disclaimer of warranties, manufacturers try to deprive consumers of rights they would otherwise have under law. The law implies, or assumes, that every manufacturer guarantees that its goods will be fit for the ordinary purpose for which they are used. That is, a saw will cut, a car will run, a gun will shoot. This is the "implied warranty of merchantability." If the seller knows of some other purpose which the buyer has in mind, the law assumes a guarantee by the seller that the product will fulfill that purpose too (thus, the "implied warranty of fitness for a particular purpose"). The disclaimer provision wipes away both of these warranties, as well as any other promise made to the buyer which does not appear in the written warranty statement. Several states, including California, Oregon, Maine, Massachusetts, and Maryland, recognize the unfairness of permitting written warranties to nullify legally granted rights, and forbid warranty disclaimers. Most other states, however, give this provision full force and effect.

No responsibility is assumed for incidental or consequential damages.

By these words, sellers seek to limit their responsibility if their defective products cause some physical or pecuniary harm. For example, if your new car breaks down and you must temporarily rent a vehicle, this provision would protect the car dealer from having to pay your rental fees. If your new refrigerator conks out without warning, spoiling $50 worth of food, this warranty term pins the food loss on you. All the manufacturers will do for you is fix the item itself—everything else is "incidental or consequential."

Warrantors don't always get away with this. When defective goods harm people, the courts ignore warranty limitations and order warrantors to compensate consumers for their injuries. This is what happened in an influential court case in New Jersey involving a car maker's warranty that gave more protection to the manufacturer than to the consumer. A woman driving her new car ten days after its delivery suffered serious injury when the car, seemingly by itself, suddenly veered 90 degrees and smashed itself into a brick wall. The court refused to give effect to the warranty provision exempting the company from responsibility, stating that to do otherwise would fail "to protect the ordinary man against the loss of important rights."

Defective parts will be repaired or replaced at our option.

This seemingly harmless, if not generous, warranty term is the cause of untold grief to consumers. Its true purpose is simple: to deprive the buyer of the right to a refund if a new product doesn't work right. While many flawed products can be made "good as new" with minor work, some cannot. These are the "lemons"—the substandard cars, appliances, typewriters, stereos, tape recorders, televisions, and so on—which cause endless despair to their owners and which their makers doggedly insist can be repaired. Auto makers are particularly noted for their unwillingness to come forth with a new car, forcing the victimized customer either to sue for a refund or to suffer inconvenience and endless trips to the repair shop.

Warranties invariably limit the buyer's remedies in this way, but when the limit works great unfairness the courts will not give it effect. In one case, for example, a Missourian's new car burned up because of a defective electrical system. Nevertheless, the dealer refused to replace it, or to refund the purchase price, relying on the warranty's promise only to repair defective parts. The dealer could not have repaired this customer's car; the fire had reduced it to worthless junk. When the buyer sued for his money back, the court ignored the warranty limitation, saying it would be "ludicrous" to adhere to the warranty as written.

In the event of a guarantee claim, mail your product, properly packaged and insured, to the nearest authorized service dealer.

Warrantors often dictate the manner in which the warranty is to be fulfilled and make it as convenient as possible for themselves. It is not easy to pack up a defective refrigerator for shipment to the factory; it is maddening to have to pay all the expenses necessary to do it. The worst warranties transfer pickup and delivery, transportation, and labor costs to the consumer, who may have assumed that all these charges would be the manufacturer's responsibility. Warranties vary a great deal as to the burdens they place on purchasers.

This guarantee does not apply to parts that might wear or accidentally be broken in normal use. It does not apply to damage caused by neglect, abuse, mishandling, or unauthorized repairs.

Arguments over warranty coverage are virtually inevitable when warranties use language like this. Too often, warrantors point to vague terms in the warranty statement to justify their refusal to remedy defective products and poor workmanship. Some manufacturers define unauthorized repairs as any repair, no matter how well performed, not done at their own factory. Others simply assume that problems are caused by customer abuse and challenge you to prove otherwise.

Consumers who insist on warranty repairs may be given the classic runaround, from retailer to servicer to distributor to manufacturer and back again. Making matters worse is the fact that service dealers authorized to do warranty repairs often have a monetary incentive to find that a particular problem is not within the warranty. Warranty work is usually paid for at a lower rate than non-warranty work (reflecting the manufacturers' superior bargaining power), so repairers avoid warranty service whenever possible. Many will seize on an ambiguous phrase in the warranty to deny coverage. The line most calculated to drive consumers crazy, however, is: "It looks like your fault—you didn't take care of it properly." Warranties properly exempt problems caused by customer abuse, but leave it up to the warrantor to decide when a product has been "abused."

Even if warranty coverage is clear, it may not be clear who is responsible. At the first sign of trouble, retailer, manufacturer, and distributor point the finger of blame at one another, while none act to satisfy the poor customer. Warranties can mean very little when the various people in the chain of distribution are falling all over themselves to evade responsibility.

NEW FEDERAL WARRANTY LAW

The problems raised by warranty abuses led Congress to enact the Magnuson-Moss Warranty Act,† effective January 1, 1977. The law helps somewhat, but leaves much to be desired in terms of adequate consumer protection.

It must first be noted that the Act does not require any seller to give a warranty. If the seller, on its own, chooses to give a written warranty, then the Act comes into play. The law divides all warranties into two legal categories: "Full Warranties" and "Limited Warranties." A full warranty grants the buyer considerable protection: all defects and materials covered must be

† 15 U.S.C. 2301.

fixed or replaced without charge, within a reasonable time, and no excessive burdens may be imposed upon the consumer (like shipping the piano to the factory). In addition, the warrantor who, after a reasonable number of attempts, cannot fix the malfunction in a product under full warranty must offer the consumer a refund or a new item (whichever the consumer prefers).

Sellers of consumer goods are free to offer only a "limited warranty," however, to which none of the above protections apply. Unfortunately, it appears that a large number of companies have decided to shun the full warranty, in order to preserve the advantages they had before the Act. The Act's sponsors had expected that the pressures of competition would induce manufacturers to give full warranties on their products, but to date this hope has been unfulfilled.

The important contribution the Act has made involves its warranty disclosure requirements. All written warranties, whether full or limited, on products costing more than $15, must include the following in clear, simple language:

- a description of exactly which parts or components are covered by the warranty.
- a clear statement of what the warrantor will do in the event of a defect, malfunction, or failure to conform with the written warranty, including the items or services the warrantor will pay for and provide.
- the length of the warranty period.
- a step-by-step explanation of the procedure which the consumer should follow in order to obtain performance under the warranty.
- the name and mailing address of the employee or department responsible for performing warranty work (or a toll-free telephone number which consumers can call for this information).
- a description of any informal mechanism the warrantor has for settling disputes with consumers.

The Act also gives the consumer the opportunity to inspect the warranty before making a purchase. In the past, warranties were always packed away in the carton with the product, rendering them unreachable until the buyer opened the box at home. Under the new federal rule, sellers must display each warranty on or near the warranted product, or else keep a binder containing all warranties in a place which is readily available to shoppers. Large retailers maintaining warranty books must keep them in each department of the store.

These provisions will help only if consumers become accustomed to reading and comparing warranties. If you find a product with a full warranty, you know you have a truly protective warranty. But when all competitors are offering limited warranties, it is something of a chore to keep track of which ones cover more parts, charge less for labor costs, and waive fewer of your rights. Only the aware, knowledgeable consumer can hope to disentangle the confusion that is warranty.

IF YOUR WARRANTY ISN'T HONORED

1. First, complain in writing to the seller and the manufacturer (look for the address given in the warranty). Send another copy of your letter to the Federal Trade Commission, Washington, D.C. 20580.

2. Next, see if the warranty contains information about a dispute settlement procedure. If so, follow that procedure.

3. Finally, if you get no satisfaction, consider suing the warrantor. Under the Magnuson-Moss Warranty Act, you can sue in a local court and, if you win, the court can order your opponent to pay your attorney's fees. If the amount involved is small, sue in small claims court.

SELECTED BIBLIOGRAPHY

Warranties: There Ought to Be a Law, pamphlet available from the Federal Trade Commission, Legal and Public Records, Room 130, Washington, D.C. 20580.

3

Speak up: how to complain effectively

> In a volatile, ever-changing world, one of the few constants on which we may still rely is the incompetence of others. —RALPH CHARRELL, *How I Turn Ordinary Complaints into Thousands of Dollars*

So says a complainer par excellence, a man who's made a second career out of seeking redress. He is atypical in many respects—better educated, more articulate, nervier, and willing to put his money where his mouth is. And he frequents the better stores and creditors, which are likely to be more reasonable. Mr. Charrell's suggested tactics include hiring an actor rather than a lawyer to represent you ("you may choose from a long list of talents that range from supercilious, pinstriped British types to shrill, overbearing dwarfs"), and we do not recommend all of them.

While most people hesitate to complain, others rent billboards to vent their dissatisfaction. (St. Louis *Post-Dispatch,* Ted Dargan)

But his tales of unmitigated gall make good reading and contain some general lessons. He is prepared for all his encounters with facts, names, and an understanding of the corporate structure, where one exists. He always acts as if he places great value on his perceptions, his rights, and his time. Furthermore, he is persistent and imaginative, and makes everyone he deals with aware of these qualities.

Irate consumers streaming into the complaint departments of stores have been the subject of hundreds of cartoons. One could conclude that American consumers are vociferous champions of their rights. But, the fact is that most people do not complain about poorly made goods, incompetent services, or broken promises. A recent study showed that people register only one third of all the consumer problems they have. And of that one third only a small number pursue the problem beyond the seller—by going to manufacturers, government agencies, or consumer groups.

Why people don't complain is an intriguing question, particularly because more than 56 percent of all complaints that are voiced result in satisfaction for the consumer. The psychic rewards of refusing to be a victim are wonderful too. Some people, however, view complaining as a daring tactic, even slightly illegitimate. And complaining is troublesome—it takes time, effort, and emotional energy. We believe in complaining, so here's how to make your complaints count.

ELEVEN GUIDELINES FOR EFFECTIVE COMPLAINING

1. Have your facts straight at all times. Don't pick up the phone or start writing a letter without being as clear as possible about dates, prices, names (substitute descriptions of people if you failed to get a name), etc.

2. Be explicit about what you want. Explain exactly what you want done—usually repair or replacement of goods or refund of money.

3. Speak firmly. Be pleasant, but talk as if you are certain of the justness of your claim, and believe that the seller will correct it promptly (until proven otherwise).

4. Act as if your time were valuable. Show your unwillingness to let the matter be prolonged indefinitely or to repeat your story countless times. Give deadlines (reasonable ones) for the action you expect to be taken.

5. Never talk (or write) to anyone who doesn't have the authority to do what you want or who won't give you his or her name and title. Remember, many salespeople don't have the authority to replace goods or refund money.

6. Keep good photocopies of every letter you send and a notation on every telephone conversation you make. Sellers usually don't do this, and your careful record may become the key factor if the negotiations are prolonged or if you go elsewhere with your complaint.

7. Begin with a telephone call.   Many complaints can be disposed of at this level, particularly if the seller is a reputable one and if you are a charge or credit customer. Determine who can help you *before* beginning your story.

8. Conclude any phone call with a restatement of what's been agreed upon.   "So I can expect delivery by Tuesday?"

9. If one or two phone calls fail, write.   See page 34 for a diagram of a successful complaint letter. You may need to make a preliminary phone call to find out who to write to. This can be a tricky business—pick the lowest-level person who seems authorized to do what you need (head of customer relations department rather than president of store or chairman of the board of parent company) first.

10. Escalate quickly.   Set brief but reasonable time limits (like ten days) on how long you will wait for redress. If someone appears unable or unwilling to help speedily, go above his or her head. You can go as far as the top of the corporate ladder. (Consult library reference books to find out who the president is. Good starting points for publicly held corporations are Standard and Poor's *Register of Corporations, Directors and Executives* and Moody's *Industrial Manual.* Your librarian may be able to suggest others.) If you get through to the corporate bigwigs (or their assistants) you may find them quite willing to dispense the corporation's money in order to preserve its reputation.

11. Find out where you can go if the seller fails to make good, and indicate your intention to do so.   Where you go and in what order depends on what's available in your area and the nature of your complaint. The choices include:

A. GOVERNMENT AGENCIES.   Complain to specific licensing boards or regulatory bodies (for banks, insurance companies, professionals, etc.) where available; otherwise contact general consumer agencies. Agencies and situations vary, of course, but as a general rule, go to local or state agencies, where they exist, first, and federal agencies after that. An abbreviated list of federal agencies is contained in the Appendix.

Many people are pessimistic about writing complaint letters to government agencies, because the complaints rarely achieve a swift, dramatic result. Although a healthy degree of skepticism about the effectiveness of government agencies is quite justified, there are good reasons to put your grievance into a coherent, concise complaint letter. First, some complaints are acted upon by government agencies quickly and decisively; you may be one of the lucky ones. Second, law enforcement agencies often prosecute chronic offenders only; your letter may help to establish a pattern of offensive behavior on the part of a seller. Finally, the mere sending of a formal complaint letter, with a copy to the merchant complained about, may induce the offender to change its position.

B. SMALL CLAIMS COURT.   Don't underestimate your ability to get action in small claims court. (See chapter 28 for details.)

C. TRADE ASSOCIATIONS. These include such organizations as the Major Appliance Consumer Action Panel (MACAP) at 20 North Wacker Drive, Chicago, Ill. 60606; the Automobile Consumer Action Panel (AUTOCAP) of the National Automobile Dealers Association, with headquarters at 8400 Westpark Drive, McLean, Va. 22102 (703-821-7000); the Direct Selling Association, for door-to-door sales, at 1730 M Street, N.W., Washington, D.C. 20036; and the Direct Mail Marketing Association, Mail Order Action Line, 6 East 43rd Street, New York, N.Y. 10017. Although industry-funded and -oriented, these groups are concerned with maintaining business' good name. You might also try a local Better Business Bureau (there are some 140 around the country). The Better Business Bureau is often mistakenly believed to have some real power to resolve disputes. It doesn't, and is not a very aggressive pursuer of consumer rights—it is a business organization, with a pro-industry stance. Nonetheless, it can sometimes be of use. The Better Business Bureau collects background information on local businesses, and in some areas it sponsors mediation boards, so that if you and the seller agree to submit your dispute to a volunteer arbitrator, you may emerge with a legally binding decision in your favor.

D. HELP OR ACTION CENTERS SPONSORED BY NEWSPAPERS OR RADIO OR TELEVISION STATIONS. Usually staffed by volunteers, many of these achieve excellent results.

E. PRIVATE CONSUMER GROUPS. Some function as complaint centers; others don't, but will pursue an occasional outrageous case.

F. NEWSPAPER OR MAGAZINE IN WHICH THE SELLER ADVERTISES. The seller doesn't want to lose the ability to advertise there (many publications will discontinue an ad after complaints), and will often give priority to a complainant who takes this route.

DIAGRAM OF A SUCCESSFUL COMPLAINT LETTER

Type this letter neatly (it won't be taken seriously otherwise) and make two clear photocopies for future use. Sending it by certified mail is a good idea, because it gives you proof that it was received and puts the recipient on notice that you mean business. Keep it brief: a single page for all but the most complicated situations.

Your Address
Date

Responsible Person (named specifically)
Seller's Address

Dear Responsible Person:
   EXACTLY WHAT HAPPENED: A brief statement of when, what, how you bought the goods or services, and what is wrong.

ANY ATTEMPTS YOU'VE MADE TO CORRECT IT: List all prior visits, telephone calls, etc. Give dates and identify (by descriptions, if not the name) people you spoke with, as well as what was said.

WHAT YOU EXPECT AND WHEN: Repair, replacement, refund, etc.

WHAT YOU INTEND TO DO IF THAT DOES NOT HAPPEN: Include this only if you know what remedies are available; if you *do* intend to pursue them; *and* if this is a second (or later) letter. The first one should express your strong expectation that the seller will remedy the situation without further action.

Your signature
Your name

DON'T WRITE LIKE THIS:

Tracy's Department Store
Shopping Mall
Iowa City, Ia.

Dear People:

After all my years of dealing with Tracy's I am truly surprised at the shoddiness of goods I have just received from you. What's the matter with you people anyway? And your young man who keeps assuring me that he'll take care of it is too much. I hope that this is an isolated occurrence and that you will rectify it expeditiously.

It was bad enough to have pajamas which cost so much ($19.95) shrink, but I refuse to pay for them. Why should I? What's even worse is that, after two telephone calls, this hasn't been corrected, although your salespeople kept reassuring me that it would be. Please take care of it as soon as possible! Or I will complain to all the consumer agencies, etc. I'm getting really annoyed because this isn't the first time Tracy's has loused something up for me or my friends. And you delivered them two weeks later (a little late, I thought, but at any rate, they arrived). I wore the pajamas only once and then they shrunk and are much too small to wear. Obviously there was something wrong with them or they wouldn't have done that. Especially for $19.95 plus tax they certainly shouldn't have shrunk after one wearing, don't you agree?

You'd better do something about this or else!

Very truly yours,
Granola Hasenpfeffer

This letter is garbled and disordered. It is wordy, but fails to include dates; description of the goods; how she paid for them; who the writer spoke with (and when); what she wants done; and her address and telephone number.

DO WRITE LIKE THIS:

326 Alabaster Lane
Sheffield Hills, Ia. 52241
March 6, 1980

Gladiola Marbleface, Chief of Customer Relations
Tracy's Department Store
Shopping Mall
Iowa City, Ia. 52240

Dear Ms. Marbleface:

*description
of the goods*

On December 4th I bought a pair of pajamas from your junior lingerie department and charged them to my account (031-48-0724N). The pajamas were made by Suzy Fluzy, were of blue pinstriped Dacron and cotton, and cost $19.95 plus tax.

*what
happened*

I wore the pajamas once and then washed them, by hand, in lukewarm water. They shrunk considerably and were no longer wearable.

what you did

Therefore, I returned them, on December 20th and was assured by Wilbur Weiss, who handled the transaction, that my account would be credited for that amount. However, my January bill arrived and included a $19.95 plus tax charge for the paja-

*attempts to
get satis-
faction*

mas. On January 20th, I telephoned your store and spoke again to Mr. Weiss, who told me to pay the remainder of the bill and assured me that the item would be removed from the next bill. Now my February bill has arrived and it shows the pajamas as "unpaid" and charges me a finance charge as well.

*remedy
requested*

I don't want to have to spend any more time on what should be a simple matter. Please remove this item from my charge record, as well as any finance charges which stemmed from my non-

time limit

payment of it. I expect this matter to be taken care of and reflected on my March bill. If it is not, I shall bring it to the at-

*what you'll
do if it
isn't met*

tention of Wendell Wormwood, president of Tracy's. If you have any questions or need more information I can be reached from 9:30 A.M. to 6 P.M. at 267-1586.

Sincerely,
Granola Hasenpfeffer

COMPLAINING TO UTILITIES: A SPECIAL CASE

If you are having a problem with a gas, electric, or telephone company, you are in a particularly difficult situation—you can't threaten to take your business elsewhere. Their monopoly status makes utility companies tough sellers to deal with. However, there are special protections—each state has its own utility laws and regulations, with an agency set up to administer

If all else fails, be imaginative. (Rapho / Photo Researchers, Inc.)

them. They are commonly called Public Utilities Commissions or Public Service Commissions and are usually located in the state capital. As might be expected, they vary in their desire and ability to protect consumers, as well as in the powers and budget they've been given to carry out that task.

Complain first to the utility company. If you are getting nowhere or if there is any possibility that your service will be terminated, write to the Public Utilities Commission (enclosing a copy of the first complaint letter).

Some public utility companies put out pamphlets about customer's rights. Consumer organizations often put out guides too. To learn more about utility companies, read *How to Challenge Your Local Electric Utility,* by Richard Morgan and Sandra Jarabek, published by the Environmental Action Foundation, 720 Dupont Circle Building, Washington, D.C. 20036.

SELECTED BIBLIOGRAPHY

CHARRELL, RALPH. *How I Turn Ordinary Complaints into Thousands of Dollars.* New York: Dell, 1973.

DORFMAN, JOHN. *A Consumer's Arsenal.* New York: Praeger Publishers, 1976. Gives names and addresses of relevant agencies in all states plus selected trade associations.

HELP: The Useful Almanac (published yearly). Arthur E. Rouse, editor and director. Consumer News, Inc., Washington, D.C. 20045. Also lists agency names and addresses (governmental and private).

STRIKER, JOHN M., and SHAPIRO, ANDREW O. *Super Threats—How to Sound Like a Lawyer and Get Your Rights on Your Own.* New York: Rawson Associates Publishers, 1977.

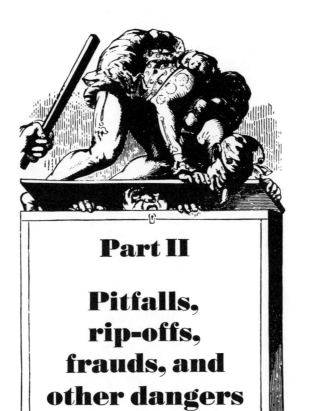

Part II

Pitfalls, rip-offs, frauds, and other dangers

4

Introduction to the vast world of frauds

The truth is usually discreditable to all concerned. — Spanish proverb

He that cheats me once, shame fa' him; he that cheats me twice, shame fa' me. — Scottish proverb

If lies were Latin, there would be many scholars. — Danish proverb

The buyer needs a hundred eyes; the seller but one. — Italian proverb

Caveat Emptor

Consider, if you will, a few case histories from the wide world of fraud:

— A young couple visits an abortion clinic to learn if the 21-year-old woman is pregnant. She has brought a urine sample for analysis. After a brief interval, the doctor solemnly reports that the test is positive and the woman is pregnant. For $125, he will perform an abortion that afternoon. But, in fact, the woman is not pregnant. She is an investigator for the New York City Department of Consumer Affairs, and the urine sample, which the doctor found positive, was not hers, but her male partner's. After two years of hearings and appeals, the doctor's license is revoked.

— Several jewelry dealers in New York's world-famous diamond district are arrested for selling "painted" diamonds to consumers. The merchants apply an artificial chemical coating to the gems to disguise flaws and improve their appearance. As part of the scheme, dealers urge consumers to have their diamonds appraised before making their purchase, and offer to refer them to an appraiser. The "independent" appraiser, receiving regular kickbacks, supplies grossly exaggerated estimates to encourage the victims to buy. An unknown number of consumers are taken in by this scheme. In court, three convicted merchants are sentenced—to pay fines of $1,000 each.

—A prominent carpet company requires its customers to sign a delivery receipt. The statement "received the above in good condition" appears on the carbon copy of the form—but not on the top page, which the customer signs.

—At a gift shop catering to tourists, an elderly woman browses among the trinkets, ornamental plates, and assorted curios. A salesman, falsely identifying himself as the owner of the store, tells her a long, involved story, ending with the sad fact that the store will have to go out of business unless the "owner" can raise money quickly. The sympathetic woman is talked into lending the store her life savings, over $5,000. As collateral, she receives merchandise worth $200. When she later tries to get her money back, she's told that the store regards the transaction as a sale—and that all sales are final.

—A literary agent solicits manuscripts from unpublished authors. A woman from the Midwest sends in a novel which is, by any literary standard, dreadful. The agent praises it effusively and says the chances of publication are excellent. Of course, he adds, the work must be properly edited. Because he's so enthusiastic about the book, he'll do the job himself—for a reasonable fee. His "careful editing," for which he charges $800, consists of slashing numerous large X's across the manuscript pages. Soon after, the agent informs his disappointed client that no publisher wants her book—but he can get it published by a "vanity press," *if* she'll pay publication costs.

—In response to his request for information, a young man receives a letter from the director of a dating service. It begins:

> Dear _____.
>
> I have your message here and I am going to handle it myself. I have definitely given thousands of people like yourself a reason for living, and can do the same for you. (YOU MUST HAVE SOMEONE TO LOVE.) My only regret is that I can't afford to give you free service. You are certainly not like the average person that contacts me and it makes me very happy to write to a person like you.

It is a form letter sent to everyone who writes to the company.

These incidents illustrate the fact that fraud and deceit can be found in a wide variety of settings and situations. Of course, every industry and trade has its marginal operators, who work at illegal pursuits on the fringes of society. But unfortunately, deceptions and unfair dealings sometimes occur among legitimate sellers as well. In 1885, Oliver Wendell Holmes wrote: "The standard of good faith required in sales is somewhat low." It is still "somewhat low" today: sales talk is untrustworthy; advertising is unbelievable; poorly made goods disintegrate before our eyes; and the burgeoning repair industry bears silent witness to the breakdown of all things large and small. There is hardly a consumer drawing breath who hasn't, at one time or another, felt tricked, cajoled, hoodwinked, lied to, fooled, or misled.

WATCH OUT FOR THESE COMMON CONSUMER FRAUDS

I heard I could earn big money as a truck driver. A fast-talking salesman made training sound simple, and jobs easy to find. So I took his training course, for $1,200. I've been unemployed ever since.

I saw an ad for "beautiful Texas wildflowers." I sent my money to "Wildflowers, Box 33, Sagebrush, Texas." That was six years ago. I'm still waiting for the flowers.

I went to a dance studio that advertised ten lessons for ten dollars. My charming instructor gave me a dance test, and raved about my wonderful rhythm. She also signed me up for $6,250 worth of lessons.

A nice young man came to my door with a "revolutionary" new vacuum cleaner. He said its price was "only $5 a week." He didn't say it would take 108 weeks to pay -- or that I could find an equally revolutionary machine in any department store for half the price.

In the following chapters we highlight specific consumer minefields. But first, we'll look at how fraud grew and why it flourishes today.

A BRIEF HISTORY OF FRAUD

The great stream of modern American trade can be traced back to the trickle of commerce in medieval Europe. As long ago as the thirteenth century, we find Berthold von Regensberg, an itinerant preacher, excoriating the early tradesmen, declaring: "There is so much fraud and falsehood and blasphemy that no man can tell it." The clothing makers "steal half the cloth"; masons paid by the day "stand . . . idle, that they may multiply the days at their work"; blacksmiths "wilt shoe a steed . . . and the beast will go perchance scarce a mile thereon when it is already broken"; wine makers "betray folk with corrupt wine or mouldy beer, or unsodden mead, or give false measure, or mix water with the wine"; tillers "lay fine corn at the top of the sack, and evil corn beneath"; bakers "bake rotten corn to bread, whereby a man may lightly eat his own death."* The litany, though seven centuries old, has a certain sound of familiarity, does it not?

Despite these strong words, it is unlikely that fraud blossomed in the Middle Ages. Merchants and traders dealt within very limited geographic bounds, with those they knew and who knew them. Sharp practices were soon discovered and known throughout the community. The medieval Church, with its considerable authority, condemned deceit and declared its motivating force, avarice, a deadly sin. At the large mercantile fairs, where groups of merchants exhibited their wares and sold to strangers, weights and measures were carefully taken and the ethical character of trade was strictly enforced by official rules.

When market towns replaced fairs as the focus of trade and commerce, strict regulation of merchandise quality and price prevailed. Violators received direct, swift, and public punishment. Cheats might be ignominiously paraded through the streets with trumpets blaring, or have their heads and hands locked in the public pillory for all to see (while their goods were burned at their feet), or be banished from the community for a year and a day. Exposure to public scorn and ridicule served to deter those tempted to give less than fair value and decent wares to their customers.

As business expanded in size and influence, the modes of trade became more impersonal and less responsive to local standards of fairness. The warning *caveat emptor*—buyer beware—began to be heard in the seventeenth century. Despite the Latin words, the phrase did not originate in ancient Rome, nor was it a legal term. It was merely a common-sense warning that, when dealing with rogues and strangers you might never see again, you had better be very careful. Some pretentious person, probably a medieval lawyer, translated the advice into Latin.

Unfortunately for the consuming public, eighteenth- and nineteenth-century English and American courts took this simple adage and elevated it into an exalted legal doctrine. The seller who misrepresented wares suddenly had a legal defense: the deceived buyer should have ignored the seller's words and independently sought out the truth. The new rule was applied in the most outrageous circumstances: in one case, a seller misrepresented 32,000 acres of rocky, inaccessible mountain land in Virginia to be rich, arable farmland. The buyer paid 25 cents an acre (a goodly sum in 1794),

* Von Regensberg's sermon on Tricks of Trade appears in G. Coulton, *Life in the Middle Ages,* Vols. III and IV (Cambridge, Eng.: University Press, 1967), pp. 57–62.

Edict of Louis XI, King of France
A.D. 1481

"Anyone who sells butter containing stones or other

things (to add to the weight) will be put into our

pillory, then said butter will be placed on his head

until entirely melted by the sun. Dogs may lick him

and people offend him with whatever defamatory

epithets they please without offense to God or King.

If the sun is not warm enough, the accused will

be exposed in the great hall of the gaol in front of

a roaring fire, where everyone will see him."

discovered the fraud, and sued for his money back. Despite the clear deceit, the court ruled for the seller, on the grounds of *caveat emptor*. Fair dealing in the marketplace lost its legal support. The new rule for sales, roughly translated, was "anything goes."

The disastrous rule of *caveat emptor,* providing legal protection to cheats and defrauders, stubbornly persisted through two centuries of American law. With the twentieth-century revolutions in technology, transportation, and communication, however, the consumer needed protection from deceit more than ever. Goods became too complicated for even the most sophisticated buyers to analyze intelligently prior to purchase. Social pressure to behave with integrity lost its effectiveness with the advent of large national corporations, manufacturing goods far from their many places of sale. The network of mass communications magnified deceptions into nationwide frauds, and the expansion of consumer credit raised the retail stakes to unprecedented heights, making fraud and sharp practice even more harmful.

A movement to protect the consumer arose, spurred by muckraking writers like Upton Sinclair, who exposed abominable conditions in the nation's meat-packing industry. The Federal Trade Commission was created in 1914 to protect business from unfair competition; it was not until 1938 that the FTC was given the clear mandate to protect consumers from unfair businesses.

Today, a certain tension exists in the law, between the reverberations of *caveat emptor* and the growing, insistent demands for consumer justice. Most legislatures have responded to the latter, enacting a variety of consumer protection statutes. Many judges, however, are still enamored of the pithy Latin phrase and do not adequately recognize or protect consumer rights. For whatever reason, the law's indulgence toward fraud is not entirely at an end. Buyer beware, however bad as law, is still good as advice.

SOME MODERN SALES TRICKS

Consumers suffer two great disadvantages in the modern marketplace. First, they are rarely as knowledgeable as manufacturers about the products they buy. A bewildering variety of complex goods confronts the modern consumer, who has neither the time nor the expertise to evaluate them intelligently. Second, sellers, unlike buyers, come to the market well prepared. Their contracts have been checked by lawyers, their promotional efforts guided by ad agencies. Most important, they know from study, observation, and experience what makes people buy. And some merchants use this knowledge to manipulate us. Subsequent chapters will examine how this is done in different trades, from home improvement rackets to the funeral industry. A number of tricks, however, are common to all trades, and here is a brief guide to some of the games sellers play.

Bait and switch.   Advertising a low-priced item (the "bait") lures customers to a store. Once they are there, salespeople try to "switch" them to purchase more expensive merchandise. In one classic case, a retailer of sewing machines advertised a "special closeout price" of $29.50 on its Magic Stitcher model. When buyers asked to see these bargains, they were told by "helpful" salespeople that the machines required oiling every few minutes; that "you need a five-pound can of grease to pack the bearings"; and that all other appliances in the house had to be turned off when the machine was in use. The clincher: you could lose an eye if the machine jammed and the needle broke. For any who cared to test it out, the Magic Stitcher was rigged so it would jam. Customers were then shown the higher-priced models, which had none of their objectionable features.

Other ways of discouraging buyers' interest in the low-priced "bait" include: displaying the goods at the back of the store, covered with dust and debris; offering unreasonably late delivery dates; claiming the item "just sold out ten minutes ago"; and loosening bolts and screws (on appliances) so they will vibrate and rattle noisily when turned on. Some sellers even deface their own merchandise. One salesman for a large department store told the FTC that his divisional supervisor once took "a big rubber mallet . . . and banged a dent in the side of a washing machine" that was advertised as on sale. Many disappointed customers, upon seeing the damaged sale machine, let themselves be talked into buying the store's more expensive washers.

Nail-downs.   A cousin of bait and switch, this scheme involves goods displayed to generate business—but which the store will never sell. In the vernacular of the trade, these goods are "nailed to the floor." Attractive nail-downs are put in the store window with low price tags, to bring in customers. Then they are disparaged, or are unavailable; they are mere props in the sell-

For information on obtaining copies of "The Victorious Victim," write to: Consumer Law Training Center, New York Law School, 57 Worth Street, New York, N.Y. 10013.

ing game. As one sales manager told his crew about a television set supposedly on sale: "Any guy who lets that set go out the door, goes with it."

Phony "sales." Words like "sale" and "bargain" are often used to mislead customers. Some merchants artificially inflate their prices one week in order to advertise large price reductions the next. The local supermarket may advertise attractive "specials" but then fail to have the items on the shelf. Another trick is illustrated by the furniture seller who featured a bargain on bunkbeds: "only $39.95." That price, however, did not include either mattresses or bedsprings. The real cost for the beds: $123.95.

Toss-over selling. In the toss-over, a hesitant buyer is turned from one salesperson to another, until he or she either decides to buy or runs screaming from the store. The sales agent who isn't succeeding with a customer simply signals for reinforcements. A new, fresh approach may work, or more sales talk may simply wear the customer down. The toss-over serves the crucial function of preventing the customer from leaving the store. As long as the consumer remains, there is hope for a sale. Sellers know that most people, out of politeness, will allow themselves to be subjected to a whole new sales pitch.

Guilt techniques. Some sellers try to make you aware of the help they've given you—and of their expectation that you will reciprocate. The way to indicate your gratitude for their time, effort, and patience, of course, is to buy. Personalizing the sale transaction forces the buyer to say "no" to another person's face—something most people hate to do. To avoid disappointing a friendly salesperson, some people will buy things they don't want, and later wonder, "Why did I ever buy this?"

"Closing" techniques. Closing a sale means finishing it—getting the customer's cash, check, signature, or deposit. Approaching the close is a delicate operation for a seller. No matter what has gone before, the consumer, faced with the need to act, may suddenly balk. A seller will not want to leave the consumer alone at this point. It is important to be there—to help the consumer fight off doubts, to support the inclination to buy, and to attack any desire to "think it over." In this critical moment, the seller will debunk careful thought as indecisiveness and gently pressure the buyer to decide right away. This is the time sellers remind consumers of the free gifts, the special discounts, and the other sundry inducements available "this time only." If a contract is involved, salespeople do their best to deflect attention from it, treating the crucial document as a mere "formality" not requiring discussion.

GOVERNMENT AGENCIES AND FRAUD

A few people naïvely believe that if they are victimized by some fraud all they need do is contact a local, state, or federal agency to resolve the problem. This is unfortunately not realistic, even when the consumer is completely in the right. Although many consumer protection agencies do obtain refunds for some consumers, they are unsuccessful in at least twice as many cases. In addition, the refunds obtained are often for much less than the consumer sought. The reasons for this vary from agency to agency, but they usually consist of one or more of the following:

Inadequate resources. Few consumer bureaus have enough staff and budget to handle thoroughly all the complaints they receive. The big-city agencies can usually resolve only a small percentage of the problems reported to them. The rest may be treated in a hasty, routine manner, and dropped if a quick resolution is not possible.

Personnel. A competent, dedicated, hard-working staff can accomplish a great deal. Too many government offices, however, are staffed by low-paid, poorly motivated, and inexperienced individuals.

Insufficient power. State anti-fraud laws are not always up to the task. They may not give the agency the ability to hold hearings, for example, or may not authorize consumer agencies to obtain refunds for the victims of fraud. As a consequence, violators of consumer laws are merely ordered to stop their illegal behavior—but not to return their illegal gains. This is the fault of the state legislatures, which pass consumer laws with great fanfare, but, yielding to the pressure of the business community, put no teeth into their enforcement.

Politicization. Government agencies are subject to political pressures from all sorts of people: governors, legislators, congresspeople, lobbyists, pressure groups, campaign contributors. Some of their requests are proper, some are improper. Not all agency officials can tell the difference, however.

Lack of consumer input. Consumer agencies are flooded with advice, suggestions, and well-presented evidence from representatives of the industries and businesses they regulate. Unfortunately, they do not receive the same kind of input from consumers, who are unable to spend hours preparing testimony, gathering expert opinions, and otherwise countering industry positions on important consumer issues. Even when consumers register complaints, they do so in a casual, unstructured, and sometimes incoherent way. This imbalance would have been corrected on the federal level by the passage of the bill to create a federal consumer protection agency. That agency would have presented the consumer viewpoint to all other agencies whose actions affect consumer interests, but to date the bill has been defeated in Congress, thanks to a massive lobbying effort by business groups.

Difficulties of proof. Some consumer agencies can act only when there is provable fraud. A seller who fails to deliver the goods to customers may be a cheat, or may be honest but incompetent. Either way, of course, consumers lose out, but the incompetent seller may escape responsibility under the fraud laws of many states. Since it is often difficult to distinguish the cheat from the incompetent, many cheats also evade punishment.

Most consumer law enforcement agencies handle only the civil (i.e., noncriminal) cases. Those that enforce criminal laws against errant merchants have an even more difficult time. A higher standard of proof (beyond a "reasonable doubt") is required in criminal cases, necessitating much more investigative work. In addition, the accused in a criminal case enjoys the constitutional privilege against self-incrimination, making evidence gathering considerably more difficult. Finally, judges often do not treat "white collar" crime seriously. After months of hard work to gain a conviction, the prosecutor may hear the judge impose a $50 fine or some equivalent "slap on the wrist" penalty. Needless to say, this does not encourage future prosecutions, a fact which is very well understood by unethical individuals in the business community.

SEVEN AXIOMS FOR AVOIDING SWINDLES

1. Don't buy something because you like the salesperson—you have to live with the product, not the seller.

2. Be suspicious of "special deals," free gifts, and other inducements to "act now." Important purchases must be carefully considered, outside the presence of salespeople.

3. Beware of sales agents who run down their own merchandise or who find excuses not to sell you their lower-priced goods.

4. Investigate the reliability of unfamiliar merchants by checking with friends, local consumer agencies, the Better Business Bureau.

5. Don't rely on verbal promises or arrangements which are not in the contract. Ask that any verbal assurances be put in writing.

6. Shop around, to compare prices and quality. Swindlers usually price their goods very high, relying on their victim's ignorance, or very low, relying on their victim's greed.

7. Be suspicious of items promoted at "giveaway" prices and of all "too good to be true" offers. Something for nothing only occurs when you give up something and get nothing.

5

Car buying

(co-authored by A. Stanley Kramer)

For many Americans the automobile was a symbol of freedom, a badge of equality, useful for transportation but essential for social intercourse and self-respect. It gave the national propensity for mobility and the restless mania for speed new and easy outlets. The automobile broke down isolation and provincialism, promoted standardization, accelerated the growth of cities at the expense of villages and then of suburbs at the expense of cities, created a hundred new industries and millions of new jobs, and required the destruction of large parts of the country to make way for roads and by-passes. It precipitated new problems of morals and of crime, and took an annual toll of life and limb as high as that exacted by the First World War.
— Samuel Eliot Morison, Henry Steele Commager, and William E. Leuchtenberg, *The Growth of the American Republic,* Vol. II

It's a lean car . . . a long-legged car . . .
  a gray-ghost eagle car.
The feet of it eat the dirt of a road . . .
  the wings of it eat the hills.
Danny the driver dreams of it when he sees
  women in red skirts and red sox in his sleep.
It is in Danny's life and runs in the blood of him . . .
  a lean gray-ghost car.   — CARL SANDBURG, "Portrait of a Motorcar"*

On July 1, 1899, the magazine *Harper's Weekly* eagerly anticipated the time when the family horse would be parked in the pasture, and the family car installed in its place. The horse, it complains, "eats from infancy to old age, he is apt to be of inferior quality, and even when good he is very perishable."† Other commentators in the first decade of the century called the horse unreliable, unsafe, a source of traffic congestion, and a willful beast with a mind of its own.

In the intervening years, the car proved itself to be as difficult as the

* From *Cornhuskers,* by Carl Sandburg, copyright 1918 by Holt, Rinehart and Winston, Inc., copyright 1946 by Carl Sandburg. Reprinted by permission of Harcourt Brace Jovanovich, Inc.
† Quoted in James J. Flink, *America Adopts the Automobile, 1895–1910* (Cambridge: MIT Press, 1970).

horse. Gas replaced oats, but poor quality, unreliability, danger, and unpredictability are still parked outside our doors. Despite all this, Americans have managed to transfer their love from the horse and buggy to the miracle of movable iron. Since the purchase of cars constitutes a major expense for consumers (and since you can't look a car in the mouth) this chapter will offer some suggestions on how to select the best car for yourself.

SELECTING A NEW CAR

There are over 250 different models of automobiles sold in America today. This implies a vast choice for the car-buying public, but the vastness is illusory. Beneath their shiny surfaces, many cars are just copies of one another. Contrary to the impression given by annual style changes, the auto industry is in fact experiencing an increasing trend toward standardization. Occasionally, different models from the same manufacturer (e.g., the Dodge Aspen and the Plymouth Volare, both made by Chrysler Corporation) are produced on the same assembly line.

In 1977 the similarity of General Motors cars was brought to public at-

The workshop where Henry Ford built his first automobile in 1893. (Ford Archives / Henry Ford Museum, Dearborn, Mich.)

tention when an Illinois man found a Chevrolet engine in his new Oldsmobile. The discovery was duplicated by thousands of other buyers across
the country, who felt cheated. While General Motors agreed to refund some
money to its unhappy customers, it pointed out that all of its 350-cubic-inch
V-8 engines are alike, no matter what type automobile they eventually in-
habit. In fact, GM continues to make engines at centralized facilities, from
which they are shipped to the various GM divisions. The company's mistake
was not in making a standard engine (or should we say, a general motor),
but in heavily advertising and promoting Oldsmobile's as a superior "Rocket
Engine." This phony claim established a clear case of deceptive advertising.
After this incident, General Motors began including in its advertising a
statement saying that its cars were "equipped with GM-built engines produced by various divisions."

Despite all the sameness in the automobile market, there are still important distinctions among cars put out by different manufacturers. Every year
a handful of cars stand out from the pack, and every year a few clunkers appear that make the rest look good by comparison. Unfortunately, the average buyer doesn't have the expertise to figure out which is which. For example, the 1971-to-1976 Ford Pintos were designed in such a way that they
posed a serious risk of fire and instant death in the event of a rear-end
collision. No consumer, of course, could tell this from looking at the car, nor
from test-driving it.

There are expert opinions available to the car buyer willing to do some
simple research. Two automotive magazines, *Car & Driver* and *Road and
Track,* test new cars and report on their findings. A more accessible source

Safety is an important factor in choosing a car. (Ralph Crane, *Life,* © 1963 Time Inc.)

of expertise for the non-auto buff is the annual April auto issue of *Consumer Reports* magazine. Here's what their experts report on:

- On-the-road performance. Test drivers evaluate engine performance, handling, maneuverability, braking power, transmission, and smoothness of ride.
- Gasoline mileage. Official Environmental Protection Agency mileage ratings appear on new-car stickers, but they are much too generous. No ordinary driver could possibly expect to match the fuel efficiency figures put out by EPA, whose ratings are based on laboratory, not road, conditions (EPA mileage ratings are useful, though, in comparing models). The magazine computes miles per gallon based on actual driving experience. Generally, among cars of a given horsepower and weight, there is little difference in fuel mileage.
- Safety. Experts check seat belts' location and ease of use, fuel-tank protection (a potentially fatal matter if a crash occurs), and effectiveness of head restraints, window defrosters, and dashboard controls.
- Predicted repair incidence. The magazine does a huge survey of its readership to determine car owners' actual repair experience. Often models exhibit the same problems year after year—an important point for new-car buyers.
- Comfort and convenience. This covers such matters as interior noise level, heater and air-conditioner effectiveness, and driver and passenger seating comfort.

Based on its findings, *Consumer Reports* indicates the cars which it believes deserve buyer preference.

IN THE SHOWROOM

After reading what the experts have to say about the new cars, plan to visit several dealers. Comparison shopping can pay large dividends in the car-buying field. Keep in mind too that 15 to 20 percent reductions can be realized by buying last year's model.

For any car you are interested in, follow these steps:

1. Find out its list price *without options* (if the list price doesn't include the dealer preparation charge, add it in).

2. Next, decide on the options you want. Buy no more than you really need, since they are expensive and add up quickly. Beware of buying cars on the sales floor—they are usually loaded with extras, to ensure that people in a hurry for delivery pay the maximum for their cars. Beware also of pressure to purchase a "package" of several options (dealers make nice profits on these "packs"). Find out the list price for each option you want (see the price stickers on the floor model or ask the dealer), and add it to the basic car price.

3. Negotiate a good deal for yourself. No one pays the list price, but dealers use it as a starting point for bargaining. The real price falls somewhere between the list and the dealer's cost. *Consumer Reports'* annual auto issue will supply you with the dealer's cost for most cars. How well you do in striking a deal depends on how insistent you are on a better price, how anxious you seem to be to make the purchase, and how fast the particular dealer is selling that particular model to other customers.

4. Once you've heard the dealer's best offer, say, "It sounds a bit high, but I'll think it over." Then see what you can get elsewhere. Call other dealers, inform them of the price you've been offered, and ask if they can better it. A few calls may save you $100 or more. And don't be surprised if the first dealer calls you back, offering a lower price.

5. Of course, price is not the only important factor in choosing a dealer. Since you will be going back for service under the warranty, you also want someone who is conveniently located and reliable. If friends and associates have had positive experiences with a particular dealer, that is a big plus, worth a higher price. Check with the Better Business Bureau and consumer protection agencies to avoid those dealerships which generate many consumer complaints.

SHOWROOM SHENANIGANS

When buying a new car, watch out for these common sales tricks:

THE LOW BALL: A salesman, seeing you have just begun shopping for a good price, quotes a very low figure he knows other dealers can't match. You leave, visit other showrooms, and return later only to find that the salesman forgot the previous offer or says he made a mistake.

THE HIGH BALL: Also a trap for the comparative shopper. The saleswoman quotes you a high figure on your trade-in car. When it comes time to close the deal, she becomes terribly apologetic, claims the car isn't worth what she thought originally, and gives you less on the trade-in than you expected.

BUSHING: Just when the deal seems complete, the salesman tells you the manager won't approve the low price. The salesman, acting more upset than you are, argues with the manager and gets the $200 increase down to $75. The manager threatens to fire him for selling cars at cost. You're out an extra $75.

BILL PADDING: Added to your bill are surprise extras you never discussed, such as waxing or undercoating which the dealer claims to have done. As a variation, the seller charges you for "options" which in fact are standard equipment on the car you ordered.

DOUBLE TICKETING: The saleswoman notifies you, at or prior to delivery, of an increase in the factory price of your car. Check the factory stickers to determine if this is true. In a few places, like New York, new laws forbid contract clauses which allow the dealer to pass on price increases to the buyer.

"Know what I'm going to do? I'm going to load you with extras!"

(*The New Yorker*)

LEMONS

Substandard cars roll off every manufacturer's assembly line. These four-wheel disasters have given a bad name to a perfectly respectable fruit, the lemon.

Auto companies and their dealers are very reluctant to refund a buyer's money or to replace a bad car with one that works. Instead, they will try to repair any defects you find. Normally this will be satisfactory, but for the real lemons, no amount of repair work is sufficient.

What can a lemon owner do? Experience has shown that, in this situation, only the toughest customers can get action. Under the law, you are entitled to "revoke acceptance" and get a refund if your new car cannot be put into good working order. You must, however, (1) inform the dealer of the defects in the car soon after you discover them (be as specific as you can about the problems, and don't leave anything out) and (2) give the dealer a "reasonable" opportunity to fix them (it is not clear how many trips to and from the shop constitute a "reasonable" number). If your car can't be fixed, you are likely to get a runaround: the dealer will tell you to complain to the manufacturer, the manufacturer will tell you to try to get it repaired again, and no one will offer you a refund. At this point, firm action is ·necessary. Some consumers have hired lawyers and brought suit to get their money back, and won. In court, judges and juries are very sympathetic to the exasperated consumer (they own cars too, after all). In addition, the mere prospect of having your case aired in court is so distasteful to the car companies that they'll often offer a refund or a replacement to avoid a trial. While lawyers' fees are expensive, you may, under the new Magnuson-Moss Warranty Act, be able to win them back in the lawsuit (see chapter 2 for more on warranties and chapter 16 for more on auto repairs).

Other embittered lemon owners have picketed dealerships and passed out leaflets describing the kind of car they received. In a few places, lemon purchasers have found one another and created "lemonstrations"—demonstrations at which they put their defective cars on public display. These tactics can be very successful, especially if they draw the attention of local newspapers or television stations. Auto dealers hate nothing more than bad publicity, and often they will immediately resolve any complaints that cause it. (For a fuller discussion of picketing and other direct action tactics, see chapter 30.)

To bring additional pressure to bear, let the seller know you are complaining to all of the following: the Federal Trade Commission (6th and Pennsylvania Avenue, N.W., Washington, D.C. 20580), the Center for Auto Safety (1223 Dupont Circle, Washington, D.C. 20036), and the National Automobile Dealers Association (8400 Westpark Drive, McLean, Va. 22101).

HOW TO FINANCE YOUR CAR

If you are not paying cash for your car, consider carefully the alternative ways to finance your purchase. Avoid the common mistake of accepting without question the dealer's offer to extend you credit. The dealer's credit may cost you considerably more than financing available elsewhere. You could lose in higher interest payments all the money you saved by comparative shopping for the car!

Check out these preferable sources of auto loans:

+ a "passbook" loan from your savings bank;
+ borrowing against a life insurance policy;
+ a credit union loan;
+ a commercial bank auto loan.

These credit sources are discussed in detail in chapter 19.

SELECTING A USED CAR

Buying a used car is a tricky business. You can get a well-maintained, moderately used vehicle at a fair price, or an old repainted taxicab driven to the point of disintegration and then carefully touched up to look fresh and healthy. Which type you get depends on how well prepared you are when you enter the used-car marketplace.

Used cars are sold by independent used-car sellers, by new-car dealers, and by private individuals. Of these, the most consistently reliable are the new-car dealers, who commonly sell relatively late model cars in good mechanical condition. These dealers sometimes receive low-quality trade-ins, but they usually unload them in the wholesale vehicle market. They have extensive repair facilities and offer the best warranties. The mechanics in any new-car dealership are experienced in reconditioning and servicing their own brand of car. In sum, when buying from the new-car seller, you may pay a higher price for a used car, but you're more likely to get a decent vehicle of reasonable quality. In a market filled with rattletraps, heaps and clunkers, this is no small matter.

Independent used-car lots carry a wide range of cars, some of which are in very poor or even dangerous condition. Often salespeople are quick to reassure buyers about the safety and dependability of a car, when in fact they know nothing of its prior history or need for repair. While some used-car dealers maintain service facilities, many do not, and most will make no effort to upgrade a vehicle in need of repair. The "bargains" on the used-car lot may seem cheap merely because several hundred dollars' worth of repairs await the unsuspecting purchaser.

Another problem in buying from used-car dealers is that they don't always stand by their backfiring merchandise. Many give no warranty at all, selling cars "as is" (a few states, such as Massachusetts, make "as is" car sales illegal). Salespeople on the lot frequently make soothing statements to the effect that "if there's a problem, don't worry, we'll take care of it," but the sales contract promises nothing of the kind, and car buyers who expect dealer servicing soon find that the unwritten warranty is worthless.

To sweeten the deal for a hesitant buyer, a used-car seller may offer a "50-50" warranty, in which the dealer promises to fix the car and to split the repair costs with the purchaser. This arrangement is usually unsatisfactory, however, because many dealers simply inflate the repair bill, to ensure that your "equal" share covers most of their share too.

Buying from a private party can be a less pressured experience. Even if the individual is trying to hide something, he or she usually lacks the dealer's skill in doing so. Because individuals don't have overhead or sales expenses, you should be able to buy at a true wholesale price. It is to your advantage to meet the previous owner, so you can make some intelligent estimation of the owner's concern for car maintenance.

There are several hazards involved in buying from private parties, however. People getting rid of merchandise normally refuse to invest any money in its upkeep. In fact, the need for an expensive tune-up or overhaul may have prompted the owner to sell the car in the first place. Since sales by private parties never involve warranties, it is important to examine the car thoroughly. The best protection is to drive it to a mechanic or diagnostic center, where for $20 to $30 you'll get an expert analysis of the car's condition. Once you know what's wrong, you can bargain for a lower price. Of course, if there's real trouble ahead, look elsewhere. An added precaution recommended prior to purchase from a stranger is a call to the local police (to see if the car is on the "hot" list).

(Photo by Elliott Erwitt, © Magnum Photos)

TIPS IN JUDGING A USED CAR

1. Never judge a car solely by its appearance. Used-car dealers have made cosmetic retouching a fine art. To conceal wear and tear, they'll shampoo the upholstery, dye the carpeting, steam-clean the engine, paint over rust, and polish the chrome. There's even a commercial spray that duplicates the *smell* of a new car.

2. Look carefully at places where wear and tear show up first: on the driver's seat, the floor mats, the pedal pads, and the armrests. Loose door handles, rust around door frames and in other nooks and crannies, and deeply etched marks on the windshield where the wiper blades pass, all represent signs of heavy use. If the car interior seems completely *un*worn, beware also—you may be looking at a much-used vehicle extensively touched up to hide its age.

3. Don't trust the seller to tell you what you need to know about a car. In a survey performed in San Diego, California, test shoppers for a public interest group, posing as ordinary customers, visited used-car dealers and took cars they were shown to professional mechanics. The shoppers then told the used-car sellers exactly what defects were found, showed them copies of the diagnostic reports, and terminated further negotiations. A second set of test shoppers then visited the dealers and expressed interest in those same cars. Seventy-six out of 101 sellers did *not* reveal the defects they knew about—even when they posed significant safety hazards. Of the salespeople that did disclose what they knew, over half could do so without a problem because the diagnoses were relatively favorable. Only a small fraction of dealers felt the moral obligation to reveal important negative information about the cars they sold. Numerous consumer complaints and investigations also corroborate that sellers often deny the existence of serious problems.

4. Don't buy at the used-car dealer's listed price. This is a figure which is set high for bargaining purposes. As a guide to the value of any used car, you should check the *National Automobile Dealers Association Official Used Car Guide* or the *Kelley Blue Book Auto Market Report*. These two compilations are commonly used in the trade, and you can find them at banks or other lenders which give used-car loans or at any used-car dealership. The prices in these books are averages, based on recent selling prices across the country. The "books" only give you a rough reference point for thinking about price. For any given car, the price will vary depending upon its mechanical condition, options and accessories, and mileage.

5. Beware of odometer fraud. Federal law prohibits sellers from setting back mileage readings on odometers,‡ but the practice doubtless still continues. Since a major factor in used-car value is mileage, a seller may stand to make $1,000 or more by setting back the odometer on a used car. Sometimes the digits on the odometer do not line up right. This is an indication of

‡ 15 U.S.C. 1981.

tampering. Don't trust a low or moderate mileage reading if the interior or exterior of the car shows signs of wear or corrosion.

The law entitles you to a statement that the odometer mileage is accurate to the best of the dealer's knowledge. If you suspect odometer fraud, steer clear of the seller and report your suspicions to the local district attorney, consumer bureau, or the U. S. Department of Transportation (400 7th Street, S.W., Washington, D.C. 20590). If you are the victim of odometer tampering, you may sue the seller for a minimum of $1,500 penalty plus your attorney's fees.

6. Don't buy a car that's been subject to excessive use by a previous owner. Some dealers will try to sell you a former police car (minus the siren and the flashing lights) if you let them. Used commercial vehicles (those owned by taxi companies, state and local governments, rent-a-car companies, and corporations) are often driven into the ground (and thence to the used-car lot).

7. Always ask the seller for the name and address of the car's previous owner. Under the federal law regulating odometers, the seller should have a signed statement from the previous owner certifying the accuracy of the recorded mileage. This statement will provide you with the information you need to locate the previous owner. Find out whether the car was ever in an accident, whether it had any serious mechanical problems, and why it was sold.

8. Examine the car on a sunny day, never in the rain or at night. It is not always easy to detect body damage, corrosion, and other evidence of overuse even in the best of circumstances. Inspections in the rain tend to be brief, and the water may hide rust, flaws in the paint job, and other problems.

9. Test-drive the car over different kinds of roads—straight, steep, bumpy, curving. Try it on a highway as well as on local streets. Note any funny noises, roughness in the engine, difficulty in shifting gears, etc. Test the brakes and all the accessories. If you find anything the least suspicious, ask an expert what it means. Sometimes a knock or a rattle means nothing, and sometimes it portends a major breakdown.

10. Watch out for cars that have been submerged under water. After severe winter and early-spring storms, plenty of water-damaged cars appear in the nation's used-car lots, usually at low prices. These cars deteriorate fast, so avoid them at any price. Check for a waterline mark, discolored fabric, a whitish coating on aluminum and chrome parts, or corrosion of copper and brass. Submersion in a flood is one of those minor incidents a salesperson may "forget" to tell you about.

11. See if the dealer pays shop mechanics "piece-rates" (by the job) or just a straight salary. If and when you need repairs, paying by the piece usually costs more and sometimes results in hurried work (since the mechanic who works quickly earns more).

12. Make sure you aren't buying a car that has been the subject of a safety or emission-control recall. Millions of cars are recalled every year

(65 million since 1966), so this is not a remote possibility. Sometimes a manufacturer's entire output for one year is recalled, as happened to American Motors Corporation when the Environmental Protection Agency ordered the recall of virtually all 1976 AMC cars because of a faulty exhaust system. Current safety investigations involve models from all manufacturers, and cover defects which could result in loss of brakes, of steering control, and of engine power. You can find out if a particular make and model has been recalled by calling the toll-free number of the National Highway Traffic Safety Administration (800-424-9393) or writing to the Office of Defects Investigation, NHTSA, U. S. Department of Transportation, 400 7th Street, S.W., Washington, D.C. 20590.

CAR MAINTENANCE

Good maintenance lengthens the life of a car, improves its performance, and increases its resale value. Your basic guide to maintenance is the Owner's Manual, which comes with the car. It contains the manufacturer's recommendations for your particular automobile. Look there for information on what type of gasoline to use, when to replace parts such as spark plugs, oil filter, and air cleaner, and how to break in the car. More extensive information appears in the Owner's Service Manual, also available from car manufacturers on request.

Here is a brief rundown of major points to monitor:

Air conditioner. If you have one, let a mechanic check the refrigerant and the system once a year, before the summer. Operate it once every few weeks during the rest of the year to keep it in good running order.

Battery. Check the water level once or twice a month; add water as needed. Watch for corrosion where the cables connect to the battery.

Brakes. These usually require little attention. If the brake pedal responds sluggishly, however, have the brake system checked right away. Brake fluid and linings generally need inspection after several thousand miles (see Owner's Manual for specific mileage).

Engine cooling system. Have the level of water or coolant in the radiator checked regularly. Add antifreeze in winter to protect the engine from the very lowest temperatures expected.

Leaks. Make a habit of checking for leaks of gasoline, oil, water, or brake or transmission fluid around the car. Gasoline and fluid leaks should be attended to immediately.

Lights. Every once in a while, check all the car lights—headlights, turn signals, brake lights, and emergency blinkers.

Oil and lubrication. Check the oil level every second or third time you buy gas. Use the type of oil recommended by the manufacturer for the climate you are in and avoid oil additives. Chassis lubrication is needed at intervals between 3,000 and 10,000 miles, depending on the car (check the Owner's Manual).

Spark plugs. These should last a long time. They are often replaced at the

10,000-mile tune-up, but on newer cars with electrical ignition systems they may last for 25,000 miles.

Tires. Check tire pressure frequently with a portable tire pressure gauge (garage air pumps are very often inaccurate). Follow the manufacturer's tire pressure recommendations carefully. Inspect the tires for uneven tread wear and for cuts and bruises. Improperly inflated tires will cause poor steering control and front-end misalignment. Misalignment may also result from driving over rough, pothole-strewn roads.

Transmission fluid. Special fluid is required for the transmission, and its level should be checked at regular intervals (there is a dipstick for this purpose under the hood). Follow the manufacturer's specifications on how often the fluid should be drained and refilled.

Waxing and polishing. A twice-a-year waxing protects against rust and keeps your car looking shiny. Use fine steel wool to ward off rusting, and polish chrome parts with one of the special liquid polishes on the market.

SELECTED BIBLIOGRAPHY

Common Sense in Buying a New Car, Common Sense in Buying a Safe Used Car, and *How to Deal with Motor Vehicle Emergencies,* available from the Office of Public Affairs and Consumer Services, National Highway Traffic Safety Administration, U. S. Department of Transportation, 400 7th Street, S.W., Washington, D.C. 20590.

Consumer Reports 1978–79 Guide to Used Cars and *Consumer Reports Annual Buying Guide* (by the editors of *Consumer Reports,* 1978).

Consumer Tire Guide, available from the Tire Industry Safety Council, Suite 766, National Press Building, Washington, D.C. 20004.

Down Easter's Lemon Guide, available from the Maine Bureau of Consumer Protection, State House, Augusta, Me. 04333.

How to Buy a Used Car, available from Book Department, Consumers Union, Orangeburg, N.Y. 10962.

"Managing Your Auto Insurance," Parts I and II. *Consumer Reports,* June and July 1977.

NADER, RALPH. *Unsafe at Any Speed.* New York: Bantam Books, 1973 (expanded edition).

NADER, RALPH, DODGE, LOWELL, and HOTCHKISS, RALF. *What to Do with Your Bad Car.* New York: Bantam Books, 1971.

"1979 Gas Mileage Guide," available from Fuel Economy, Pueblo, Colo. 81009 (published by the U. S. Environmental Protection Agency).

6

Now you see it, now you don't: con games

A fraud is not perfect unless it be practiced on clever persons.

— Arab proverb

Con man and credit trimmer Richard Town had so incurred the wrath of his high-placed victims that in London, on May 23, 1712, he was hanged. . . . Town's open-air execution before a cheering multitude was highlighted by the fact that the day was his birthday. This suave con man stood coolly on the scaffold and shouted in a stentorian voice: "My friends, this is my birthday. I see you have come to help me honor it." To an attractive lady nearby he remarked: "Madam, my compliments, and thank you for coming to my adventure." True to the unruffled demeanor that was to hallmark those of his miscreant trade, Town then adjusted the cap over his head and cavalierly signaled the drop to fall.   — JAY ROBERT NASH, *Hustlers and Con Men*

Many people think of con artists as sly-looking sharpies or carnival hustler types who operate shell games for foolish passers-by. In fact, successful con artists are often honest-looking, friendly, sincere, and conservatively dressed. Many are women, a testament to the equal opportunity nature of the profession. They often work in pairs, although members of a team will pretend to not know each other during a con game. Their victims are drawn from all ranks of society, not just from the uneducated. Many swindles trap well-to-do members of the middle class, who generously support all sorts of cons.

Confidence games come in all shapes and sizes. Some, called "big cons" in the trade, are elaborately planned hoaxes which net thousands of dollars for their perpetrators; other (the "little cons") are quick deceits to gain five or ten dollars, or whatever cash the victim has on hand.

Despite their incredible variety all confidence games have two features in common. First the victim (or "mark") must be persuaded that the confidence man (or woman) is an ally. Second, the mark must be given a reason to participate. Usually it is the promise of a cash reward. Occasionally, it is merely the psychic satisfaction of doing a good deed—helping someone in need or rendering a service to the community. Consider the methods and motivating forces behind the following ruses commonly in use today: the Bank Examiner Swindle, the Pocketbook Drop, and the Handkerchief Switch.

The Bank-Examiner Scam, by Larry Williams

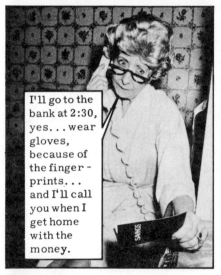

(Originally published in *New York* magazine, January 30, 1978.)

THE BANK EXAMINER SWINDLE

Two practitioners of this scheme, arrested in New York City a few years ago, fleeced elderly widows of over $400,000 in a single six-month period. Widows are a popular target, and can be easily found since they characteristically list themselves as "Mrs. John Smith" in local telephone directories.

Other victims may be spotted in a bank, followed home, and then contacted by telephone. The caller poses as a police detective working with the "State Bank Examiner." He informs the victim that employees at her bank are suspected of stealing from depositors' savings accounts or safe-deposit boxes. The detective asks for the victim's cooperation to catch a suspected teller (sometimes offering a reward for doing so). The victim, carefully warned not to tell anyone what she is about to do, is instructed to go immediately to the bank, visit the teller's window, withdraw all her money, and place it in a plain envelope. Because the money will have the suspected employee's fingerprints on it, she is told, it must be analyzed at a police laboratory. The examiner (or the police detective) will be at the bank to get the envelope. The victim is sometimes told to wear gloves—so her own fingerprints won't be on the money!

The more drama the con artist works into the scene, the more credible it appears to the victim. When the swindler accepts the victim's money at the bank, he may even give her a "receipt" for it, and commend her for her great public spirit, before he disappears forever. The whole scheme is planned to take place quickly, so the victim cannot reflect upon the fact that the police don't ask members of the public to help catch embezzlers, and that embezzled funds are lost not by depositors but by the bank.

THE POCKETBOOK DROP

In this scheme, a stranger, usually a woman, starts up a casual conversation in the street with the victim. Soon another stranger (also a woman) appears, and asks directions. Suddenly she spies an envelope nearby. She asks them what to do with it, and the first stranger suggests they open it. Upon doing so, they find it is full of cash. A note inside indicates the money is from gambling, numbers running, or some other illegal activity. The victim and the two strangers discuss what to do. One of the swindlers says she works for a lawyer in the neighborhood, whom she will consult about the problem.

She leaves and soon returns, stating that her boss said they should divide the money equally since they all know about it, but they must hold on to the money for ninety days before it is legally theirs. The lawyer will give each lucky finder one third of the money, but first they must prove that they won't spend any of the found money for 90 days, by showing the lawyer they possess money of their own. The two swindlers urge the victim to show the lawyer a large sum of cash, and offer to go to her bank with her to make the necessary withdrawal. They do so, and the lawyer's employee volunteers to take the victim's savings to her boss. She leaves, returns, and says the lawyer, now counting her money, wants to talk to her. The victim is given a fictitious name and address for the nonexistent lawyer, and left to go off on a wild-goose chase.

THE HANDKERCHIEF SWITCH

The New York City Police Department describes this ingenious scheme as follows:

> A man is seeking a hotel or rooming house, he can't read or write and asks for your help. He is either a seaman or visitor from another state, settling matters of a deceased relative. He shows a large sum of money and offers to pay for your assistance. Another man will approach, and caution the stranger to put the money in a bank. The newcomer says the hotel sought is demolished, but he knows of a room. The seaman does not trust banks, and suggests you hold his money until he gets the room. You tell him to put the money in a bank. He says he doesn't trust banks, but if you prove you can make a withdrawal, he would put his money in a bank. You go to the bank and make a withdrawal. He insists you hold the money. He gives you his money tied in a kerchief and begs you to be careful. The second man suggests you place your money in the same kerchief for safety. The seaman opens the kerchief and puts your money in with his and ties it up. He will show you how to carry it, under the arm or in the bosom. He may open his jacket or shirt and insert his hand with the kerchief, at this time switching the kerchief for another, identical one. The strangers leave and you examine the handkerchief only to find you can have pieces of newspaper. You have given your money away.

These schemes all have one common element: they present their victims with a dramatic situation which demands immediate attention and requires them to withdraw money from their bank accounts, on the request of a seemingly honest stranger (the con artist). While the swindles may take various forms, their success depends upon the conner's ability to gain quickly the trust of the intended victim. Once the victim's confidence is secured, the rest is generally easy. The scheme may appeal to the victim's good nature (as in the Handkerchief Switch) or to the less noble desire "to get something for nothing" (as in the Pocketbook Drop). Many times too, the swindlers appeal to the victim's desire for company and friendship, and the excitement of a shared adventure.

Not all cons are as elaborate as the ones described above. Some are simple ruses, like the infamous "three-card monte." This is a version of the old shell game. The dealer puts three cards face down on a table; one of them is an ace. Passers-by are invited to bet on their ability to find the ace after the dealer mixes the order of the cards in front of their eyes. A confederate of the dealer, pretending to be just one of the crowd, selects a likely victim, makes some friendly remark, and says the game is easy to win because, unknown to the dealer, the back of the ace is slightly nicked on one corner. To prove the point, the stranger makes a bet or two, and wins. The victim then steps up to the table, makes a larger bet—and loses. The dealer merely palms the nicked card, and substitutes another one with an identical mark on it. Victims can hardly complain about cheating, since they themselves tried to cheat the dealer.

Whether a con game puts the victim "on the send" for more money, or simply goes after the cash he or she is carrying at the time, one thing is almost always certain. Once money is lost in a confidence scheme, there is little chance of its return. Even criminal prosecution (*assuming* the culprits can ever be found) may not turn up all the money lost. The best advice here is: beware and be wary.

A CON GAME FROM THE NINETEENTH CENTURY

Edgar Allan Poe admired the crafty ingenuity of the swindles which prevailed in the nineteenth century. In an essay entitled "Diddling Considered as One of the Exact Sciences," he described some of these con games. The following is an excerpt from that essay:

Again, quite a respectable diddle is this: A well-dressed individual enters a shop; makes a purchase to the value of a dollar; finds, much to his vexation, that he has left his pocket-book in another coat pocket; and so says to the shop-keeper—

"My dear sir, never mind!—just oblige me, will you, by sending the bundle home? But stay! I really believe that I have nothing less than a five dollar bill, even there. However, you can send four dollars in change with the bundle, you know."

"Very good, sir," replies the shop-keeper, who entertains, at once, a lofty opinion of the high-mindedness of his customer. "I know fellows," he says to himself, "who would just have put the goods under their arm, and walked off with a promise to call and pay the dollar as they came by in the afternoon."

A boy is sent with the parcel and change. On the route, quite accidentally, he is met by the purchaser, who exclaims:

"Ah! this is my bundle, I see—I thought you had been home with it long ago. Well, go on! My wife, Mrs. Trotter, will give you the five dollars—left instructions with her to that effect. The change you might as well give to *me*—I shall want some silver for the Post Office. Very good! One, two—is this a good quarter?—three, four—quite right! Say to Mrs. Trotter that you met me, and be sure now and *do* not loiter on the way."

The boy doesn't loiter at all—but he is a very long time in getting back from his errand—for no lady of the precise name of Mrs. Trotter is to be discovered.

GLOSSARY

bajour: a gypsy term for a big score.

baron: a well-dressed swindler who has stores and merchants put charges on his bill at a fancy hotel; either the hotel or the sellers or both are left holding the bag.

big con: an elaborate scheme to obtain not just the victim's cash on hand but also bank savings or other possessions.

bunko squad: the police squad dealing with con games.

christen: to mark cheap jewelry "14K."

dress a roll: to carry a roll of money with large denominations showing on top and smaller ones beneath.

flimflam: any con game generally.

green goods worker: a swindler who sells phony securities.

gully miner: a swindler who dupes small investors.

kissing the dog: working face to face with the victim.

little con: a brief scheme aimed at getting whatever money the victim is carrying at the time.

mark: the victim.

pigeon: another term for the victim.

put on the send: to induce the pigeon to go and get more money to put into the swindle.

roper: the con artist who makes the initial contact with the victim.

shill: a confederate of the con artist, who feigns interest in the con game in order to induce others to participate.

sting: the point at which the victim's money is taken (hence the title of the popular movie of the early 1970s whose plot hinged on an elaborate con game, *The Sting*).

sucker bait: the winnings of a victim, given to spur a greater investment of money.

7

Door-to-door sales

I hear you knocking, but you can't come in . . . — Popular song

In a classic comedy routine, an aggressive door-to-door salesman approaches a small country cabin. He knocks on the door, pushes past the woman who answers, and before she can say anything, he empties a bag of sooty black dust all over her living-room floor.

"If I can't pick up all that dust with this miraculous new machine, madam, I'll eat it!" the salesman cries. "Where can I plug it in?" The housewife stonily replies, "We don't have electricity here, sonny." In the final scene, we see the salesman on his hands and knees, reduced to eating his own bag of dust.

Why do people enjoy this scene? Probably because we know what it is like to deal with a high-handed, aggressive seller, and we relish the thought of the consumer, at least once, getting the upper hand. In reality, few people ever get the best of a hard-selling, smooth-talking door-to-door salesperson. Every year door-to-door sales are high on the list of consumer complaints filed with state and local consumer protection bureaus throughout the United States. The volume of complaints is particularly revealing because the entire industry accounts for only 3 percent of all national retail sales. Thus, despite the presence of reputable companies in the field, like Fuller Brush and Avon cosmetics (which sell relatively inexpensive items), con-

Beware of chinchilla sellers. (Courtesy the American Museum of Natural History)

sumers must be extremely wary of buying expensive products from door-to-door sellers.

Virtually anything from encyclopedias to memberships in lonely hearts clubs can be—and is—sold door-to-door. It is sold by an outwardly friendly but grimly aggressive sales army: one that never stops smiling, but won't take "no" for an answer. And like any good soldiers, they don't know the meaning of the word "surrender." These smooth talkers can make a worthless correspondence course sound like a Harvard education. They are masters of exaggeration, of false implication and misplaced emphasis; of the hidden condition and the critical omission.

Door-to-door salespeople make even the most preposterous schemes sound attractive. A few years ago, dozens of midwestern residents were talked into investing thousands of dollars to breed chinchillas in their own homes. According to the sales pitch, chinchillas could be raised right in the basement or in a spare room of the house. By spending only thirty minutes a day, the average breeder could expect to make annual profits of "over $10,000." The chinchillas cost $2,000 (not including the cages, animal feed, and special heating equipment). They arrived at their new homes, all right, but raising them proved a bit trickier than expected. Chinchillas, being very nervous animals, tend to chew on their fur when conditions are not precisely to their liking. The inexperienced chinchilla breeders found their profits being literally chewed up.

SALES TRICKS

Examples of fraud and deceit in door-to-door selling are legion. Each year thousands of consumers wind up paying for unwanted magazines, inferior home improvements, worthless vocational school training, and expensive encyclopedias they don't really need. Why is the door-to-door salesperson so successful, even with sophisticated buyers? There are many reasons. First, he (or she) comes prepared. Companies which rely on door-to-door sales spend days rehearsing their representatives in their sales pitches. The presentation is meticulously planned, right down to the salesperson's appearance, gestures, and even jokes. Virtually nothing is left to chance. One sales manual goes so far as to tell the seller to step back five feet after ringing the doorbell. It explains that when a woman opens the door and sees someone that far back, she will instinctively open the door wider. (The assumption is that the victim will be a woman; housewives are the door-to-door seller's most common target.)

Because people are reluctant to invite sellers into their homes, the industry has invented a number of standard ruses to assure a friendly welcome. A telephone caller says "you've been specially selected" to receive a free gift. A woman visitor says she's come to describe a "new program in your community." A pleasant, mild-mannered man says he's "taking a survey," or that your neighbors—whose names he has just read from the mailboxes—suggested he call. These tricks, known as "door openers" in the trade, serve one crucial purpose: to get the seller past the doorstep and into the house.

Once comfortably inside, the seller digs in, ready to stay as long as necessary to make the sale. One door-to-door vacuum-cleaner salesman makes it a point never to leave his victims until they either sign a contract or forcibly throw him out. Whether out of timidity, or a sense of politeness and hospitality, few people threaten to have him physically removed. After four or five hours of his sales talk, many people sign a contract just to be rid of him.

Taking advantage of human nature in this way is the seller's stock in trade. Written into almost every sales pitch are efforts to befriend you, to arouse your sympathies, to play upon your hopes, to exploit any emotional weakness you may have. To curry favor and gain trust, instruction manuals tell salespeople to find something in the house to flatter: the furniture, the draperies, the children, anything. A false sense of friendship is fostered by the use of first names. Sympathy is garnered by letting you know how far the salesman or saleswoman has come (and under what miserable conditions or at what personal sacrifice). If young, the sellers is inevitably "working to win a scholarship."

Some products lend themselves to fear or anxiety ploys. Representatives of a company selling teaching machines told suburban parents that everyone in their children's class had bought the machine; any child without one would be unable to compete effectively in school. Hearing this, otherwise sane and reasonable people parted with $495 for a poorly designed, cheaply made device which educators later found to be virtually worthless.

If creating anxiety doesn't work, there is always guilt. Parents resistant to buying children's books have been asked this question: "Can't you put away this small amount every week for your child's education?" A seller of vocational training courses prods reluctant buyers with: "Get out of the rut you're in—if not for yourself, then for your family."

If salespeople want you to overestimate the quality of their product, they want you to underestimate its price. A common trick is to state, not the total price, but only the deceptively low weekly or monthly charges. Another way sellers minimize the total price is by accepting a trivial down payment. Customers of one vacuum-cleaner seller were surprised to find that their 95-cent down payment secured a $400 purchase.

What might have saved many of these often intelligent consumer victims is simple: taking time to *think* before agreeing to buy. The door-to-door seller will always try to force the prospect to decide *immediately*. "This special offer won't be good tomorrow" is a classic refrain. A free dictionary may induce you to buy a $600 encyclopedia without careful thought. But any "special" offer will always be there tomorrow—and it probably won't look so special then, either.

Fast-talking door-to-door sellers don't give their victims time to reflect. Their carefully rehearsed chatter is designed to produce an ill-considered, immediate and emotional response.

ROTHCO
ORIGINAL

"NOW HERE'S A BRUSH WHICH, WHEN PURCHASED,
GETS RID OF ME."

YOUR LEGAL RIGHTS

What legal rights do consumers have against the door-to-door army? Proving fraud—a specific lie told by the salesperson—is costly and difficult to do in court; it is usually just your word against the seller's. High-pressure tactics by themselves are not illegal.

However, because abuse is so common, and protection for the consumer so ineffective, the Federal Trade Commission recently gave buyers an important new right—the right to cancel any door-to-door sales contract within three days of signing it. No reason is needed: just a written notice to the seller canceling the contract. The law covers all sales made at the buyer's home, office, or other place not the seller's place of business. The seller must give the consumer a printed form which can be used to effect cancellation. The form is a convenience; any writing, including a simple letter saying, "I cancel my purchase from you," signed by the buyer, will effectively cancel the sale. It is best to send any cancellation letter by registered or certified mail if possible.

Upon cancellation, the seller must refund any money paid and return any traded-in goods. The consumer must permit the seller to retrieve the merchandise: if the seller doesn't do so within twenty days, the consumer can keep the merchandise too. While some states give added protections, the basic rights outlined here are afforded to all consumers in the nation.

THE BEST PROTECTION

Often the three-day cancellation right is no protection at all. Salesmen frequently work with samples, or just pretty pictures; your merchandise might not arrive until after the three days have expired. Or you may not use the product for a few days, only to discover its flaws too late. The best and only sure protection is not to be victimized by door-to-door salespeople in the first place. Remember that this is usually the most expensive way to buy any item. Goods sold door-to-door often cost two to three times the price of comparable merchandise sold in retail stores. Furthermore, if a problem with the product develops, there is no readily accessible store to go to complain. Finding the salesperson again is usually impossible.

Finally, door-to-door selling brings into your home a total stranger—one who appears friendly at first, but who may later annoy, harass, or even threaten you to make a sale.

In the area of door-to-door selling, the best protection is simple. Don't buy.

DOOR-TO-DOOR SALES CAPERS

A woman reported to the New York City Department of Consumer Affairs that when she told a vacuum-cleaner salesman she wasn't interested in buying, he argued, cajoled, pleaded, and finally broke down and cried, telling her that his wife was sick, he had five children, and if he didn't make this sale he would lose his job. He seemed to cheer up when she agreed to buy.

A burglar-alarm-company salesman told a customer that a $750 alarm would ring in the nearest police station as well as in the owner's apartment. The alarm went off by accident in the man's apartment. It was so low it could not even be heard outside the apartment, and it was never connected to any police precinct. A Fire Department inspector found that the alarm was worth no more than $75. "No one but the burglar could hear it," the chagrined customer complained.

An experienced saleswoman of educational materials advised a novice: "Play on the mother's sympathy. You're this poor, hard-working young girl, trudging around in the rain or the heat, just trying to make an honest living."

At a sales meeting, a supervisor says, "Don't ask women to 'sign' our contract, because husbands tell their wives not to sign things. Just tell them to 'O.K.' it. And don't call it a 'contract,' call it an 'application form.'"

Instructing a new saleswoman, a veteran huckster of medical books for nurses says, "Work in the hospitals. Just walk in. If you happen to get caught, stay calm, don't panic. Someone says: Who are you? What are you doing here? You selling books? Say: 'I'm with the AMA.'"

A seller of karate lessons refused to take "no" for an answer from a lady who answered the door. He grabbed her arm, pulled it behind her back, put his leg in front of her, and knocked her to the floor. Friends came to help and the salesman fled.

An FTC Administrative Law Judge found an encyclopedia company had falsely represented that its product was endorsed by Pope Paul.

POSTSCRIPT

The following is a narrative of a fictional door-to-door sale which has been broadcast over radio stations and used as a teaching device. Can you pick out the falsehoods, tricks, and psychological appeals made by the salesman in this short sales pitch?

ANNOUNCER: Henry and Emma Singalong were sitting at home one evening, when the doorbell rang.

(Doorbell rings.)

HENRY: Yes?

BOB: Mr. Singalong, I'm Bob Craig, and I work for the Reader's Information Bureau. We're taking a survey of reading habits in this neighborhood, and if you'll take a minute to answer a question, I'm authorized to give you a valuable free gift I know you'll enjoy. May I step in?

(Pause.) (unctuously) You have a lovely home here, Mrs. Singalong.

EMMA (flattered): Why, thank you.

BOB: Now, Henry and Emma, I have one very important question to ask you. If you had your choice of reading any two magazines from this list, which would you choose?

HENRY: Well, let's see. (Slight pause.) I guess *Playboy*—Emma loves that —and *Sewing for Fun & Profit*. . . . I like to do a little knitting now and then.

BOB: You do? That's wonderful. For your cooperation, we will send you, *at our expense,* free subscriptions to the two magazines you've chosen, plus another subscription to a new bimonthly, *Carousel Review.* All of this, absolutely free, for the next sixty months, with no obligation whatsoever on your part.

EMMA: Oh!!

HENRY: That's great!

BOB: I guess you're wondering why we're doing this. It sounds crazy, right?

EMMA: Well, a little. (Chuckles lightly.)

BOB: Every year, Emma, we send out thousands of copies of these magazines to sophisticated people like yourselves. By doing this, we increase our circulation, and so we get more money for our advertising. So you see, we can give free subscriptions to specially selected people, because it all comes out of our advertising budget! All *you* have to do is simply take care of the small publisher's service charge of 89 cents a week. Isn't that great?

EMMA (uncertain somewhat): It sounds good. . . . but I'm sort of confused. Who do you work for, the magazines, or . . . ?

HENRY: And what do we have to do, exactly?

BOB: It's an advertising promotion. You can cancel whenever you want, but why would you want to? As a special bonus, if you decide *tonight* to help in our special circulation campaign, I'll throw in, absolutely free, this beautiful 300-page edition of Harrod's *The History of the Western World!* Take a look at that. But you've got to accept tonight. This offer won't be good tomorrow. (Pause.) I can see you're very discriminating readers. Now I'll just fill out this receipt for the book. My boss needs that, and you just sign right here. (Pause.) That's fine. Well, folks, I've got to be going to our next lucky couple! Congratulations, and enjoy your gifts!

Scene two: One Week Later

EMMA: Any mail, dear?

HENRY: There's a bill here from Reader's Information Service for $231.40!

EMMA: What!

HENRY: For magazines, it says here, "pursuant to your contract with us."

EMMA: You mean we signed a contract? Where's that paper the salesman left us?

HENRY: I've got it here someplace. (Pause; rustle of papers.) Here it is. It says "contract" right on it, and that we owe $231.40!

EMMA: That man lied to us. It wasn't a receipt!
HENRY: Why didn't you read it Emma before we signed it!
EMMA: Why didn't you???

ANALYSIS

The magazine huckster in this story used some of the most common door-to-door sales tricks to get Mr. and Mrs. Singalong to sign an expensive five-year contract. First, he did everything he could to disguise the fact that he was a salesman. He came to the door claiming to be taking a survey, for an organization that didn't sound like a selling company. He used the bait of a free gift to get inside the house. The insignificant 89-cent-a-week charge adds up to the grand total of $231.40. If the Singalongs had merely taken a moment to figure out the total cost, they would have known it wasn't inexpensive, much less "free."

Bob Craig made a particular effort to flatter Mr. and Mrs. Singalong, and to call them by their first names. This is a calculated attempt to gain the confidence of the couple, to overcome their natural wariness, and to play on their basic belief that a friendly person won't lie.

One common lie is to call a contract a receipt, or something else not as important. The Singalongs fell for this trap.

Finally, Craig resorted to one of the oldest tricks in door-to-door selling: attempting to force his prospects to decide immediately. Don't be pressured to sign a contract by a "today only" offer. If the salesman says you must decide right away away—throw him out. It's the best decision you'll ever make.

8

Food for thought

There is no love sincerer than the love of food.
— GEORGE BERNARD SHAW, *Man and Superman*

Over the last fifty years the food that Americans buy has changed as dramatically as the stores from which they buy it. Storekeepers used to buy from local farmers and butchers, so the food available to a shopper varied according to location and season. But America's food supply has passed from the hands of local growers and manufacturers into the control of national companies. This has meant more long-distance shipping of food and more availability of out-of-season or non-regional foods. It has also led to the development of foods which have a long shelf life and travel well (the famous tasteless, cardboard-like American tomato will soon be available in an even more packable square shape).

(Copyright © by Richard W. Golden, 1978)

Long shelf life and universal appeal have been gained by the use of a wide variety of chemicals. Animals are fed antibiotics, hormones, and other drugs so they'll live longer, grow fatter, and breed better. Fruits and vegetables are sprayed to combat insects, to change their colors, and to preserve them. Numerous foods are injected and treated with flavor enhancers, preservatives, stabilizers, emulsifiers, fillers, extenders, and other miracles of modern chemistry. Consequently, all foods are less natural than they once were. An explosion of additives has permeated our food supply.

Another way our food differs from that of our grandparents is seen in the great increase in precooked foods. People cook less than they used to— because more of us work outside the home, because cooking has become devalued, and because alternatives are available. Prepared and partially prepared foods occupy an increasing proportion of the market, with "convenience" foods gaining in popularity even while home economists decry their low food value and inflated prices. The typical supermarket offers 8,000 to 10,000 separate items today, but surveys show that the American diet is considerably worse than it was twenty years ago and that knowledge about nutrition has gone down too.

THE DANGERS OF ADDITIVES

The problem of potential harm caused by additives in food is a complex one and largely beyond the scope of this book. There are now more than 3,000 additives used in manufacturing our food; both the direct additives and those used in producing, processing, or packing the food which wind up inside it. Not all food additives are listed on labels. Many of them are totally unnecessary, added to make food last longer than is required or to give what the industry thinks is greater appeal. Thus, manufacturers put coloring in pet food to please the owners, and additives in baby food to make it taste better for the adults spooning it out (the babies can't tell).

There is considerable evidence that many food additives can be dangerous when ingested over a long period of time and in conjunction with other substances we eat, drink, and breathe. More and more chemicals which were "proved" or assumed to be safe have turned out to have carcinogenic properties. Since it generally takes twenty years for cancers caused by a new chemical to develop (and another twenty to thirty years to see the last of them after the substance is removed), there are compelling reasons to believe that the government has done a totally inadequate job of protecting us.

There are a myriad of federal laws and regulations which deal with the labeling, advertising, production, and content of food. Government regulations are exquisitely detailed (they take up 3,634 pages of fine print in the Federal Register and deal with such precise topics as low-sodium Colby cheese), but they fail to keep out all harmful substances and are of little practical use to the consumer. They are complemented by a battery of state and local laws and regulations which deal with other sale-of-food issues.

(*The New Yorker*)

One book which examined the subject in depth, *Eating May Be Hazardous to Your Health,* by Jacqueline Verrett and Jean Carper, put it thus:

> The overriding question is, considering the crudeness of our testing methods, the near-impossibility of discovering harm from human experience, and the frivolous use of food additives: Why take the risk? What harm can there be in a conservative approach to protection, as Congress intended? Government officials often rationalize their laxness by saying that precipitous action against food additives would be rash on the basis of "so little evidence." Considering everything, it is not caution that is rash but the government's failure to stringently enforce the law and to protect us against possible future catastrophe.

There's an attractive poster put out by the Center for Science in the Public Interest (CSPI) which describes and rates the most common food additives as "safe," "to be used with caution," or "to be avoided." You can order a copy of the Chemical Cuisine poster from CSPI at 1755 S Street, N.W., Washington, D.C. 20009, for $1.75 apiece.

CONVENIENCE FOODS

And now a word about convenience foods—those combination packages, boxed, canned, or frozen, designed to save time and effort. Each year more and more of them are sold, so there must be something about cake mixes, TV dinners, and hamburger-helper-type foods that has great appeal to Americans. Buy them if you wish, but be aware of two drawbacks. They are usually much more expensive than the ingredients bought separately; you are paying dearly for the "maid service." And they are often high in additives as well as price.

You can obtain convenience foods free of those drawbacks by making your own. Cook extra soups, stews, casseroles, and meats and freeze them in individual-sized containers; mix a jar of salad dressing to keep in the refrigerator; add grated cheese and herbs to plain bread crumbs and use as you need it for a filler or stuffing.

HOW TO BE A SUCCESSFUL SUPERMARKET SHOPPER

The benefits of supermarkets (convenient locations, cleanliness, wide assortment of foods, promotional contests, and sales) are such that there are few people who don't do much of their shopping there. Because supermarkets have become big business, an enormous amount of money and energy goes into discovering and implementing marketing techniques which will cause the supermarket shopper to buy more than he or she needs. Scores of market research firms and publications are dedicated to this end, and it's been said that the American supermarket shopper is the most "studied" creature ever. The key to the whole scheme is motivating "impulse buying": leading the shopper to buy items which he or she had no intention of buying on entering the store. The plan is successful—it's been estimated that impulse buying now accounts for 50 percent of an average supermarket shopper's purchases.

It requires attention and time to buy food well, plus vigilance toward whatever sales gimmicks the food industry is concocting. Here's a rundown of some of the basic devices used to make you buy more.

1. Store layout.   Essential foods are placed far away from each other, so that you must walk through the entire store even if you only want meat and potatoes. Typically the meat counter is against one wall, the dairy on another, and produce on the third. Displays are also arranged to encourage the purchase of complementary (but unneeded) items; thus salad dressing (often the more expensive kind) is displayed next to lettuce and talcum powder next to diapers.

2. Check-out counter.   Shoppers are a captive and bored audience when waiting on line to pay. So the check-out counter is loaded with displays of

(Photo Researchers, Inc., © F. B. Grunzweig, 1976)

such nonessentials as film, candy, and magazines to entice you. Some of these items cost considerably more then they would in a discount drug or dime store; almost all of them are bought by people who didn't plan to make these purchases.

3. Height-sight factor.   The level at which an item is displayed has been shown to have a tremendous influence on sales. Therefore, stores place high-markup items at eye level, while putting the lower-priced essentials at less visible heights, since people will search them out anyway.

4. Child manipulation.   This is a particularly effective technique, evil though it is. Children can exert considerable pressure to buy on the adults who take them shopping, *if* items they like are visible to them. Those items are often the low-nutrition, heavily sugared, and overpriced goodies pushed so relentlessly on children's television. Not by accident, the cereals, cookies, and sodas are put on children's eye level and are often close to one another (so that the adult who resists the first entreaty or two begins to feel like a monster and eventually gives in).

5. Holiday atmosphere.   Supermarkets capitalize on everyone's desire to be a good provider and to make holidays "special" for oneself or one's family. Creating an atmosphere of celebration can help boost sales by 15 to 20 percent, so it's often a festive time in the supermarket. When there isn't a major holiday looming, the store may celebrate the change of seasons with decorative bunting. To help supermarket managers make the most of this phenomenon, they were given this advice in a book called *Modern Super-market Operation:*

> Spring offers the following promotion themes: National Baseball Week, National Garden Week, Nationally Advertised Brands Week, National Donut Week, National Pickle Week, National Baby Week, Iced Coffee Week, National Dairy Month, and many others. Special days include Army Day, Daughter's Day, Arbor Day, May Day, Moving Day, Mother's Day, and Memorial Day. There are many local or regional activities such as blossom festivals in orchard areas which offer merchandising themes.*

6. Misleading displays.   A little less cheery are end displays or overflowing bins which contain items which are *not* reduced in price but are placed so as to convey the impression of a "sale."

7. Misleading statements.   Hand-lettered signs saying "Featured," "New," and "Special" don't promise bargains, but they do *imply* them. Similarly, superlatives on labels, like "Our Finest" and "Susie Q's Best," are empty phrases, providing no basis for comparison.

8. Misleading pricing.   It is a psychological fact that prices which end in "9" (99¢, $1.19, etc.) seem lower than they are. Multiple pricing can also create an illusion of savings (e.g., "four for a dollar"). "Bargains" that save a penny or two ("four for 99¢") can lead the unwary to buy more than they can use.

9. Recipe planners or weekly meal plans.   Billed as "services," these schemes serve the store, not the customer. The plans rid the store of slow-

---

* Dr. Edward A. Brand (New York: Fairchild Publications, 1963), p. 84.

CONSUMER LAW TRAINING CENTER

moving cuts of meat and other items. Even if one ingredient is on sale, the recipes require you to buy many others which are not.

10. Family packs. Preselected combinations of meat are no bargain. "This Week's Selection" of prepackaged meat often costs more than if the contents were bought separately.

TIPS

To help you chart an economical course through the perilous maze of supermarket buying traps, we offer a few suggestions.

◆ Make a list and stick to it. If you can, avoid shopping when you're hungry (you'll buy twice as much) or when you have children with you.

◆ Comparison-shop the supermarkets near you periodically, by comparing several different kinds of goods, to see if one store is cheaper overall. Often none will be, because in some areas supermarkets avoid price competition, vying instead for choice locations, snazziness of interiors, and added services or bonuses.

◆ Read labels for contents, quantity, and price. If unit-pricing stickers are required in your state, use them to learn the price per pound, ounce, quart, etc. If not, bring a pocket calculator or some scrap paper with you if you want to know what you're paying. Larger sizes are usually (but not always) more economical than smaller ones, if you can use the larger quantity. In some places food labels must indicate the dry or drained weight of canned goods (the weight of the food minus the water or syrup in which it is packaged). This enables meaningful comparative shopping, since you eat only the corn niblets, not the water.

◆ Check for freshness by reading open dating (open date labeling) where it's available. These regulations require the packager of food to include understandable information about the freshness of the food. It can indicate when it was packaged; how long it should be good; or when it should be removed from the shelf. This information is already provided in code (different ones for each producer), so that stores know when to remove merchandise. However, unless open dating laws exist, the ordinary shopper can't tell when the items are due to be retired.

◆ Try the house brands of canned and packaged foods (which may cost 10 to 22 percent less than nationally advertised versions) and the house brands of cleaning and paper products (averaging 33 percent and 25 percent less, respectively). They are often identical to the name brands you've been selecting.

◆ Don't buy non-supermarket goods in a supermarket. More than half the toothpaste and aspirin bought in the United States is purchased at supermarkets, as is one third of all the first-aid equipment and 10 percent of all phonograph records. It usually costs more for the convenience of buying such items in the supermarket.

◆ Stock up on sale items if they will keep and you have the room to store them.

◆ If the store runs out of an advertised sales item, see if it offers rain checks. Required in some places, rain checks from stores give any disappointed customer either substitute goods at the "sale" price or a written guarantee that he or she can buy the item at the sale price as soon as the store restocks it.

SUPERMARKET ALTERNATIVES

The shopper who is disenchanted with supermarkets can utilize small, more specialized stores (groceries, butchers, produce stores). Another possibility is to join a buying club or food cooperative to find lower prices and better quality. That option is discussed at length in chapter 31.

THREE RIP-OFFS TO AVOID

♦ There's one way of "saving money" that often results in a big loss of it—investing in a combination freezer-food plan. Typically, the hype tells you that you are being "given the chance" to buy a freezer full of meat at less than the freezer itself would cost. It sounds like an irresistible bargain, *except* the "price" of the freezer is usually grossly inflated, as are the accompanying finance charges. The freezer itself is often too big for ordinary household use. And the food frequently turns out to be inferior to what was ordered. All in all, a poor deal. If you want to buy a freezer, comparison-shop for the best cash price and best borrowing terms. And buy the food you want, when you want it, after checking around.

♦ Buying beef in bulk (a side or half a side) is another deal fraught with peril. Often the meat shown to you or pictured is superior to what you receive (even when you've "chosen" a particular piece of meat). Representations about yield after cutting and trimming are frequently inflated, so that the price per pound is higher than what you would pay in a store. Bait and switch sales presentations are common. So check others' experiences with a particular seller before you buy meat in bulk.

♦ Beware, too, of unhealthy "health" foods. The current interest in eating more natural foods has led, inevitably, to frauds. There are misrepresentations as to produce being "organically" grown (i.e., without man-made chemical fertilizers, sprays, etc.). Your only recourse here is to check the seller's sources and try to buy from someone you trust. A number of large cereal manufacturers have introduced their own lines of "natural" cereal. The problem is that many of them contain substantial amounts of sugar ("natural" or "turbinado" sugar is just about as nutritionally deficient as white) and are no better than ordinary breakfast cereals. Other products laden with artificial flavorings and colorings are marketed as "preservative-free" or "health" foods. So read the labels. Remember, too, to compare prices of items sold in supermarkets and health-food stores—the same goods are sometimes available for substantially less in the supermarket.

NUTRITION AND LABELS

What can you do? Since you are going to be eating for the rest of your life, it's really advisable to invest a little time in researching what you are eating. If you don't have a basic understanding of nutrition and are unclear about what this cholesterol crisis is or why so much sugar is bad, read up on it. There is an overabundance of materials around; good starting points are *A Diet for Living,* by Jean Mayer (New York: David McKay Co., 1975), and some U. S. Department of Agriculture booklets: *Nutrition: Food at Work for You,* and *Nutrition Labeling—Tools for Its Use* (Agriculture Information Bulletin No. 382), which explains how to read the nutritional information on labels and evaluate foods for nutritional value. Both are available from the Superintendent of Documents, U. S. Government Printing Office, Washington, D.C. 20402. For an explanation of how American eating habits affect the world, coupled with alternative recipes, see *Diet for a Small Planet,* by Frances Moore Lappé (New York: Ballantine Books, 1971).

Learn how to read labels too. Here's what to look for:

◆   Name and net weight of contents, on the front. Where the contents are both solid and liquid (i.e., canned fruits and vegetables), the liquid is included in the net weight.

◆   List of all ingredients, in descending order of amount. There are two problems with this. First, there are about 300 standardized products, such as

(Photo by Cliff Ratner)

flour, ice cream, and catsup, for which ingredients do not have to be listed. So you can't tell if those products contain additives or things which you are allergic to or wish to cut down on. Second, the quantity or proportion of the ingredients isn't shown. A Houston Veterans Administration analysis of 78 breakfast cereals discovered that 11 contained more than 50 percent sugar, and another 24 of them had between 25 and 50 percent. This is a double rip-off—both nutritionally and economically—since sugar (and salt) can usually be added to foods when served, at less cost.

◆   A serving (or portion)—for the purpose of the nutritional information offered. This is often a smaller quantity than the average person would eat.

◆   Nutritional information for each serving. Labels indicate the quantities of nutrients and the percentage of U.S. Recommended Daily Allowance. A label cannot claim that a food is a significant source of any nutrient unless it contains at least 10 percent of the recommended daily allowance.

◆   Often, calories per serving.

◆   If food is an imitation.

VOCABULARY LIST FOR READING LABELS

NUTRIENT   **A basic natural substance in foods which supplies one or more of these: body fuel for energy; materials for the building or maintenance of tissues; or substances that regulate body processes. There are three essential nutrients, all necessary components of a healthy diet:**

◆   *Protein*   **The main nutrient responsible for building and maintaining body tissues. High sources of protein are meat, poultry, fish, seafood, milk and its products, and eggs. Other good sources are legumes (dried beans, peas, soybeans), peanuts, and other nuts.**

◆   *Carbohydrates*   **The nutrients which supply energy. There are three types: starch, sugar, and cellulose (which gives bulk or roughage). Important sources of starches are cereal grains, rice, and vegetables such as potatoes; sources of sugar are fruits, honey, and molasses; and sources of cellulose are fruits, vegetables, and whole-grain cereals.**

◆   *Fat*   **The nutrient providing the most concentrated sources of energy. Weight for weight it supplies more than twice as much energy as carbohydrates or protein.**

UNITED STATES RECOMMENDED DAILY ALLOWANCE **(U.S. RDA)   The estimated daily amount of protein, vitamins, and minerals that one should eat to stay healthy (according to the government health officials). People of different sex, ages, and sizes vary in what they need, so these amounts are designed to be adequate for all healthy people and are overgenerous for many. Because it is more difficult to assess the required amounts of calories, carbohydrates, and fat, no RDA for them has been specified.**

CALORIE   **A measure of energy, expressed in terms of heat. The energy is used to maintain the body and is expended in physical activity. Excess calories are, of course, stored as fat.**

HOW TO COMPLAIN

If you've bought food which is spoiled or short-weighted, take it back to the manager of the store where you bought it. A state agency which has responsibility for sanitation or weights and measures may also be interested, as might some local agencies with similar responsibilities.

If you find a canned or packaged food that is impure or contaminated, also contact your local U. S. Food and Drug Administration office to alert them to the possibility that there are other such packages. It is essential to do this if the food makes you sick. You can also write to the manufacturer or packer (indicated on the label). If you do, the time involved in finding out the name of the president of the company usually pays off, as your letter may be taken more seriously and responded to more promptly.

If the food is meat, poultry, eggs, or anything else overseen by the U. S. Department of Agriculture (which stamps this fact on the food), contact that agency.

And if false or misleading advertising (not labeling) is involved, contact the Federal Trade Commission.

In all cases, save as much of the food as remains (and is savable), as well as the label, and sales receipt if you have it.

(Photo Researchers, Inc., © F. B. Grunzweig, 1974)

SELECTED BIBLIOGRAPHY

LAPPÉ, FRANCES MOORE. *Diet for a Small Planet*. New York: Ballantine Books, 1971.

MARGOLIUS, SIDNEY. *The Great American Food Hoax*. New York: Dell, 1971.

MAYER, JEAN. *A Diet for Living*. New York: David McKay Co., 1975.

Midget Encyclopedia of Food & Nutrition (five very appealing booklets: *The UN-greasy Spoon; The Food Biz or Whatever Happened to Farmer Brown; Chemical Cookery; A Five-Minute Course in New-trition;* and *What's Left to Eat—A Public Service for Bored Tongues*), available from the Center for Science in the Public Interest, 1755 S Street, N.W., Washington, D.C. 20009.

VERRETT, JACQUELINE, and CARPER, JEAN. *Eating May be Hazardous to Your Health*. Garden City, N.Y.: Anchor Press, Doubleday & Company, 1975.

9

In the final analysis: funerals

We have, in the United States and Canada, an amazing custom of displaying dead bodies in a costly and elaborate manner. Each year, in response to this custom nearly two million American families put themselves through an emotional ordeal and spend upwards of two billions of dollars doing so. — ERNEST MORGAN, *A Manual of Death Education and Simple Burial*

Pompous funerals are a homage to the vanity of the quick, rather than a tribute to the memory of the dead.   — DE LA ROCHEFOUCAULD, *Maxims*

"Mourning Picture for Polly Botsford and Her Children." (Courtesy Abby Aldrich Rockefeller Folk Art Center)

In 1963 Jessica Mitford wrote a best-selling exposé of the funeral industry titled *The American Way of Death*. Fourteen years later she commented in an article in *McCall's,* "The Funeral Salesmen":

> . . . I may have opened up the subject . . . but it was the media, the churches, the growing consumer movement that took up the cry against what the funeral industry refers to as "the traditional American funeral." By this, the funeral men mean the full treatment: display of the embalmed and beautified corpse reposing on an innerspring or foam rubber mattress in an elegant "casket"; "visitation" of the deceased in the mortuary "slumber room"; an open-casket ceremony at which the mourners parade around for a last look; a burial vault that allegedly affords "eternal protection"; elaborate "floral tributes" from family and friends; a "final resting place" in a "memorial park" or mausoleum. . . .
>
> This "tradition," first conceived by the embalming-fluid salesmen and then tenderly nurtured by the undertakers, is not exactly hallowed by time, nor does it stem from the teachings of any religion.

The death of a relative or friend did not always set off a lavish ritual of ceremony in this country, nor does it elsewhere. Families used to care for their dead with some assistance from neighbors and church members, at a minimum of cost and without great emphasis on viewing a better-than-lifelike corpse. But a group of specialists arose who parlayed their willingness to handle an unpleasant task into an entrenched and aggressive "profession."

People arranging funerals are the most defenseless of consumers. They are compelled to make a major purchasing decision with little or no prior experience, in a short period of time. Furthermore, they are emotionally distressed, often disoriented, and barely capable of dealing with the mundane details of life. Some feel guilty about not having treated the deceased person well enough. The combination of these feelings (temporary though they may be) makes the purchaser putty in the hands of a manipulative funeral director.

And there are many desperate funeral directors. The American funeral industry is in serious trouble today. There are 22,000 funeral homes in the United States, most of which maintain a costly physical plant (including an embalming room, viewing rooms, a chapel) and a full-time staff, usually available twenty-four hours a day. The majority of them, however, handle fewer than 100 funerals annually. This is enormously cost-inefficient and accounts for the high cost of American funerals. Into each funeral price is built a high overhead fee. The funeral industry survives in its present form only because of the substantial profits gained from the "traditional" American funeral, and it has fought fiercely against any changes in that tradition.

The industry is now being challenged in two ways. First, a growing number of Americans are rebelling against the morticians' expensive concept of the proper way to treat the dead. Over the past fifteen years there has been an expanding trend toward simplified, less expensive funerals and toward cremation. An illustration of the trend is found in the fact that memorial societies (nonprofit groups dedicated to education about death and to simplification of burials and cremation) have grown in total membership from 17,000 families in 1963 to over 750,000 in 1978.

Second, the Federal Trade Commission has been concerned over the last few years with the misleading and coercive practices which its staff believes to be widespread in the industry. After lengthy hearings, the Commission has taken action. (Unfortunately, its action will probably be appealed by the funeral industry, so it may be several years before the regulation comes into effect.)

SELLING TRADITIONAL FUNERALS TO THE PUBLIC

Despite these challenges to the industry, its members continue to pressure consumers to choose lavish funerals. Here's an example, as described in a letter published in the New York *Times,* May 1, 1978:

> To the Editor:
> Every few years the press highlights the high cost of getting buried. New laws are enacted, ignored, the public continues to be fleeced and now, once again, "The Federal Trade Commission . . . will soon recommend that undertakers be regulated as never before." And here we go once more!
> No matter how many laws are passed there will be one item never to be regulated. How can the consumer go bargaining for the price of a funeral? You can't. By the time one sits talking to the smooth salesman, his establishment already has the body. You are now a captive audience.
> I know what it feels like. While the smoothie was talking me into buying a package I could not afford and which the religious convictions of the deceased did not allow, a man looking like a character out of Dickens interrupted our important conference to say that "the body does not fit into that particular coffin ordered." It would have to be a more expensive box. It was a great surprise to us as the body of the deceased had wasted away during the final illness and could not have weighed much. However, his next line (superbly rehearsed) told the story: "But we can shove her in." One of the family nearly fainted and the sale of a more expensive coffin followed.

> EUGENE WEINTRAUB
> New York, April 23, 1978

PRESSURE TACTICS

One of the authors spent more than a week at the FTC hearings listening to funeral director after funeral director testify. She came away convinced that many of them truly believe that *they* know best what funeral arrangements their customers should have and need, in order to "handle their grief well." Morticians have coined the phrase "grief counseling" for the self-delegated role of telling customers how to make the "appropriate" arrangements. Not surprisingly, they are only too ready to urge customers to select the more expensive items, in order to "show respect" and "express your love" for the deceased.

Customers who express concern about prices are accused of having little affection for the deceased. Preferences for simplicity, and concern about price by those whom the undertakers believe "could do better," are treated as miserliness. It is a trade custom to refer to the simplest caskets as "boxes," "rowboats," or "orange crates." The tactic of responding to an inquiry about less expensive caskets with an "Oh, you mean the *welfare* coffin? Would you really consider that one?" has caused countless people to make more expensive "choices" than they wanted to.

Caskets are usually the single most expensive part of a funeral, with the entire funeral cost generally based on the price of the coffin selected. As a rule, display rooms are designed to actively discourage purchase of the lower-priced caskets. These are difficult to find or may even be absent from the main, well-lighted display area and shown only to the inquiring consumer in a basement or closet. Rarely are cloth-covered pine boxes, an attractive, inexpensive alternative, displayed at all. The less expensive caskets are sometimes nicked or scratched, partially obscured by cloth or other merchandise, or, on occasion, resting in a pool of water. However it is done, the implication is clear—this is inferior merchandise for an uncaring purchaser.

Undertakers also discourage cremation, even when customers request it because of the expressed desire of the deceased. They view the growing interest in cremation as a dangerous challenge to the full-dress funeral, and thus to their livelihood. Although rarely refusing to provide cremation services when demanded, they disparage their purchase and have increased the profit on them. When customers insist on cremation, many funeral homes still try to sell them an expensive coffin, sometimes misrepresenting that coffins are required by law.

Tactics similar to these are used by business people in other trades, of course. But funeral directors deal with a captive clientele, especially since the law requires that their services be used. Unfortunately, many undertakers consciously play on common feelings of remorse to make a larger sale.

LACK OF INFORMATION

It is almost impossible to obtain price information about funerals over the telephone, the only realistic way to comparison-shop for such services. Although price surveys have shown wide variation for the identical funeral or cremation services, funeral homes prefer to discuss such matters only in person (knowing how unlikely one is to negotiate wisely in such a situation). In a survey of New York City funeral homes conducted in 1974, 63 percent of the funeral homes contacted flatly refused to give any price data or required persistence and coaxing before they would do so.

Nor is price information usually available in advertisements. Funeral establishments frequently advertise that they exist to serve you with dignity, but don't tell what that dignified service will cost. The trade associations have strongly discouraged price advertising, claiming that the public is not interested in it. Even when they can be obtained, the price data are confusing. Funeral homes offer (and usually sell) "complete" funerals, which include a wide variety of services tangential to the care and disposition of the body. Many funeral homes will sell less than the "complete" funeral, but only if the customer affirmatively asks for this. Otherwise, the assumption is that all the unnecessary extras are wanted. Funeral directors do not regularly provides lists of services and costs before funerals are arranged, except in those very few states (California and New Jersey, among them) which require them to do so.

MISINFORMATION

Misrepresentations by funeral directors about legal (and sometimes religious) requirements, as well as about the quality of the merchandise, are common. Undertakers may believe the misrepresentations made to them by the casket manufacturers. But, knowingly or innocently, many purchasers of funerals are misled. Major misrepresentations include:

- *Embalming is required by law, for health reasons.* It rarely is: embalming is commonly required only when burial is put off for several days, if a body is shipped from one state to another, or if the deceased had a communicable disease.
- *Embalming will preserve a body longer.* Certain embalming fluids will do that (witness the Egyptian mummies), but those fluids cause the skin to turn hard and leathery and therefore are not used by American embalmers. The embalming done to prepare corpses for viewing is a cosmetic, not a preservative, measure.
- *A casket is required for direct cremation.* In fact, simpler and much less expensive containers (of cardboard, plywood, and wood) are available for cremation and for burial.
- *The costlier coffins, described as "airtight" or "watertight" or "sealer coffins" will preserve the corpse longer.* This aspect is played up in casket manufacturers' advertising and in funeral directors sales pitches. The coffins are marketed as having such qualities as "enduring protection," and one line is touted as "the invincibles, they have withstood the test of time." There is no proof that this is true. In fact, whatever the merits of seeking to prevent the decomposition of a dead body, keeping out air or water probably does not do it. The bacteria which cause the decay may actually flourish in the absence of air and water.

HOW THE GOVERNMENT DOESN'T NOW BUT MAY SOON PROTECT YOU

All states have funeral regulatory boards or agencies which are charged with licensing and regulating the behavior of funeral directors. Unfortunately they are usually composed entirely of funeral directors, often the very same individuals who are active in the trade associations. As might be expected, these boards have shown a much greater concern for the well-being of their industry and its members than for consumers.

Funeral directors have lobbied long and hard for their occupation to be

regarded as a "profession" rather than a business, and have sought the en-
actment of a network of state laws which provide great benefits for the funeral business, all in the name of "protecting" the public. For example, the
states require that funeral directors be involved in (and paid for) the disposal of *all* bodies, even those merely transported from a hospital bed to a
nearby medical school. In Florida, a provision that no cremation can take
place until forty-eight hours after death is coupled with a requirement that
all bodies kept more than twenty-four hours be embalmed. In other words,
no direct, low-cost cremation is possible. Other laws require that each
branch of a funeral establishment chain have its own embalming room,
which serves only to drive up prices. The FTC hearing officer, who spent
three months listening to witnesses and reading documents, concluded that
"state regulation against unfair or deceptive funeral industry practices have
been dominated by industry interests to the detriment of the consumer."
(Report of Presiding Officer Jack E. Kahn on Proposed Trade Regulation
Rule Concerning Funeral Industry Practices, July 1977.)

Because the states have not curbed funeral-home abuses, the Federal
Trade Commission began action to regulate the industry. After much
research, it issued a proposed rule and held hearings around the country in
the spring and summer of 1976. The National Funeral Directors Association (NFDA) and its local affiliates mounted a vigorous and costly opposition to the proposed rule, viewed as a major threat to the $4 billion funeral
industry. The opposition was as colorful as it was vehement. One past director of the New York State Funeral Directors Association saw the rule as "a
threat to the American way of life" (quoted in *The American Funeral Director,* December 1975); a trade magazine editorial opined that the "FTC
are trying to force their agnostic, atheistic ways on the God fearing, traditional family-oriented American" (quoted by Jessica Mitford in her
McCall's article, from *Mortuary Management*).

The outcome of the FTC rule is unclear, but it has already served to
publicize the problems; to spur some states to take local action; and to put
undertakers on notice that they will be held to higher standards of ethical
business behavior.

If upheld, the FTC rule would make it easier for consumers to make true
choices in arranging funerals. Directed at undertakers and funeral homes
only (not cemeteries or sales firms offering funeral insurance), it would:

◆ prevent disparagement of a consumer's concern for price;
◆ require written itemization of all components of a funeral before a customer agrees to it;
◆ prevent the giving of misleading information about embalming, the preservative value of caskets, and the need for coffins for cremation;
◆ prevent interference with memorial societies or direct cremation services;
◆ prevent profiting on so-called "cash advances" for florists, obituary notices, etc.;
◆ allow unfettered advertising of funeral prices.

Since the rule faces a series of court challenges, the state boards are the only place a disgruntled consumer can lodge a complaint about mistreatment in the meantime. Some of them have been improved as a result of the attention given to the issue. The clearer the abuse and the better-documented the case, the better your chances are of prevailing there.

WHAT YOU SHOULD KNOW ABOUT FUNERALS BEFORE YOU ARE FACED WITH ARRANGING ONE

FUNERAL COSTS

If you are an average American, the biggest purchases you will ever make are a home, a car, possibly a college education, and a funeral. In buying a car you are not likely to end up with a Cadillac when you wanted only a Volkswagen; nor will you buy the Hearst mansion if you can only pay for a

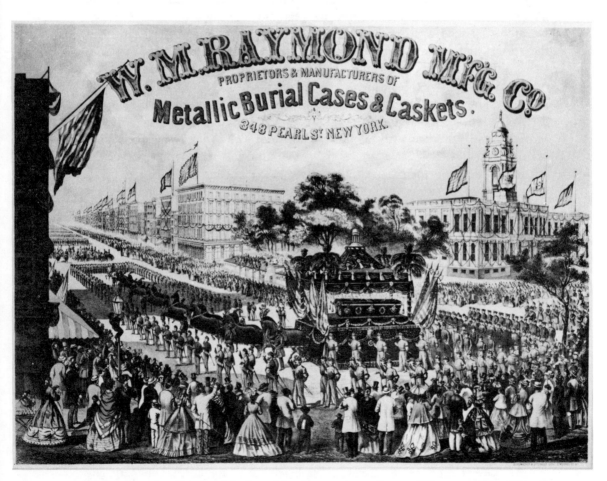

What was appropriate for Abraham Lincoln may not suit you. (Museum of the City of New York)

small split-level house. But if you arrange for a funeral, you may wind up purchasing one well beyond your pocketbook or tastes.

A complex bundle of individual goods and services are purchased as part of a typical American funeral. Most people are unfamiliar with these components, and thus have little chance to decide which they want. The average cost of death today (for funeral and burial) is over $2,000. The major expenses are for funeral-home services and goods (including a coffin); plus a coffin enclosure, burial space in a cemetery, and a grave marker. Beyond the requirement that an undertaker be involved in transporting dead bodies to their ultimate destination, the other services and goods are optional. You can decide to forgo any of them, but be warned—not all undertakers respond happily to attempts to substitute your judgment for theirs.

It is not merely economic motives that make morticians suggest costly and lavish items. "It is also because of an ideal they want to see expressed in the funeral ceremony. They have their own sense of the fitness of things. Undertakers consider funerals their 'creations,' rituals that must be arranged in an appropriate manner, using the best materials available." (*Funerals: Consumers' Last Rights,* by the editors of *Consumer Reports,* 1977, pp. 64–65, discussing an observation made by Leroy Bowman.) Thus funeral directors customarily size up their customers' finances (by looking at their car, clothes, occupation, home address, reaction to casket prices, etc.) and urge them to buy a funeral "in keeping with" (or above) that style.

There is every reason to be guided into an expensive funeral, if you want one. But for those people who don't, or who want to be sure they are getting a fair deal on their funeral, here is a guide to what you typically pay for and which items can be made to cost less.

FUNERAL-HOME GOODS AND SERVICES	ALTERNATIVES
(For Traditional Funeral)	

GOODS

1. **Coffin: The price range available from any undertaker is generally quite wide, although they are reluctant to show you the less expensive models.**	**There are pine boxes with cloth covers available at a low price—you must ask for and insist on one, though.**
2. **Coffin enclosure: Grave liner or grave vault.**	**Be sure the cemetery you will be using requires one (not all do), and see if it offers lower prices than the undertaker (most do).**
3. **Burial clothes**	**Bring decedent's own clothes, which is more personal at any rate— streetwear or pajamas and robe.**

4. Flowers	**Eliminate, or provide your own.**
5. Memorial prayer cards	**Eliminate.**
6. Acknowledgment cards	**Send your own, if you wish.**

SERVICES

7. Embalming	**A closed-casket ceremony eliminates the need for embalming, as does immediate burial followed by a graveside or memorial service.**
8. Preparation-room use	**This is eliminated if the body is not embalmed.**
9. Use of funeral-home facilities for two or three days	**Shorten the period (the charge is per day) or eliminate it by arranging for immediate burial with a graveside ceremony or a subsequent memorial service in someone's home.**
10. Limousine(s) to church or cemetery	**Eliminate them; mourners can go in their own cars.**
11. Flower car	**Eliminate, and ask mourners to omit flowers (perhaps to contribute to a specified charity instead).**
12. Maintaining guest register	**A friend or relative can see to this.**
13. Hiring pallbearers	**Let friends and relatives do this task.**
14. Death notices in newspapers	**Arrange for these yourself.**
15. Music	**Eliminate or have friends supply it.**
16. Clergy honorarium	**Pay it yourself. There are numerous documented instances in which honoraria paid to funeral homes never reached the clergypeople.**
17. Transcripts of death notices	**No alternative: you will need these to arrange for death benefits.**
18. Arranging for death benefits	**Do it yourself (see later section in this chapter).**

If you are faced with arranging a funeral, there are measures you can take to improve your chances of getting what you want. If at all possible, select an undertaker before the death occurs—ask friends for their experiences and call or visit for information. Decide on what aspects of the "full, traditional" funeral you want and which you don't. And take a trusted friend, adviser, or relative, *one who is not emotionally involved in the decision,* with you when you make arrangements. Your task will be easier if you have thought through the issues before death is imminent.

CEMETERY COSTS

It is possible in some places to bury a body or remains on private land, although most people prefer to use cemeteries. Cemetery arrangements can be made before they are needed, and often are. The money paid is usually not refundable or transferable, but as long as you are fairly certain that you will still live in the same area (or will want to be buried there), advance arrangements are fine.

Cemetery costs usually include:

- ◆ plot or crypt (underground burial chamber);
- ◆ coffin enclosure, if not bought from the funeral home;
- ◆ opening and closing the grave or crypt;
- ◆ memorial (marker or monument);
- ◆ other services, including "perpetual care" of the grave (a lump payment for unending custodial care of the marker and paths) or annual fees for the same. Some cemeteries charge for but do not actually give much custodial care—a walk around the cemetery, particularly the closed sections, should give you an idea of how well taken care of it is.

The plots or crypts vary in price according to size and placement. The only other item whose price you can control is the grave marker. There is no need to choose one at the time of the funeral if one hasn't already been purchased. Memorials range from small, simple, flat or upright slab engravings to elaborate mausoleums, with a commensurate price variation. It's a good idea to postpone any decision to buy an expensive one until several months after the funeral. This will enable you to shop around, compare the goods and prices of independent dealers with those of the cemetery, and make the decision in a calmer state of mind.

BUYING TIP

For complete information about funerals, burial, and cremation, an excellent paperback reference book is *Funerals: Consumers' Last Rights,* **by the editors of** *Consumer Reports,* **1977, available from bookstores and from Consumers Union, Mount Vernon, N.Y. 10550.**

LONG-RANGE PLANNING

Some people attempt to make arrangements for their own death long before it is imminent. For them it is simply a way of making decisions in an orderly fashion, analogous to writing a will. Others think of making arrangements when they become seriously ill or quite old.

As sensible as the idea of arranging in advance seems, it is fraught with problems. It is particularly hazardous to conclude funeral or crematory arrangements much in advance of need.

Pre-need plans for funerals are often sold by sales firms which do not themselves provide the funeral or burial services. They frequently solicit door-to-door, advertise heavily, and have a poor record for reliability. Some don't deliver what they promise or consistently confuse buyers as to what they'll receive. Others are fly-by-nights, gone before most of their customers need to cash in. Avoid them.

When dealing directly with a funeral home, particularly a well-established one, you are on safer ground. But the funeral industry has, in general, sought to discourage pre-need arrangements (which are often less expensive than those made by next of kin). Many undertakers prevail on grieving relatives not to honor the arrangement by the deceased; to "do better" for him or her. There is a further problem of the seller claiming that the price has been raised since the arrangement was made—make sure you have a clear, *written* understanding of what the payments cover.

Generally, it is best simply to leave an understanding of what you want done with your body with your survivors, rather than with a funeral director or sales firm. Putting it in writing too helps the survivor resist guilt and pressures to do otherwise. A constructive way of facing the issue and thinking it through is by joining a memorial society.

Pre-need arrangements for cemetery space and markers are often made satisfactorily, although there are dangers there too. You must be certain that you will be remaining in that area, or will want to have your body shipped back there (at a significant cost). There is also the possibility that your payment will not be considered a complete one if prices go up—check the contract for an "escalator clause" and be sure you know how much more your survivors may have to pay (for the plot or in fees or upkeep). If you buy a plot while relatively young and healthy, compute the interest on the money you have paid out—you might be better off putting it in a special account or trust fund for your survivors.

MEMORIAL SOCIETIES

The problem of securing simple, low-cost funerals and cremations led to the development of memorial (or "funeral") societies: nonprofit cooperatives which help members learn to arrange for such services. The societies make information on alternatives available to members, and often negotiate directly with local funeral homes and crematoria to secure low-cost alternatives for them. (They do not make arrangements for individual funerals or cremations, however.) Memorial societies can sometimes arrange for funerals that may be otherwise unavailable to their members, or can obtain lower prices.

The societies vary in size and in the services they offer. All are run as cooperatives and staffed by volunteers. Lifetime membership fees are low (usually in the $10–$15 per family range).

There are now 170 individual societies, all of which stress simplicity and dignity in funeral arrangements. They are all loosely linked into one umbrella organization—the Continental Association of Funeral and Memorial Societies, 1828 L Street, N.W., Washington, D.C. 20036, which will tell you where the society closest to you is. The guidebook of the memorial societies, which presents a moving statement of reasons for choosing an untraditional American funeral and provides detailed information on the other options, is *A Manual of Death Education and Simple Burial,* by Ernest Morgan, now in its seventh revision (available for $1.50 from the Celo Press, Route 5, Burnsville, N.C. 28714, or from the Continental Association).

ALTERNATIVES TO TRADITIONAL FUNERALS AND BURIALS

CREMATION

Cremation is being selected by more people around the country, and has been rising at a particularly fast rate on the West Coast (where, in 1976, 40 percent of the dead were cremated). This trend has seen the development of direct cremation chains, which pick up the deceased from hospital, home, or nursing home and provide all cremation services for a total fee of about $250. They began in California and have spread to Florida and New York. In all three states the chains have faced formidable opposition from the funeral industry, in court and legislative challenges. Nonetheless, they've thrived.

DONATION OF ORGANS OR BODY FOR MEDICAL OR RESEARCH PURPOSES

Medical and dental schools need bodies for teaching and research purposes. In some places the need is severe—although Harvard and Yale medical schools have more donations than they can use, many of their less glamorous counterparts suffer from a shortage.

Patients with kidney, eye, and heart problems are awaiting transplant donors all over the country. Many will die or live out their lives blind or tied to a dialysis machine for lack of enough appropriate donors.

People who donate their bodies or organs can do so before a funeral and have a funeral or memorial service afterwards or they may choose to do

---

UNIFORM DONOR CARD

OF _____
PRINT OR TYPE NAME OF DONOR

In the hope that I may help others, I hereby make this anatomical gift, if medically acceptable, to take effect upon my death. The words and marks below indicate my desires.

I give: (a) — any needed organs or parts

(b) — only the following organs or parts·

_____
SPECIFY THE ORGAN(S) OR PART(S)

for the purposes of transplantation, therapy, medical research or education.

(c) — my body for anatomical study if needed

Limitations or
special wishes, if any: _____

Signed by the donor and the following two witnesses in the presence of each other:

_____
Signature of Donor   Date of Birth of Donor

_____
Date Signed   City and State

_____
Witness

_____
Witness

This is a legal document under the
Uniform Anatomical Gift Act or similar laws.

For further information, consult your physician or:

KIDNEY FOUNDATION OF NEW YORK
432 Park Avenue South, New York, N.Y. 10016

24 HR. EMERGENCY
DONOR TELEPHONE 212 – 861- 7370

without one. But it is essential to let next of kin, as well as medical personnel, know of the intention to be a donor. Most states now recognize the legal validity of a decision to become a donor. This intention is most easily expressed by carrying a completed Uniform Donor card (signed, in most instances, in front of two witnesses). A card is available from the American Medical Association, 353 North Dearborn, Chicago, Ill. 60605, or from any of the organizations discussed below. For more information about becoming a donor, write to the two nonprofit groups which supply information about body or organ donations: The Living Bank, P.O. Box 6725, Houston, Tex. 77005 (713-528-2971), and Medic Alert, 1000 North Palm, Turlock, Calif. 95380 (209-632-2371).

Eyes can be donated to a local eye bank (usually listed in the phone book under Lions Eye Bank, or contact Eye-Bank Association of America, 1111 Tulane Avenue, New Orleans, La. 70112). Other parts of the body which can prolong others' lives are kidneys (contact the National Kidney Foundation, 116 East 27th Street, New York, N.Y. 10010); pituitary glands, for children suffering from serious growth problems (National Pituitary Agency, Suite 503, 210 West Fayette Street, Baltimore, Md. 21202); and blood (Red Cross or local hospital). Researchers are in need of inner ears (Deafness Research Foundation, 336 Madison Avenue, New York, N.Y. 10017) and skin tissue (Naval Medical Research Institute, Wisconsin Avenue, Bethesda, Md. 20014).

DEATH BENEFITS

There are a number of kinds of cash payment death benefits which may be available to the survivors and which regularly go unclaimed. It is an excellent idea for every adult to keep a current list of benefits and give copies to the next of kin. However, most people don't do that, so a survivor or funeral director should check the following sources:

Social Security. All recipients, as well as everyone who has worked at a job with coverage for at least eighteen months of the last three years, are eligible for a payment of up to $255.

Veterans Administration. All veterans are entitled to $250 toward funeral costs; free burial in a national cemetery or $150 toward burial costs; and a free headstone or monument.

Life insurance
Workmen's Compensation (for an injury-related death)
Trade union
Credit union
Fraternal organization

AFTER-DEATH SWINDLES

After arranging for the disposition of the deceased, survivors sometimes find themselves the victims of a particularly loathesome group of con artists.

These swindlers read obituary notices and contact widows and widowers, often pretending not to know about the death. They may send bills or COD items or demand "final payment" on loans or insurance policies supposedly contracted for by the deceased. Their success is premised on the emotional vulnerability of their victims, plus the fact that few people know all the financial involvements, especially if small, of their next of kin.

The swindlers are often imaginative. A few years ago, one built up a thriving business in which he posed as an army sergeant, contacted families of soldiers killed in Vietnam (from lists published in a local Spanish-language newspaper), and offered to sell them special coffins in which to view the soldiers' remains. Once the $100 per coffin was collected from a community, he disappeared.

Bogus insurance brokers contact a widow and tell her about a life insurance policy which her late husband took out as a "surprise." She is entitled to all the money, *if* she'll just make the last, overdue payment.

Protect yourself by asking for identification from everyone who contacts you; demanding proof of any agreement or contract signed by the deceased; and paying only on receipt of any merchandise or dividends. A legitimate businessperson won't be troubled with these requirements—a con artist may flee.

GLOSSARY

burial vault: a four-sided coffin enclosure which prevents earth from caving in. Most cemeteries require a burial vault or grave liner.

casket: coffin.

columbarium: a building or wall which accommodates cremated remains (usually in urns).

cremation: reduction of a corpse to bone and ashes or *cremains* at a crematory. *Direct cremation* involves taking the body from place of death immediately to the crematory. *Indirect cremation* follows a funeral.

embalming: temporary preservation of the deceased by means of injecting chemicals into the body. The primary reason for embalming is to keep the body presentable for viewing—it is unnecessary for closed-casket funerals or cremations. The embalming fluids used in this country preserve corpses for viewing, but do not prolong decomposition of the body to any substantial degree.

funeral: commemorative service for deceased person held in the presence of the corpse (with the casket open for viewing or closed).

funeral director: mortician, undertaker. "Funeral director" is the term preferred by the practitioners. Interestingly, it removes the connotations of mortality and burial present in the other words; it makes the handler of dead bodies sound more like one who oversees a theatrical production.

grave liner: a simple, three-sided concrete container for a casket which prevents earth from caving in, required by most cemeteries. Serves the same purpose as a *burial* (or *grave*) *vault,* which is more expensive and possibly preserves the casket somewhat longer.

mausoleum: aboveground structure which houses the corpse or remains.

memorial service: a commemorative service for a deceased person held after the corpse is removed (and buried or cremated).

pre-need arrangements: plans for a funeral or cemetery plot made before death occurs.

urn: a container for cremated remains; it is buried, placed in a columbarium, or given to survivors to keep or to use to scatter the remains.

urn garden: a cemetery area where urns are buried.

SELECTED BIBLIOGRAPHY

Funerals: Consumers' Last Rights, editors of *Consumer Reports,* 1977. Available from Consumers Union, Mount Vernon, N.Y. 10550.

MITFORD, JESSICA. *The American Way of Death.* New York: Simon and Schuster, 1963.

———. "The Funeral Salesmen." *McCall's,* November 1977.

MORGAN, ERNEST. *A Manual of Death Education and Simple Burial.* 8th ed.; Burnsville, N.C.: Celo Press, 1977 (1st ed., 1962). $1.50.

The Price of Death: A Survey Method and Consumer Guide for Funerals, Cemeteries and Grave Markers, Consumer Survey Handbook 3, Seattle Regional Office, Federal Trade Commission, 1975. Available from the FTC, 2840 Federal Building, Seattle, Wash. 98174.

10

Keeping mind and body fit: health clubs, dance studios, etc.

Now! Your way to an instant new figure. You can be Bikini Slim in Only 60 minutes. Introducing ONE HOUR European "Quick Figure". LOSE up to 15 inches in just one hour during your first treatment . . .

It's easy as 1. You spend 5 minutes in the whirlpool mineral spa. 2. Then you are ever so carefully wrapped with our exclusive tape wrap, moistened with the European "Quick Figure" solution. 3. You do nothing but relax, nap or read a book for one hour while you are inched away . . . from the woman you are to the woman you want to be. —Ad for a Texas health club

The Legislature declares that the purpose of this title is to safeguard the public against fraud, deceit, imposition and financial hardship . . . in the field of health studio services by prohibiting or restricting false or misleading advertising, onerous contract terms, harmful financial practices, and other unfair, dishonest, deceptive, destructive, unscrupulous, fraudulent and discriminatory practices by which the public has been injured in connection with contracts for health studio services. —California Health Studios Act, Calif. Civ. Code, §1812.50

Mrs. John P. Boyd, a 56-year-old widow, sold her home and used the proceeds of her husband's life insurance policy to pay for 2,438 hours of dancing lessons that cost her $27,000. . . . "I was lonely," Mrs. Boyd says in explaining her actions. —New York *Times,* December 13, 1973

Dance studio contracts were the product of intense, emotional and unrelenting sales pressure. . . . The record is replete with trick advertisements to draw prospects, sham dance analysis tests . . . promises of social status and companionship, psychological sales techniques. . . . Many were reduced to tears. One woman begged from her knees to be allowed to contract. —Opinion of the court in *Arthur Murray Studio of Washington, Inc.* v. *F.T.C.* 458 F. 2d 622, 625 (5th Cir. 1972)

Wonderful things happen when you know how to dance. —Fred Astaire Dance Studio ad

The urge for self-improvement comes to all of us at some point, and we usually manage to resist it successfully. The marketplace, however, offers many ways to build a better you. Nowadays there are lessons available in everything from ballroom dancing to transcendental meditation. To satisfy your yen for physical fitness, there are health clubs, figure salons, weight reduction centers, and body-building courses.

While lessons and club memberships are often beneficial, they sometimes pose serious problems for consumers. A principal difficulty is that when people sign up for these services they can't be exactly sure what they'll be receiving for their money. The karate lessons, for example, may be taught by an expert, or by an incompetent who's one chop ahead of the class. Once you're committed to a long-term contract, however, it is difficult to get out, even if there is a good reason.

Apart from dissatisfaction with the seller's performance, there are many reasons to stop attending lessons or to discontinue memberships. Your initial enthusiasm may quickly wane. Or you may fall ill or have to move. The seller usually collects your money at the outset, and may refuse to give it back no matter what subsequently occurs. For that reason, it is best never to pay for services far in advance of when you use them.

The number of self-improvement offerings are considerable, and discussing them all would be impossible. Instead, the two industries which have generated the greatest number of customer complaints—health spas and dance studios—will be highlighted.

HEALTH CLUBS

It is not easy to decide what to do with flab—you can hide it under loose-fitting clothes, tuck it into a tight-fitting girdle, put a belt around it, or just give up on it. Or you can do what thousands of Americans did last year: take it to a health club.

Although their advertisements often claim members can shed pounds and inches in no time, health clubs—or "spas," "gyms," and "salons," as they are also called—are used not only to lose weight. Many health-conscious consumers, tied to desks and offices all day, go to the clubs to exercise and to keep in shape. Physical fitness for its own sake has become a new national pastime, with just about everyone running, stretching, lifting, or pulling (in addition to the usual pushing and shoving).

What every potential health club member should know is this: the odds are great that no matter how long your membership runs—one year, two years, or a lifetime—*you probably will stop using the facilities within 60 days of signing the club's contract*. For a variety of reasons, consumers rapidly become disenchanted with these places, sacrificing hundreds of dollars in membership fees. This mass disappointment is a fact which the clubs turn to their advantage, by collecting full payment from their "dropouts" while recruiting many more customers than they could handle if all members used the facilities. As one health spa chain stated in a report for stockholders:

(Wide World Photos)

Nearly all memberships are sold under agreements providing for 24 equal monthly payments. Members are obligated to make payment on their membership contracts regardless of their use of the company's facilities. Approximately 75% of all new members cease to use such facilities to any material extent after the second month of their membership.

Thus, health club members might well fit the classic theater owner's description of the audiences for a failing play—"they're staying away in droves." But the non-participation of paying health club members costs them money, so we can safely assume the problems involved are serious. To forewarn those about to jog to the nearest physical fitness salon, the principal drawbacks of these establishments are listed below.

1. Overcrowding of facilities. This is a common problem in urban locations, where many individuals have similar work schedules and limited free time. Clubs often take on all prospective customers, regardless of the strain on the equipment and facilities at hours of peak use. Numerous clubs claim that membership is "exclusive" or "limited," but these are often false verbal promises not contained in the contract.

2. Poor maintenance. At some spas, exercise machines are always inoperable, the pool closed for repairs, or the sauna condemned by the Board of Health. It is commonplace for clubs to spend more on advertising their facilities than on maintaining them. After a few frustrating visits to a club with one or another of its principal features out of order, it is not surprising that members drop out.

3. Restrictive rules. Some clubs' own rules limit access to the facilities to certain hours of the day or to specific days of the week. The gym may be open to men only half of the time, and to women the other half. Or special programs and classes may pre-empt general use of the facilities for several hours each week. Not all consumers are made aware of these limitations before they enroll, although the restrictions may make use of the club extremely inconvenient.

4. Overblown promises of weight loss or body improvement. Some consumers place great faith in claims that they can become slim and trim in a few weeks, or even days, following the simple program of some health spa. But the countless "scientific plans" and programs for body improvement devised by the spas are of dubious medical validity, administered by people with little, if any, medical knowledge. Some involve diets which are unsuitable or even unsafe for certain individuals. Others just reflect the latest fads, and turn out to be worthless.

Many weight-reducing plans feature "passive exercise" machines (e.g., vibrating chairs, tables, and belts), advertised as the effortless way to lose weight. In reality there is no easy, lasting weight-loss technique, and these claims merely play upon the anxieties generated by our weight-conscious society. Relying on overblown claims of health spas can be foolish and even dangerous.

5. False promises of "personalized" instruction. Consumers are lured into enrolling in some clubs by promises or personalized training and attention from body-building experts. But the program supposedly designed "just for you" may be a standard set of routine calisthenics and exercises given to everybody. Few clubs have enough experts to give personalized attention to individual members.

6. Unfounded health-care claims. Too many health club employees act like amateur doctors, assuring people who enroll that they can get relief from ailments ranging from high blood pressure to constipation. The promised cures rarely come to pass. One woman with varicose veins was told they would disappear, along with her lifelong curvature of the spine. "To hear them tell it, I was going to end up with the body of a young girl, all in proper proportion, and without dieting." Of course, her body remained the same, although her purse was a little lighter when she left the spa.

7. Curtailment of spa activities. Contracts sometimes provide that if the spa doesn't provide some essential feature, customers may use the facilities of another of its branches. This may be used to justify a cut in services at a neighborhood location, forcing patrons to travel greater distances and discouraging them from frequent participation. Owners of health club chains have been known to close down local branches entirely, informing customers that there's an open branch only twenty-five miles away.

A variation on this theme occurs when a club solicits members before its facility is ready for use. Consumers are offered "pre-opening price discounts" to enroll early. But construction delays, or unrealistic calculations of when "opening day" will be, lead to consumer victimization. Ironclad contract clauses do not permit the customer to cancel because of the delay, and those consumers who lose interest, or move, or make other plans, find they have obliged themselves to pay even if the spa opens one or two years late.

8. Use of high-pressure tactics. Spa employees cajole consumers into long-term commitments by the use of flattery, pressure to decide immediately, and offers of phony "discounts." Customers lured by ads which promise "10 free sessions" discover the free sessions are part of a two-year package costing $250. The spa manager may offer a "special discount" if the customer enrolls that same day—without taking time to think it over. Relays of fresh salespeople may alternate in pressuring the prospect to sign. The consumer who asks to take the contract home to read is told that this is against company policy. Reluctant customers may be falsely told the "application form" is not a binding contract, or that it is cancelable at any time (although the small print says the opposite). These tactics are quite effective. Once in the sales manager's muscular grip, few consumers escape without signing.

9. One-sided contract terms. Health club contracts are routinely harsh and grossly one-sided. Consumers who must discontinue use of the club for personal reasons—pregnancy, illness, job transfer or relocation to another city—are usually not allowed to discontinue their memberships. Neither do the clubs make much effort to screen out persons who are unable to take advantage of the spa's programs because of medical problems.

The clubs typically do not even take responsibility for injuries which they inflict on members. Contract clauses excuse the clubs from liability for negligent acts by employees. Thus, injuries caused by improperly maintained equipment or strains suffered as a result of suggested exercises too strenuous for the individual involved do not require the club to take any corrective action or to pay for the harm done.

WHAT YOU SHOULD DO BEFORE JOINING A HEALTH CLUB

1. Know yourself physically. **The President's Council on Physical Fitness strongly advises that no one over 35 start strenuous exercise without having a doctor's checkup, including an electrocardiogram taken under physical stress. Those under 35 should be warned that they too may have hidden ailments and that a complete physical examination is a good idea, especially if you are a stranger to exertion.** *Also, if your exercise program involves a diet, let your doctor prescribe it.*
2. Look for a club with facilities for vigorous, active exercise such as a swimming pool, jogging track, and dance classes. **Avoid clubs that offer weight-loss guarantees, vibrating belts, spot reducing, and other passive motorized machines.**
3. Visit the club's facilities during the hours you are likely to attend. **Club attendance can be very high during certain hours and can prohibit you from obtaining full use of the facilities if those are your only available times.**
4. Consider cheaper, more reliable ways of reaching your fitness goals. **Many public recreation departments and especially YMCA's (Young Men's Christian Associations) offer quality fitness programs for**

men and women with well-trained instructors. (YWCA's are being
phased out as YMCA's open their programs to women.) They require
medical certificates and cost much less. YMCA's require you to purchase
an annual membership, which varies in cost but is generally much less.
While membership involves signing a contract, you can at least obtain a
refund if you cannot continue with the program.

5. *Ask yourself whether you will be able to attend the club regularly
and obtain your money's worth.* In any case, sign up for as short a period as is possible, since your expectations may not be met or your life
style may change over a period of time. Ask about club policy if you are
injured or become pregnant; some will extend your policy for the length
of time you are unable to attend.

6. *Don't fall for pre-opening "specials" or "discounts."* Join a club
that is already operating so that you can visit it first.

7. *If possible, take the contract home and read it before signing.* If it
involves a great deal of money or if you can do so easily, have a lawyer
read it. Look for clauses in which the club waives responsibility for injury to you while on the premises. If you sign such a contract, be sure
you have a good personal health insurance plan. Finally, make sure you
understand what happens if you decide to cancel your membership.
There are many different and confusing refund policies. Under present
collection practices some health clubs can still harass customers and
may sue for the full contract price, even if the member never used the
club's facilities.

8. *Ask about the instructors' qualifications in physical fitness.* Too
many clubs hire attractive, well-built instructors who may not have the
necessary training for teaching or supervising physical fitness activities.
Some clubs do require all of their instructors to participate in at least a
24-hour training program conducted by club personnel.*

DANCING IN THE DARK

One of the most cynical of all consumer swindles takes place in the nation's dance studios, where consumer abuse is set to music. In a warm and
friendly atmosphere, dance studio instructors charm their struggling partners into long-term contracts, endless lessons, and near bankruptcy. Elderly
men and women have contracted for hundreds of hours of lessons, far beyond their physical endurance (and sometimes far beyond their life expect-
ancies). The carefully rehearsed, subtly performed dance lesson scheme is
very instructive indeed—as a step-by-step lesson in consumer fraud.

Unscrupulous dance schools give a unique twist to the most common
selling tricks. "Bait" advertisements promise a free introductory lesson, or a

* Reprinted from: New York Public Interest Research Group, Inc., project director Joseph
Krasevec, *Consumer's Guide to Queens Health Clubs* (1975).

short series of lessons for a few dollars. In the studio, however, consumers are gently maneuvered into much more expensive commitments by instructors who attempt to create an emotional tie between themselves and each new student. The means used are those of friendly persuasion: a warm smile, personal attention, generous praise, compliments. Dancing, of course, offers the perfect opportunity to develop a personal and intimate male-female relationship. The play upon the customer's emotions is no accident. Studio managers know that people often come because they are lonely. As one woman who signed up for 2,500 dance lessons said: "My husband passed away. I had no social life, and when I went to this studio they were friendly and loving, and in an intimate atmosphere, they would tell me, 'You want to be a great dancer? You are going to be the best!'" The flattery of an attractive, experienced partner, delivered with an air of utmost sincerity, is difficult to resist.

Some patrons are led to believe they will be dancing in international competitions. Studios nurture this sense of unreality by planning phony dance "tests." The student and instructor, observed by the studio's manager or filmed on videotape, dance together. The manager and assistant manager then confer privately to "judge" the performance. The student sits with the instructor (sometimes holding hands), waiting for the results. After letting some tension build, the "judges" emerge and announce that the student has done outstandingly well. In the midst of congratulations and good feelings all around, the student is urged to go for the "Silver Medal" of the "Gold Trophy," or some other symbol of achievement. To do so, of course, requires more lessons. Any student who resists may find the usually friendly instructor becoming cold, angry, or hurt. The manager adds to the pressure by threatening to fire the instructor for "inability to inspire your students." The unwitting consumer victim is caught in a cross fire of pleadings, appeals, and threats, all leading to the same result: more lessons.

These scenes can be emotionally wrenching. One woman, who underwent a series of such sales appeals, told the FTC:

> The constant battering, it never let up. Two weeks at a time was about all they would let you go without being approached for some little additional something. . . . I was a nervous wreck there most of the time.

Keeping students on the upward path to terpsichorean glory (and dance studio profit) necessitates an elaborate structure of goals. A Florida judge described the various achievement levels created by one dance studio to coax a 51-year-old woman out of $31,000 worth of lessons:

> At one point she was sold 545 additional hours of dancing lessons to be entitled to the award of the "Bronze Medal," signifying that she had reached "the Bronze Standard," a supposed designation of dance achievement by students of Arthur Murray, Inc. . . .
>
> At one point, while she still had to her credit about 900 unused hours of instruction, she was induced to purchase an additional 24 hours of lessons to participate in a trip to Miami at her own expense, where she would be "given the opportunity to dance with members of the Miami Studio. . . ."
>
> Later, while she still had over 1,000 unused hours of instruction, she was induced to buy 151 additional hours at a cost of $2,049.00 to be eligible for a "Student Trip to Trinidad," at her own expense, as she later learned. . . .
>
> On another occasion, while she still had over 1,200 unused hours, she was induced to buy an additional 175 hours of instruction at a cost of $2,472.75 to be eligible "to take a trip to Mexico."
>
> Finally, sandwiched in between other lesser sales promotions, she was influenced to buy an additional 481 hours of instruction at a cost of $6,523.81 in order to "be classified as a Gold Bar Member, the ultimate achievement of the dancing studio."

The studio no doubt bought gold bars to celebrate this ultimate achievement.

A sales trick used by sellers everywhere is the phony "discount." This is raised to an art form by the suave dance masters. Instead of offering "discounts," they offer "scholarships." A $1,500 scholarship enables its unlucky winner to take $3,900 worth of lessons for "only" $2,400. The scholarship, which merely reduces the cost of lessons to the studio's regular price, appears to the victim to be not only a price discount but also a reward for past achievement. How could anyone be so ungracious as to turn down such a generous—and flattering—offer? And so, round and round the dancing victim goes, and from contract to contract, and award to award, in a whirl that would make any consumer dizzy.

TIPS FOR TAKING LESSONS
—WITHOUT BEING TAKEN

Not all social dancing schools employ the artifices described above. But it is best to keep them in mind when considering signing up for dance lessons. Here are some points to remember:

1. Do *not* believe that the nationally known names in the dance business are above such tactics. Their studios are frequently franchises which may or may not be very reliable.

2. All studios have the monetary incentive to keep you as a customer for as long as possible. *You* must decide when you've had enough—and be prepared to meet resistance to your desire to quit.

3. Don't be fooled by false praise and glowing compliments. These are tendered to keep you a happy, and paying, customer.

4. Never sign a long-term, expensive contract for lessons. If you are asked to, refuse to make any commitment longer than six to eight weeks, and do so only after a trial period in which you can terminate lessons at any time.

5. Don't be fooled by bronze, silver, and gold trophy courses which require many lessons—they are only sales devices to obtain long-term commitments.

6. Don't join a studio just for companionship. It is very expensive, and you can find truer friends elsewhere (whom you won't have to pay).

7. Don't make payments far in advance of the lessons you will take. Payments should correspond to the number of lessons taken.

Remember that you are in charge—if the studio does not permit you to take the limited number of lessons you want, find another one. When you threaten to do so, the studio may suddenly "change its policy" to accommodate you.

Women's self-defense class in 1906. (Photographs by Byron, the Byron Collection, Museum of the City of New York)

LEGAL RIGHTS

A few states have taken measures to regulate health spas, dance studios, and others offering extended services to consumers. The laws generally group all of these businesses together under the rubric "future services" because they require the consumer to agree in advance to pay for services which will be rendered in the future. California pioneered the unusual and effective regulatory step of clamping a $500 limit on health spa contracts, and a $2,500 limit on dance studio deals. Further, under California law if the consumer must stop attending a club or studio because of physical disability (or worse, death) the contract is automatically canceled. Following California's lead, Illinois put a $2,500 ceiling on all future-service contracts and prohibited agreements which last for the "lifetime of the buyer." Wisconsin law allows any consumer to cancel a future-service arrangement, without penalty, within three days of the seller's performance under the contract. The seller may not collect more than a year's payment in advance (a merchant who receives full payment long in advance has little incentive to maintain the quality of its services).

Despite the variety of rules designed to curb the excesses of these sellers, the misrepresentations and unfair practices described in this chapter still persist. The Federal Trade Commission has proposed a nationwide rule which would require all health clubs and gyms to limit their contracts to two years; to provide reasonable refund policies for patrons who discontinue their membership; and to give all customers a three-day "cooling off" period during which they could cancel their contracts without obligation. This rule, originally proposed in 1975, has not yet been enacted, and some or all of its provisions may change before it appears in its final form.

Given the unrealistic expectations raised by the operators of health clubs, reducing salons, body-building courses, and all the rest, much consumer disappointment is inevitable. In the world of self-improvement, it is best to practice careful consumer self-defense.

11

Home improvements

> Hi! We just finished blacktopping a driveway in the neighborhood, and we've got some extra materials left over. If you like, we can do your driveway too, for *half price*. Our boss will think we used up all the materials on the first job, and you'll do us a favor by not making us drive back to the office with this load.

So begins one of the time-honored frauds in the home improvement field. Some blacktoppers collect their bargain fees, go back to the truck—and just drive away. Others stay to put down a black, oily concoction which washes away with the next rain, leaving a mucky residue on the front lawn.

A variation on this scheme has the seller offering a remarkable bargain "if you will merely allow our company to use your home as a model to show your neighbors and to display in our advertising." The offer may be to install a new roof, to remodel a kitchen, to sell aluminum siding, or to waterproof a basement. The job either is never begun or is abandoned as soon as a substantial payment is received. In some cases, the work is performed, but with such cheap materials and shoddy workmanship that even the "bargain" price is a rip-off.

Some "home improvers" can more accurately be termed "house wreckers." Consumers dealing with one New York contractor were left with gaping holes in their walls, plaster falling from the ceilings, and debris coating their floors. Others found themselves cooking their meals on portable stoves for months, because the home improver had disconnected the gas lines. One woman, who wanted a bathroom renovated for her elderly sick mother, was reassured by a promise to complete the job "immediately." Five weeks later nothing had been done and the woman called to complain. "That same day a worker arrived and took the bathroom apart," she said. "Then everyone disappeared again."

Purchasing a home improvement job from an itinerant worker is very risky. While reputable businesses usually maintain offices in the community, shady characters frequently operate solely out of a truck, and can never be located when the victimized homeowner realizes what has happened. Government officials have become particularly familiar with the handiwork of one notorious band of gypsy con artists who travel in caravans throughout the country, cheating homeowners with an endless variety of home repair rackets. After going through a community, the clan picks up and moves on, before homeowner complaints bring out the authorities.

Primping on Pennsylvania Avenue. (Thomas McAvoy, *Life*, copyright 1945 Time Inc.)

Scare tactics are common in these rackets. Sales agents for one furnace company, posing as government safety inspectors, told furnace owners that "old Betsy" was about to blow and probably destroy the entire house. The "inspector" made this ominous diagnosis after totally disassembling the homeowner's furnace. With the furnace on the floor in a thousand pieces, even the most reluctant homeowners agreed to buy the new model recommended by the phony inspector.

CHOOSING A CONTRACTOR

These outright frauds are just the most flagrant examples of abuse in the home repair field. Millions of people are disappointed with the quality of work performed by hired contractors who do incompetent work, who fail to give reliable cost estimates, or who choose low-grade, inadequate materials. Because of this, it is important to choose a home improvement contractor with care.

First, think carefully about what you want done. An outside contractor may not be needed at all. Many jobs can be done with the help of do-it-yourself manuals, some of which are provided free or at low cost by the federal government (write to the U. S. Department of Agriculture Extension Service, Washington, D.C., 20251 and to the U. S. Department of Housing and Urban Development, Washington, D.C. 20410). At a minimum they will give you an idea of how much work is involved and what is a reasonable fee for doing it. Local utility companies also issue advice on home insulation and other energy-saving tips (an excellent booklet is *How to Save Money by Insulating Your Home,* available in New York from Consolidated Edison, Consumer Affairs Department, 4 Irving Place, New York, N.Y. 10003).

For complicated tasks, it is best to seek out a local contractor with a proven reputation. A good way to begin is to ask for recommendations from people who have lived in the community and from friends who have had work done in the past. Do *not* rely on the local Yellow Pages or on newspaper ads.

Ask several contractors for price estimates. Beware of markedly low estimates and unbelievable bargains—these may indicate general incompetence, the intended use of cheap materials, or fraud. Visit the contractor's place of business. Is it a real office, preferably one that's been there for a while, or is it the back of a truck? Ask prospective contractors for a bank reference and for one or two customer references (good contractors will be happy to have you examine their prior work). Check with the Better Business Bureau or local consumer affairs office to make sure there's no backlog of complaints about the contractor, particularly if it's a major job. For very substantial projects, such as adding to an existing structure, consider hiring an architect, who will choose the contractor for you, design the addition, and supervise the work. As a source of professional advice and planning, an architect may well be worth the additional cost.

In many cities and counties, home improvement contractors must be licensed in order to operate. Contact the local consumer office or the state attorney general's office to see if this is the case in your area. If so, ask to see the contractor's license number. A license is no guarantee of honesty or competence, but it guarantees a minimal compliance with the law and will provide you with a place (the licensing agency) to go with complaints. Unlicensed dealers may be "fly-by-nighters" with no ties to the community; avoid them at all costs. Before hiring the licensed contractor, see if the licensing agency has any negative information about it in its files.

PAYING THE CONTRACTOR

Always get a written agreement before giving someone money to begin work. That contract should provide for payment in installments which are scheduled to coincide roughly with the amount of work performed. The larger the final payments are, the more incentive the contractor has to finish the job on schedule. The completion date and the amount of each payment should be specified in the written contract. The contract should also specify the exact job to be done and the materials to be used (listing them by brand name and model numbers wherever possible). You may want to consult with local building supply dealers or home improvement experts in a local consumer agency to ensure that the materials suggested are of reasonable quality. Never make final payment until the job is done to your satisfaction: it's your only leverage.

Many state laws create "materialmen's liens" on a homeowner's house or property. This is a legal right which gives suppliers of materials (such as siding, roofing, and lumber) the right to seize your property if their bills are not paid. While the general contractor will hire and pay subcontractors to supply materials, a dishonest general contractor may abandon the job and leave you stuck with the subcontractors' bills. The existence of liens is an important reason to make sure the contractor is financially responsible and of good reputation. It is wise to consult a lawyer before undertaking an expensive transaction involving your home, to ensure that you are not placing what is probably your most valuable asset in jeopardy. This can be remedied by putting a clause in the contract requiring the contractor to provide you with an affidavit that all materials suppliers and laborers have been paid before final payment is due the contractor.

SEVEN DANGER SIGNS

Beware of any home improver who:
1. **Has no license (where law requires one).**
2. **Asks you to sign a Certificate of Completion before the work described in the certificate is performed.**
3. **Maintains no permanent business location.**
4. **Claims to be working "in the neighborhood" and has extra materials left over.**
5. **Offers to make yours a "model home" in the neighborhood.**
6. **Will not supply names of previous customers whom you can call for references.**
7. **Pressures you to decide quickly or lose the chance to get the work done.**

YOUR LEGAL RIGHTS

Many cities, counties, and states require home improvers to meet minimal standards of honesty and fairness in performing their work. Even where no laws specifically regulate this field, consumer agencies can act under the general anti-fraud statutes which exist in all states. It is important to note, however, that, as a practical matter, most agencies have a difficult time *proving* improper behavior by a home improver. Most cases require the testimony of an expert who can evaluate the quality of the work done and determine if the job contracted for was adequately performed. Few consumers and few consumer agencies have access to this kind of expertise. As a consequence, many legitimate complaints go unresolved because of lack of legally sufficient evidence. Small claims court lawsuits by consumers are often unsuccessful for this very reason. Nevertheless, the court or a consumer agency may be able to mediate some mutually acceptable compromise, so they should not be ignored by dissatisfied consumers. But here, as elsewhere, avoiding trouble in the first place is the only sure remedy.

Before you sign any contract, take two important measures. First, check the contract for the fourteen points listed below. Second, take your time—don't sign until you've had a chance to think about it, to comparison-shop, and to show it to someone whose judgment you trust.

HOMEOWNER'S CHECKLIST

Before you sign the contract:	Yes	No
Does the contract heading clearly state the contractor's name, address, telephone and license number?	———	———
Is the date of the contract filled in?	———	———
Does the contract clearly state when the job will begin and how much time is estimated for completion?	———	———
Are all advertised or verbal representations, guarantees, and warranties spelled out and made a part of the contract?	———	———
Is every item of the repair or renovation clearly printed or typed in? Quantity——— Quality——— Brand name——— Model number———	———	———
Are both labor and material guaranteed against defects or poor workmanship? For how long?———————	———	———
Does the contract contain a clause to the effect that shortcomings and defects in both material and labor will be corrected without charge?	———	———
On brand name items, will the contractor provide manufacturer's warranty cards for you to complete and mail in? Don't rely on the contractor to send these in. All products manufactured after July 4, 1975, must state whether warranty is "full" or "limited." Which type is on the product the contractor intends to use? ———————	———	———
Will there be any hidden charges used as a device to disguise the actual cost of the job?	———	———
Will the contractor procure all permits required by law?	———	———
Is there any charge for procuring these permits?	———	———
Does the contractor have a performance bond?	———	———
Are his or her Workmen's Compensation, Public Liability, and Property Damage insurance in force?	———	———
Don't let work begin until the contractor provides you with certificates of insurance. Does the contractor or salesman try to rush you into signing?	———	———

—Source: New York City Department of Consumer Affairs.

SPECIAL NOTE: TERMITE EXTERMINATORS

The termite is the homeowner's natural enemy. So is the termite exterminator who offers to make a free termite inspection and *always* finds the little devils, whether they're there or not. It is important for the homeowner to know something about termites before calling in a professional, to avoid paying for the elimination of nonexistent termites.

First, termites are easily confused with flying ants. Both insects swarm in large numbers in the spring (and sometimes in the fall). They look alike, but upon close examination you can tell them apart. The ant has two large wings and two small wings; the termite's four wings are equal in size. The ant may be colored brown, red, or yellow, while the termite is black. Finally, the ant's body is in two sections connected by a narrow channel; the termite's body is of an even thickness. It is not difficult to catch one of these insects in flight and examine it for telltale characteristics.

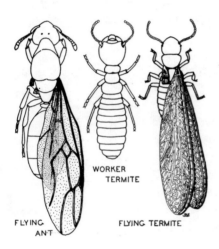

WORKER TERMITE

FLYING ANT

FLYING TERMITE

Flying cousins. (Nassau County Cooperative Extension)

Never feel rushed to find a termite exterminator. Termites do not destroy a house in a few days. In fact, they take several years to seriously damage wooden structures. They live in the soil and build up a large, complex colony. If food is not at hand, they'll go looking for some, and, wood lovers that they are, they may find an edible home nearby. A feeding group will hollow out the inside of some item of wood. They will avoid piercing the outside of the wood, which protects them from the inhospitable dryness of the air. The termites don't work incessantly; their need for moisture causes them to return to the soil each day. This means that they can be exterminated by poisons placed in the soil surrounding the house. The poisons must be carefully and thoroughly distributed, however, to prevent the termites from finding any usable pathway into and out of the house.

Proper extermination is thus a big job, and usually requires a professional exterminator. But beware of those experts who claim your house is in imminent danger of collapse—it never is. Take your time, compare prices, and check the references and reputation of the exterminator. Don't skip these steps because one firm advertises a "free inspection." That may simply be a device to entrap not termites, but customers.

SELECTED BIBLIOGRAPHY

Protecting Your Housing Investment, a 32-page booklet available from the U. S. Department of Housing and Urban Development, Washington, D.C. 20410.

12

---

43 million do it every year: home moving

When Thomas M. Edwards was transferred to New Jersey from California two summers ago, the telephone company executive figured he had about 8,000 pounds of household goods to move. So when Valley Moving & Storage of San Jose calculated the weight at about 10,000 pounds, Mr. Edwards was puzzled and a little suspicious.

But state and federal investigators weren't puzzled at all. They were taking pictures of the move with a hidden camera, and as Valley employees secretly loaded nearly 2000 pounds of junk metal onto the moving van, the camera recorded it all. — *The Wall Street Journal,* September 15, 1978.

We are a people on the move. One out of five Americans moves each year, and the rate is increasing. If it keeps up, evolution may ultimately have to outfit us with wheels instead of toes, a set of high-beam headlights, and ample trunk space in the rear. For the time being, however, we must rely on the home-moving industry, which has passed the one-billion-dollar-a-year mark in sales and eagerly looks forward to the job of disassembling and reassembling over 3,000 American homes a day.

Moving is usually a physical and psychic trauma. Although no consumer advice can change this fact, there is some information which can help you keep the confusion, commotion, and chaos down to a minimum.

Moving companies which transport household goods across state lines are regulated by the Interstate Commerce Commission (ICC), a federal agency. Specific ICC rules govern some, but not all, aspects of the transaction between the consumer and the mover.

SELECTING A MOVER

In choosing a mover, two factors are most important: price and reliability. For large moves, prices may vary considerably, so get price estimates from several different movers. Cost, however, should not be the sole determining factor in selection. When you are moving all your worldly possessions to a distant location, it is crucial to find a reliable, trustworthy mover.

To help consumers in their choice of a mover, the Interstate Commerce Commission requires all interstate moving companies to compile data on their performance, and to make this information available to all consumers. These performance reports indicate how many claims for loss or damage were made against the mover; how many shipments were delivered late; and how often the mover incorrectly estimated the final cost of shipment.

(*The New Yorker*)

Figures compiled in 1977 for the twenty largest moving companies show that substantially incorrect estimates (either 10 percent more or 10 percent less than final cost) were given more than half the time. One company underestimated its charges in over 30 percent of its moves.

Failing to meet promised delivery dates was also a major problem. Several

1977 PERFORMANCE DATA—TWENTY LARGEST** MOVERS

PREPARED BY THE INTERSTATE COMMERCE COMMISSION DATA OBTAINED FROM THE LISTED MOVERS 1977 ANNUAL PERFORMANCE REPORTS —UNAUDITED—	SHIP-MENTS	ESTIMATES			ON-TIME PERFORMANCE		
	shipments moved for individual householders who paid charges at delivery (COD)	shipments moved on which estimates were prepared	percent of estimates which were over estimated 10 percent or more	percent of estimates which were under estimated 10 percent or more	percent of shipments picked up more than 5 days later than specified in order for service	percent of shipments picked up 1 to 5 days later than specified in order for service	percent of shipments delivered more than 5 days later than specified in order for service
Average—20 movers listed	419,001	245,193	27.5	23.7	1.3	3.1	5.3
Aero-Mayflower Transit Co.	71,230	43,889	33.6	25.7	1.3	2.1	7.1
Allied Van Lines, Inc.	90,117	46,134	26.5	26.4	1.4	3.3	2.6
American Red Ball Transit Co.	8,651	5,447	26.9	27.4	1.6	2.9	11.1
Atlas Van Lines Inc.	20,838	12,651	28.2	29.4	1.1	1.9	9.2
Bekins Van Lines Co.	56,217	26,773	37.9	23.7	1.0	3.0	6.1
Burnham Van Service, Inc.	2,498	1,123	29.0	21.4	0.3	0.3	9.2
Engel Van Lines	1,906	1,370	12.6	18.8	0	0.3	3.2
Fogarty Van Lines, Inc.	5,914	5,034	29.4	22.3	0.2	0.4	0.5
Global Van Lines, Inc.	14,008	10,231	22.4	24.1	0.3	1.6	7.5
Ivory Van Lines, Inc.	2,091	1,084	27.6	26.8	0.9	2.4	1.2
King Van Lines, Inc.	3,842	3,317	12.8	15.5	5.0	5.9	1.3
Lyon Moving & Storage Co.	7,103	2,471	22.2	26.1	0.3	0.6	4.5
National Van Lines, Inc.	6,237	2,723	26.7	28.7	1.0	1.5	19.3
North American Van Lines, Inc.	59,638	40,278	24.4	20.1	1.4	4.7	3.0
Pan American Van Lines, Inc.	3,161	2,401	32.0	21.7	0.9	0.2	2.4
Republic Van Lines, Inc.	6,186	5,016	22.7	24.5	0.1	1.2	3.5
Smyth Van Line, Inc.	4,907	3,152	19.9	31.9	0.7	0.6	9.1
Trans American Van Service	2,082	1,895	10.1	13.6	0	0.6	8.3
United Van Lines, Inc.	43,859	26,732	21.5	19.6	2.2	5.5	5.1
Wheaton Van Lines, Inc.	8,516	3,472	19.6	11.3	0.4	0.6	7.8

**Based on Total COD Shipments Delivered—1977

| | HANDLING OF LOSS–DAMAGE–INCONVENIENCE CLAIMS | | | | | | | | |
percent of shipments delivered 1 to 5 days later than specified in order for service	percent of shipments on which a $50 or greater claim for loss or damage was filed	percent of shipments on which a claim was filed for expenses resulting from delay by mover	average number of days required to settle loss and damage claims	percent of claims settled within 30 days after filing	percent of claims settled between 31 and 60 days after filing	percent of claims settled more than 60 days after filing	percent of claims settled during year prior to institution of law suit by the shipper	percent of claims settled during year after the institution of a law suit but prior to settlement by the court	percent of claims settled during year following a final decree by a court after shipper brought suit
8.1	17.8	1.4	28	69	16	16	99.2	0.8	0.2
9.1	22.7	0.7	32	66	12	22	99.7	0.3	0.0
4.9	14.8	.7	39	61	17	22	98.0	1.8	.2
9.9	15.8	2.1	32	57	29	14	100.0	0	0
11.6	23.1	1.7	24	67	19	14	99.7	0.2	0.1
8.9	18.4	2.7	25	75	14	11	99.2	0.4	0.4
8.7	15.8	1.2	13	88	11	1	99.8	0.2	0
11.4	11.1	0.8	41	34	26	40	100.0	0	0
1.2	25.5	0.3	28	71	17	12	99.7	0.1	0.1
10.9	8.8	1.2	24	77	18	4	100.0	0	0
3.2	14.5	0.3	14	76	11	13	99.0	1.0	0
7.9	13.6	0.7	57	27	26	47	96.5	0	3.5
7.3	14.5	0.9	20	78	20	2	99.9	0	0.1
16.2	20.7	2.6	34	58	29	13	99.2	0.5	0.3
8.9	20.4	2.1	20	76	15	9	99.3	0.6	0.1
6.2	14.9	0.1	21	75	20	5	99.0	0.5	0.5
6.9	20.6	2.1	33	59	29	12	98.5	1.4	0.1
8.7	6.4	1.4	45	43	25	32	90.1	9.4	0.3
1.3	11.6	.01	38	31	44	25	97.3	0	2.7
8.4	14.6	0.9	23	78	8	14	99.0	0.1	0
8.1	14.5	1.5	27	67	21	12	99.9	0.1	0

large companies missed delivery deadlines 20 percent of the time or more. Finally, many companies had numerous damage claims filed against them. The statistics show a great deal of difference between companies, however. Frequency of damage claims ranged from 25.5 percent of all moves for one company to 6.4 percent for another.

Similar data are available for all 2,500 interstate movers. The information is on file at ICC headquarters (at 12th and Constitution Avenue, N.W., Washington, D.C. 20423) and can be reviewed through a computer system at ICC regional offices in Atlanta, Boston, Chicago, Fort Worth, Los Angeles, Miami, New York, Philadelphia, and San Francisco. Each moving company is also required by ICC rules to furnish a copy of its most recent performance report to any prospective customer.

The ICC also publishes a very useful guide, titled *Summary of Information for Shippers of Household Goods*. The 33-page booklet contains helpful advice on preparing for the move, packing, and dealing with the mover, and provides handy checklists. Movers are required to provide you with a copy of this publication. However, it is best to write to the ICC, Household Goods Branch, Washington, D.C. 20423, for a copy of the guide as soon as you decide to move.

MOVING BRIGHTON BEACH HOTEL, CONEY ISLAND, WITH LOCOMOTIVES.

By B. C. MILLER & SON, House Movers, 979 and 998 Bergen Street, Brooklyn, N. Y.

One alternative to careful packing. (Museum of the City of New York)

ARRANGING FOR THE MOVE

Interstate movers use an *order for service* form which specifies the pickup and delivery dates, the estimated charges, the method of payment, and the location of the scale to be used in weighing your shipment. It is up to you and the mover to agree on pickup and delivery dates.

The rates charged by movers are filed with, but not set by, the ICC. All will charge a rate based on the *weight* of the goods you are shipping and the distance they must travel. To give you an estimate of the cost, the mover must approximate the weight of your furniture and other goods. This may be a rough guess, and often the actual weight is substantially different. Under current ICC rules, the mover's estimate is *not* binding in any way. A proposal now under consideration by the agency would change this, but now no error in estimation, no matter how gross, will affect the final bill.

The actual weight of the shipment is determined by a certified weighmaster or by use of a certified scale. The moving van, loaded with your goods, is driven onto a large platform scale, and the weight recorded. This figure, minus the weight of the unloaded van, yields the net weight of your goods.

It is important for you to be present at the weighing of your goods. The mover must notify you of the location of the scale; make sure to ask if you aren't told. If you are not there, funny things may happen—like the throwing in of a few concrete blocks for added measure. At the weighing, the loaded moving van, the driver, and the necessary equipment (dollies, handcarts, etc.) should be on the scale. The moving crew should *not* be (watch for this—sometimes four hefty movers jump aboard, adding 800 pounds to your bill).

You are entitled to copies of two *weight tickets*. The first shows the weight of the vehicle without your shipment (the "tare" weight). The second shows the weight of the vehicle after loading your shipment (the "gross" weight) and, by a simple subtraction, the weight of your goods ("net" weight). Make certain that your copies contain the same figures as the original tickets.

At the time your goods are picked up, the mover will give you a *bill of lading*. The bill of lading is the contract of transportation, and should state the place of delivery, where you can be reached in case of delays, and the terms of the mover's liability for loss or damage. It will also have on it the tare weight of the vehicle. Later, when you get the weight tickets, check to see that the tare weight recorded on the bill of lading is identical to the tare weight written on the weight tickets.

If several customers' goods are being shipped on the same van, you can ask to see the *vehicle-load manifest* (which the driver must carry and show you upon request). The manifest contains the gross, tare, and net weight for your shipment and for anyone else's on the truck. Thus, to ensure complete accuracy, check the weight information on all these documents—weight tickets, bill of lading, vehicle-load manifest—to see that they correspond. Report any inaccuracies which are not immediately corrected to the nearest ICC office.

If you request it, the mover must reweigh the van at your destination. Where there is a difference in weights, the lower of the two measures is used. You may be billed for the reweighing (usually from $20 to $30), except when the reweigh shows a drop of more than 120 pounds from the original weighing or when the actual weight exceeds the estimated weight by 25 percent or more.

Occasionally, there will be no scale either at the place of origin, or en route, or at destination. In this case, the trucker will compute the bill based on an assumed, or "constructive" weight of seven pounds per cubic foot of van space used. The ICC requests that all use of constructive weight be reported to its offices.

PICKUP

Before loading your goods onto the truck the mover must prepare an *inventory,* describing the nature and condition of your goods. This is a crucial document, since it will be referred to if you later claim the mover lost or damaged anything. Check to see that the inventory accurately describes the condition of your property. Usually the mover will use a code, such as the following:

SAMPLE MOVER'S CODE

BE — Bent	**MO** — Moth-eaten
BR — Broken	**PBC** — Packed by Carrier
BU — Burned	**PBO** — Packed by Owner
CH — Chipped	**R** — Rubbed
CU — Contents & Condition	**RU** — Rusted
Unknown	**SC** — Scratched
D — Dented	**SH** — Short
F — Faded	**SO** — Soiled
G — Gouged	**T** — Torn
L — Loose	**W** — Badly Worn
M — Marred	**Z** — Cracked
MI — Mildew	

You will be asked to sign the inventory. Look at it carefully, and if you do not agree with the mover's assessment, ask that it be changed. If the driver refuses to do so, then make your own notation next to the particular item.

If you have any items of unusual value, carry them with you if possible. Any antique furniture or other item of extraordinary value entrusted to the mover should be specifically listed, in your handwriting, on the bill of lading. Most moving companies have provisions on their printed forms which deny liability for such items if they are not listed on the bill of lading.

DELIVERY AND PAYMENT

The terms of payment will be specified in the bill of lading. Generally, the mover's bill must be paid in cash or by certified check, money order, cashier's check, or traveler's check. Personal checks are not acceptable, a fact which has unpleasantly surprised many homeowners. If you are unprepared to pay the bill in this way, the mover will not unload your goods. Where the charges exceed the mover's estimate by more than 10 percent, however, you can pay the estimate plus 10 percent, have the goods unloaded, and pay the balance in fifteen days.

At delivery, make sure all items on your copy of the inventory are given to you. Don't sign any receipt until you have counted your possessions and ascertained that they are in the same condition as when you shipped them. *If there is something missing or damaged, note this on any delivery papers you are asked to sign.* Don't accept any assurance from the driver that you can make your claim later. The claim you make later will be founded upon the notations you make at the time of delivery.

CLAIMS

In the event of loss or damage to property, you must file a *claim* with the mover. After noting the damages on the delivery receipt, leave the item in its carton and contact the moving company offices (or the company's "destination agent," if one is listed on the bill of lading). Do this as soon as possible. When discussing the problem, ask for a company claim form.

In filling out the claim form, give reasonable values for your goods. The company is not required to accept your appraisal, and may discount your claim entirely if it appears inflated. A company representative may ask to inspect the damaged goods. If possible, get repair estimates or independent appraisals. They will provide useful support for your claim.

Movers must acknowledge claims within thirty days of receipt. If you need assistance in making the claim or in obtaining a response from the mover, contact the ICC's nearest local office or its headquarters. Bear in mind, however, that the ICC cannot force the mover to accept your claim. It may help in clarifying your rights and the mover's liability, but if you are not able to reach a satisfactory settlement with the mover, your only recourse is to sue. A minor moving catastrophe can be handled in small claims court.

LIABILITY

The mover's maximum responsibility in case of loss or damage is determined according to one of three formulas, to be chosen by the consumer.

◆ Under the first formula, the consumer pays nothing, and the maximum liability is computed at 60 cents per pound for each container shipped. This is totally inadequate, unless you happen to be shipping a householdful of dry cereal.

◆ Under the second option, the maximum liability is $1.25 multiplied by the weight of the entire shipment. Thus, if the shipment weighs 5,000 pounds, the mover's maximum responsibility is set at 5,000 times $1.25, or $6,250. The consumer must pay for this coverage at the rate of 50 cents per $100 of liability.

◆   Under the third option, the consumer may set the upper limit of liability at any sum greater than $1.25 times the shipment weight. Again, the consumer is charged 50 cents per $100 of coverage. This option should be chosen when the second option provides inadequate coverage for the value of the shipment.

There is a special place on the bill of lading for customers to indicate which option they choose. This coverage, it should be noted, is not insurance automatically payable upon loss or damage. It is merely the highest sum the mover will pay when actual damages equal or exceed the maximum limit.

CUTTING THE COST OF MOVING

1. Travel light. Many people carry everything they've ever owned with them from place to place. This can become really expensive, so don't transfer unused possessions from one attic or closet to another—get rid of them. Go through every closet before you move, and decide what you really want and what you don't. The rule here is: when in doubt, throw it out. Follow this rule, and your moving costs will shrink considerably.

2. Sell or dispose of some heavy items which you can replace at your new location. Items such as bricks used in bookshelves, furniture you don't particularly like, and fragile articles that may not survive the move fall into this category.

3. Consider alternative means of transporting items. Books and other heavy items may be shipped by common carrier. Valuables should be taken with you rather than sent with the mover if at all possible.

4. Do your own packing. Movers will pack for you, but this costs more. So pack your own books, clothes, etc. You may, however, want to leave the packing of certain fragile items such as dishes and glassware, large mirrors, and major appliances to the movers. Discuss special packing needs with the mover before the moving day.

5. Keep records of moving costs, including the costs related to buying your new house and selling the old. Under certain circumstances, these costs are tax-deductible (since tax rules change and are complicated, ask your accountant or the IRS for current information on deductibility of these expenses).

INTRASTATE MOVES

Moving within a state or within a single city is much cheaper and less complicated than interstate moves. You do not, however, have the benefit of ICC rules described above. The local mover's rates may be based on a per-hour basis, liability limits may be different, and licensing may or may not be required. In these circumstances, it is doubly important to hire a mover upon the personal recommendation of someone you trust, and after discussing rates and terms with several movers. Get estimates of the cost, and find out if local consumer agencies have records on the company. A number of states, usually through departments of transportation, regulate movers. So do some municipalities. Contact these agencies for information on your legal rights and the mover's responsibilities.

Because local movers may be subject to little or no regulation, it is important to make your agreement with the mover completely clear and in writing before the move takes place. During the move, you should be present to supervise both pickup and delivery.

SELECTED BIBLIOGRAPHY

The following are available free from the Interstate Commerce Commission, Washington, D.C. 20423:

Summary of Information for Shippers of Household Goods.
Public Advisory No. 1—Householders' Guide to Accurate Weights.
Public Advisory No. 2—Arranging Transportation for Small Shipments.
Public Advisory No. 3—People on the Move.
Public Advisory No. 4—Lost or Damaged Household Goods.

The ICC also maintains a toll-free hot line, 800-424-9312, to answer questions and offer other help.

13

Realty and reality: land sales

Give me land,
lots of land
'neath the starry skies above
Don't fence me in . . .

—COLE PORTER*

Lots are frequently advertised at extremely low prices. When a prospective buyer appears he is told that the low-priced lots are all sold and then is pressured to buy one that is much more expensive. If the cheaper lot is available, it may be located on the side of a cliff or in another inaccessible location. If accessible, it may be much too small for a building lot or have other undesirable features. —U. S. Department of Housing and Urban Development, *Buying Lots from Developers*

When Americans think of land, they envision wide-open spaces, green and fertile valleys, blue skies and red sunsets. When Americans buy land, they often wind up with a dusty piece of the great western desert or some choice acreage in a Florida swamp. Some find a pleasant enough spot, but one lacking such amenities as running water and electricity. A few can see their land only from the air: without public roads, there is no way to get there.

Too often, prospective land purchasers let their dreams get the best of their judgment. Sellers of undesirable real estate are experts in making their homesites sound as if they'll fulfill any dream. Buying land is a complicated task which should not be undertaken without careful consideration, consultation with a lawyer, and an on-site inspection of the property. Unscrupulous land developers attempt to convince buyers to skip these steps and to sign a contract at the first meeting with the developer. Some invite prospects to free steak dinners, often at posh hotels or restaurants. While the prospects eat, salespeople urge them to buy land, sight unseen, in distant states. The dinner is used to foster a sense of obligation, and to create a captive audience for a three- to five-hour sales presentation. In addition to sales agents hounding diners while they eat, a series of speakers, slides, and films also urge them to buy. A speaker may construct vivid verbal images of a retirement paradise or an investment bonanza, but usually the spiel bears little resemblance to reality. Even films can be doctored in order to show an unattractive area to the best advantage. One land company was accused of painting grass bright green and placing artificial pine cones on its trees for just such a promotional film.

Consumer disappointment with land purchases is very common. Here is a brief sampler of the problems innocent purchasers have encountered:

◆ A boating enthusiast bought land sight unseen in Virginia. The seller described the many waterways and "intercoastal canals" which crisscrossed the development, making it ideal for boating. After signing the contract, the buyer discovered that the "canals" were few in number—and less than a foot deep.

◆ A woman from out of state bought land near Tampa, Florida. When she went on her first visit, she found her lot—at the bottom of the Hillsborough River. The seller had subdivided the river bottom and sold it in neat parcels to all comers.

◆ A West Virginia firm promoted its property as a relaxing campsite community, complete with full recreational facilities. The facilities were there, but the seller had sold so many small lots that the lot owners could hardly get near them. At the pool, for example, the army of owners rotated seating rights every twenty minutes according to an alphabetical plan, to give everyone an equal chance.

Selling land sight unseen is an old racket. Here, in New York's Grand Central Station in 1959, a salesman hawked Florida homesites. (Wide World Photos)

◆ A man bought land in Arizona. The salesperson told him the lot was 50 feet by 150 feet. This was technically correct, but since he had bought the side of a cliff, his 50 feet was straight up.

Anyone who buys land without visiting the property beforehand is asking for trouble. No glossy brochure or sales film can substitute for a personal examination. Many developers encourage a visit, but then see to it that a sales agent is with the visitor every moment. You need time to walk around the property by yourself, free of distracting sales talk. A common tactic used to deny buyers this opportunity is to require all visitors to park their cars and be escorted around the property by company representatives. In the car, a two-way radio may be blaring with such phrases as "Hold lot 47! Hold lot 50!" This is intended to convey the message that lots are being sold rapidly. The sales agents then urge their prospects to buy right away, before the best parcels are taken. Of course, the "Hold" routine is a charade, used to pressure prospects to buy hurriedly.

Contrary to the sales pitch, the opportunity to buy expensive property will not disappear overnight. The best thing to do after the visit is: go home.

Rio Rancho Estates

RIO RANCHO ESTATES, NEW MEXICO 87124

Dear Friend:

This month Rio Rancho Estates celebrates the new season with a series of gala holiday banquets.

You are invited to attend as our complimentary guest without any obligation whatsoever.

A delicious, full-course dinner will be served. Included in our entertainment plans is the screening of our latest Southwest color film "Your Golden Future." You'll see and hear how an entirely new city offering a new way of life is being created. You'll be given valuable information on low-cost vacations—a fascinating presentation including land sales, business, recreational, retirement and other exciting opportunities now unfolding here and in neighboring Albuquerque.

Your evening should be delightful and memorable.

It is necessary that we have your reservation as soon as possible, so that we can complete seating arrangements for each couple.

Please mail the enclosed postage-free card today. You'll be glad you did.

Sincerely yours,

W. C. Hardy

Rio Rancho Estates

Send your regrets for this one. (From the collection of D. V. Ackerman, Esq.)

Don't sign anything until you've thought about it, talked it over with friends, and obtained legal advice.

LAND BUYER'S CHECKLIST

When considering whether to buy land, there are a number of important factors to think about.

1. Is the land going to be significantly changed by the developer? A wooded forest, for example, which you see on a site visit may be slated for demolition. Homesites may be planned right next to one another. Power lines may be about to crisscross your property. Beware of this sort of overplanning. On the other hand, some developers' plans are too skimpy. They may leave out such vital things as roads and sewer lines. Do *not* depend upon verbal descriptions of the seller's plans. Ask to see the *property report,* and study it carefully on your own.

2. If you want to build a house on the property, check on the local zoning rules. These laws may significantly limit the placement and size of homes. Other local laws may also affect your plans, by requiring expensive sewage treatment systems, and sometimes by totally prohibiting building (where, for example, soil conditions will not support permanent structures).

3. Check on the financial stability and reliability of the developer. Some land sellers take in large amounts of money and disappear, or go bankrupt, leaving the lot owners stuck with the costs of building community facilities. Your accountant or lawyer can evaluate financial information given by the seller in its property report. As a further precaution, call the complaint office of the U. S. Office of Interstate Land Sales (202-755-6713) and ask if other consumers have had problems with this seller. Also call your local consumer affairs office and Better Business Bureau for their complaint information. A few phone calls in the beginning can save you a great deal of time and grief later. With a financially unstable developer, the planned tennis courts may remain a weedy field and the future "Olympic swimming pool" a muddy puddle.

4. Have a lawyer examine the contract carefully. Many unexpected and grossly unfair terms may be found in it. Some contracts, for example, require you to exchange your lot for a different, smaller one if you plan to build. Others grant the seller the right to cut down all your trees for lumber. Because of the complexity of the legal language used in these agreements, it is usually important to enlist a lawyer's help.

5. Make sure water is accessible. This may be a serious problem in semi-arid spots. Where water is available, find out how expensive it will be— don't assume it is free.

6. Determine if utilities are in place. If the area is not currently served by a utility company, find out what plans exist for coverage (unless you don't mind living without electricity and heat).

7. Talk to present lot owners about their experience. Some may tell hair-raising stories about problems you never dreamed existed. If you are buying land in a development, ask the developer for a list of lot owners. If you are buying a single lot, talk with neighbors and community officials about the land and living conditions. Never rely solely on the word of the seller in such matters.

8. Find out about all the fees you may have to pay. These can include: local taxes, annual maintenance fees, special assessments, homeowner's association membership, sewer, water, and trash collection fees, and insurance. The developer's property report and local authorities can inform you about what to expect to pay.

9. Check with local real estate brokers to compare land prices in the area. Often buying from a developer means paying top prices, in order to cover the developer's high sales commissions and advertising costs. As with all major purchases, it pays to comparison-shop.

10. Don't expect your purchase to be a great "investment." You are buying on the retail market, and if you want to resell, you will be in competition with many others, including the developer you bought from. Furthermore, your purchase contract may contain limitations on your right to resell. Land developers often claim their lots are fine investments, but if you try to resell you may discover contract provisions which make it difficult or unprofitable to do so.

As the Indians who sold Manhattan Island learned, few land sales are inconsequential. (Courtesy the American Museum of Natural History)

LEGAL RIGHTS

With minor exceptions, the sale of land which is subdivided into fifty or more parcels is governed by the federal Interstate Land Sales Registration Act.† This law entitles the prospective buyer to receive a detailed *property report* from the seller prior to or at the time the purchase agreement is signed. The report contains information about the existence of mortgages or liens on the property; availability of water, utility services, and recreation facilities; soil conditions which could cause problems in construction or in using septic tanks; financial background of the seller; and other vital facts. An even more detailed *statement of record* must be filed by the developer with the U. S. Department of Housing and Urban Development, and is available for public inspection at HUD headquarters (451 7th Street, S.W., Washington, D.C. 20410). These reports, although required by law, are prepared by the seller and *not* approved or checked for accuracy by the government.

This law aims to give buyers the facts about the property before they make any purchase. But the law does not control the price which may be charged or the quality of land which may be sold. No government inspection of the land is made. In short, the law does not guarantee that the land is valuable or that the dealer is honest. A buyer who does not read the property report, investigate the facts, look at the land, consult a lawyer, *and* take time to think about the purchase, is likely to make a substantial and costly mistake.

Many states also have laws regulating land developers. Some of these require developers to register and obtain permission from the state to sell or advertise parcels of land. In Michigan, a strong Land Sales Act gives the buyer the right to cancel any contract with a developer within five days after receiving a copy of the contract and the property report. Any buyer who does not receive the property report before signing the contract has a continuing right to rescind the transaction and obtain a full refund. Fraudulent sellers may lose the right to sell in the state, be fined up to $25,000, and be imprisoned for up to ten years. Victimized consumers can sue for return of their money plus interest and their attorney's fees.

Other states, including Arizona, Illinois, and New York, also provide for registration of land developers, and even threaten criminal penalties for fraudulent practices by them. The problem for the consumer, however, is that the state agencies enforcing these laws often lack the power, or the will, to force unethical developers to return money to dissatisfied buyers. A defrauded consumer will usually have to hire a private lawyer and prove deception in court in order to recover the purchase price of the property. Even the states which theoretically can seek criminal sanctions against a developer almost never bring any such cases. Thus, in this, as in so many other

† 15 U.S.C. 1701.

areas, the only assured protection against fraud is avoiding victimization in the first place.

COMPLAINING

The consumer with a complaint against a land developer should send a letter detailing the problem and the requested action to (1) the seller; (2) the Office of Interstate Land Sales Registration, 451 7th Street, S.W., Washington, D.C. 20410; (3) the real estate regulatory agency, if any, for the state in which the land is located or in which you live. These state agencies have various names—for example, the Real Estate Commission (Colorado), the Department of Registration and Education (Illinois), and the Department of State (New York). If you are in doubt as to the right place to write, contact the state attorney general's office for the name and address of the proper agency.

Complaints to government agencies may lead a developer to resolve your problem, and may spur the agency to initiate a wider investigation if it has other similar complaints on file. But don't be surprised if you are simply advised to take your claim to court—this is a standard reply for many agencies.

SELECTED BIBLIOGRAPHY

ALLAN, LESLIE, KUDER, BERYL, and OAKES, SARAH L. *Promised Lands,* Vol. I: *Subdivisions in Deserts and Mountains.* New York: Inform, Inc., 1976.

"Buying a Homesite? Beware the Promised Lands." *Consumer Reports,* May 1978, p. 283.

Get the Facts Before Buying Land. U. S. Department of Housing and Urban Development, Washington, D.C. 20410 (free).

PAULSON, MORTON C. *The Great American Land Hustle.* Chicago: H. Regnery Co., 1972.

WOLFF, ANTHONY. *Unreal Estate.* San Francisco: The Sierra Club, 1973.

14

Buying by mail

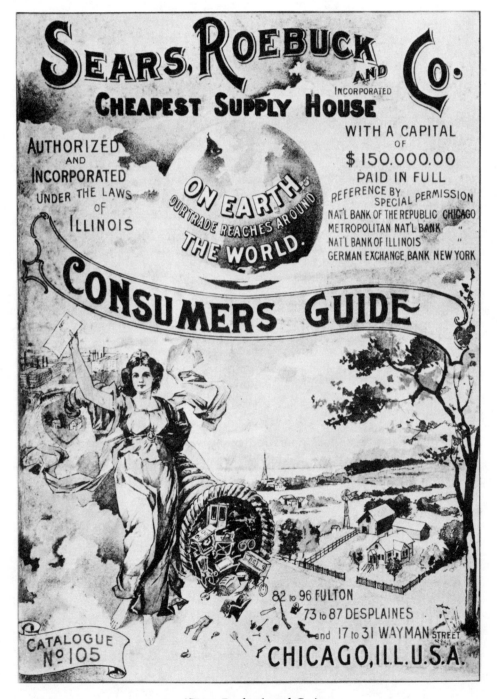

(Sears, Roebuck and Co.)

Buying by mail can be fun. Browsing through a thick catalogue on a rainy afternoon, you can imagine yourself buying everything. Even if you can only afford a few odds and ends, it's pleasant to see the marketplace spread before you so invitingly. And so in homes and offices throughout the land Americans can be found happily snipping out mail order coupons. They are very good at it too—on an average day, over $150 million worth of merchandise is sold through the mails.

"*Most of our business is done over the phone.*"

(*The New Yorker*)

Can this huge "pen pal" operation really work, with buyers and sellers who never see one another confidently exchanging enormous sums of money and merchandise? Somehow it works very well indeed, and the mail order industry is a thriving one, containing some of the giants of American retailing in its ranks.

But two major consumer problems have plagued the mail order field. First, it has become a haven for fly-by-night promoters. Some of them sell worthless junk, others operate with little capital and no inventory, and still others conduct fraudulent schemes masquerading as legitimate sales offers. Cheats find the mails congenial because it preserves their anonymity and permits them to keep a good, safe distance from their victims. A few of their most notorious schemes are described later.

The second problem, of failing to deliver ordered merchandise on time, is less serious, but more widespread. Even the most reputable companies drive their customers to rage when occasionally they cash checks promptly but then lose track of orders, miss promised delivery dates, and fail to acknowledge customer inquiries. The shoddier businesses make a regular practice of it. In fact, one executive of a mail order house testified: "There are those who will promote an item by mail—without *any* inventory and will accumulate customer orders when received—and *then,* and only then, initiate action to *procure* merchandise—since at this point no inventory risks are involved. Obviously, months of delay in receiving merchandise and shipping customer orders may be involved." Such merchants will send out postcards saying, "You may expect shipment within three–four weeks." A year later, customers are still waiting.

In 1975, the FTC asked the public to tell it what problems existed in this area. The response was overwhelming: more than 10,000 pages of recorded testimony documenting consumers' complaints about mail order sales, plus hundreds upon hundreds of complaint letters. The majority of gripes dealt with delays in delivery or outright failure to deliver ordered merchandise. Consumer frustration over extreme delays and utter disregard of their inquiries by sellers was intense. As a result, the FTC enacted a Trade Regulation Rule on Mail Order Merchandise, which provides that:

- ◆ All orders received by mail must be filled within the time promised or, if no date is specified in the seller's ad, within thirty days.
- ◆ If the order cannot be shipped within this time, the company must notify the consumer, offering a refund or a new delivery date. The choice is the consumer's, and the seller must provide a postage-paid card on which a preference for one or the other can be indicated.
- ◆ If the consumer chooses a refund, the seller must return all money paid within seven business days.

The rule does not apply to COD deliveries, to magazine subscriptions and other serial deliveries, to mail order seeds and growing plants, or to services such as mail order photofinishing.

If you deal with a mail order seller who violates this rule, contact: Director, Bureau of Consumer Protection, Federal Trade Commission, Washington, D.C. 20580. The Commission uses the complaints to determine whether a pattern of noncompliance with the rule exists. If so, it will initiate its own action against the seller. It will also forward a copy of each consumer complaint to the U. S. Postal Inspection Service, which can attempt to obtain satisfaction for you.

MAIL FRAUD

Outright frauds and slipshod business practices mingle together freely in the mail order field. The real thieves simply advertise a great bargain, supply a mail address, and wait for the orders—and the checks—to pour in. When enough money is accumulated, they cash in, deposit the customers' orders in the nearest trash can, and leave town. One way to avoid being taken is to order only if you see a full name and street address of the firm.

In one recent case, a mail order con artist offered digital watches at great prices. He gathered in $1.7 million, without delivering a single watch. Fortunately, he was caught, tried, and the judge gave him the time—eight years. But this is the unusual case—most shady promoters disappear before the authorities can find them.

A wide assortment of bogus offers may find a home in your mailbox. Prominent ones to look out for are:

Bargains that sound too good to be true.   They usually *are* too good to be true. Mail cheats will play upon the universal desire to get something for (almost) nothing. Consider the case of the phony coin dealer who knew that offering a rare 1913 nickel for $10 (it was worth five times as much) would drive collectors crazy. Hundreds mailed in their $10 checks, only to find that the nickel was indeed as rare as they had thought—they never saw one.

Chain swindles.   The chain letter, in which you are asked to send money to the person whose name appears at the top of a list in exchange for having your name go on the list, is the granddaddy of mail fraud. Some of the letters threaten to call evil spirits down upon you if you ignore the request. Promoters put their own names (and several aliases) at the top, to ensure that all payments come to them. It is a complete gyp, with no hope of success, but it is kept alive and well by the gullible. A variation on the scheme is the "chain referral"—a promise by a seller to pay consumers for bringing in new customers. The consumer who pays $150 for a sewing machine, expecting to earn that money back in "commissions" paid for new customers, is in for a rude shock. New customers are hard to come by, especially when the company salespeople have already blanketed the area.

Fake contests.   The mail sometimes brings good news, but the news that you have won a contest which you never heard of isn't good. It usually involves a so-called "prize" not worth having. One seller's prize was a "check" good only at the seller's store, as partial payment for overpriced merchandise which the seller couldn't get rid of any other way.

Missing-heir schemes.   A few years ago a clever swindler sent official-looking documents to thousands of people named Kelly. He offered to provide information to aid the recipient in establishing a claim to a $50,000 estate left by one "Mary Kelly." The information would cost only $10. Taking a chance that they might be the lucky missing heirs, and convinced by the legitimate appearance of the solicitation, thousands of victims sent in their $10—which then became the only matter truly "missing."

Sale of worthless vanity items (missing-hair schemes).   Men, do you need an elixir to bring back your hair? Ladies, would you like to add two inches to your bust line? All sorts of devices, pills, and miracle techniques are available claiming to do this and much more. Mail order products to increase sexual potency, take off weight, remove skin blemishes, cure all manner of diseases (real and imagined), are sold to trusting but foolish souls every year. For more on this type of quackery, see chapter 26.

Charity solicitations.   Charities regularly solicit contributions by mail. So do swindlers, working for "charities" with worthy-sounding names but the unworthiest of causes (themselves). Don't contribute to organizations you never heard of.

Unordered merchandise.   Unwanted and unordered goods sometimes arrive in the mail. If such a package comes to you, federal law* permits you to treat it as a gift. You have no obligation to return it or to store it for the sender. Use it, burn it, file it, or throw it in the garbage. Just don't pay for it. If you are sent bills or collection notices, report the company to the FTC.

Money-making schemes.   Investments, franchises, small businesses, and other money-making opportunities are regularly hawked through the mail. These are some of the most unreliable, baseless claims peddled to the consuming public. Claims of "easy money," "guaranteed incomes," and "solid investments" particularly hoodwink the elderly who have time or money to invest and unemployed people eager for any source of income. These are discussed in detail in chapter 15.

Mail order insurance.   Mail order insurance is a very risky purchase indeed. The coverage is attractively advertised, but frequently the policy itself contains numerous limitations, exclusions, and other trapdoor clauses that take away the coverage you think you're getting. Some of these policies, for example, cover hospitalization but define "hospital" in such a way that more ᵗhan 80 percent of the hospitals in the nation don't qualify to give treatment. Some brochures boast of substantial benefits at cheap prices, but there's always a catch. One company claimed "maximum policy benefits for hospital care $5,000." The policy, however, limited the coverage to a total of only $500 in any one year.

Don't be fooled by the fact that no medical exam is required. The application form will ask you to report any medical attention you've received in the last five years and to list all physical ailments. The company may later refuse to pay if you leave out anything, or it will claim you had a "pre-existing condition" which isn't covered. Policy benefits often will be reduced at age 65, and the fine print may impose other severe limits on benefits.

Low premiums are a popular come-on, but they disguise important facts. The premiums may be increased at a later date. This is a common ploy—if you're considering purchasing a policy, write to the company for a full schedule of premium payments to check. Low premiums may also simply mean that the company does not pay out on claims. Whatever the reason, there's no great bargain for you—insurance companies charge for good coverage, and giveaways are always illusory.

Some companies attempt to make their offers appear to have the endorsement or approval of the U.S. government. The prominent use of the word "Medicare" may confuse the careless reader. Policies aimed at veterans or

* 39 U.S.C. 3009.

members of the armed forces may look impressive and be accompanied by an official-looking letter, but beware. The U.S. government does offer low-cost life insurance, but not by mail—it is purchased directly by the serviceperson through his or her military unit and premiums are paid by payroll deduction. Parents recruited to buy life insurance for their children in the armed forces should recognize this ruse employed by private companies charging higher than government rates.

If, after all this, you are intent on buying a mail order policy, make sure the company is licensed by your state Insurance Department. If it isn't, don't deal with it. There will be no recourse for you if a dispute arises between you and the company.

For further information on the pitfalls of mail order insurance, write to the FTC for its "Consumer Bulletin No. 1, Mail Order Insurance."

WHERE TO COMPLAIN ABOUT MAIL ORDER COMPANIES

The U. S. Postal Service polices the mails and investigates complaints against mail order sellers. It is important to realize, however, that the Postal Service has relatively few inspectors to handle the avalanche of 170,000 complaints a year. Although criminal prosecution is possible, it is highly improbable, due to the high standard of proof required and the difficulty of proving fraudulent intent (required under the federal mail fraud law). The postal authorities are also empowered to stop mail delivery to and from chronic offenders.

Before turning to the Postal Service, try one or both of these.

1. Inform the newspaper or magazine in which you saw the company's

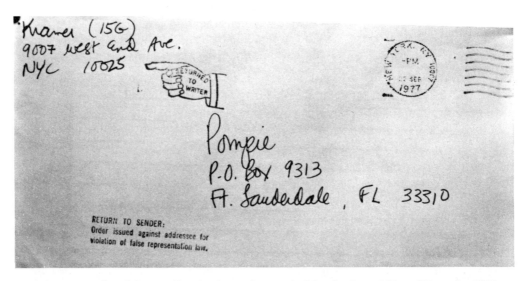

A letter to a fraudulent mail order house intercepted by the Post Office. (Photo by Cliff Ratner)

advertisement. A mail order seller that depends heavily on a particular magazine to generate sales will respond quickly to complaints forwarded by the magazine. For this reason, it is important to note the name and date of the publication carrying the mail order firm's ad. Keep a copy of the ad for this identification (and also to check for differences between the advertisement and the product).

2. Send your complaint to the Direct Mail Marketing Association, 6 East 43rd Street, New York, N.Y. 10017. This is an industry group which attempts to resolve consumer disputes. Although it lacks formal power, it is sometimes successful in prodding a legitimate company to act fairly and promptly.

NOTE ON MAILING LISTS

If you are an Expectant Mother, a Wealthy Widow, or a Left-Handed Person (or perhaps all three?) you are no doubt on a mailing list with thousands of others of your kind. You also receive unsolicited mail from marketers who specialize in selling to your group. Many people welcome this mail; others hate it. For the latter, there's an industry-sponsored program which permits individuals to have their names removed from commercial mailing lists. To take advantage of it (or to have your name *added* to mailing lists) write to: Mail Preference Service, 230 Park Avenue, New York, N.Y. 10017. The Service will send you a form for use in excising your name from the mailing lists of its members (which include 2,700 industry firms) or adding your name to existing lists in any of twenty-three different categories.

15

Mind your own business:
money-making opportunities

The business of America is business.   —CALVIN COOLIDGE

Would you like to make $406,900 in the next 50 days?   —Business opportunity ad

THE WESTERN BOY

OR,

THE ROAD TO SUCCESS.
By Horatio Alger, Jr.

Horatio Alger wrote about poor honest boys who made large fortunes. In reality such stories are few and far between. (From *Horatio Alger, Or the American Hero Era*, by Ralph Gardner, published by Wayside Press.)

Whether you want to be rich or famous (or for the piggish, both rich *and* famous) there's a promoter somewhere who, for a price, will tell you how to do it. The secret of success may cost anywhere from $1 to $10,000; the secret itself may be a cheap booklet full of platitudes about starting a mail order business, or a costly investment gamble whose chances of success range from slim to none.

In a nation where workers want to own their own business, waitresses yearn to be on the stage, and retirees dream of making small killings, it's easy for slick operators to peddle, in various forms, the "opportunity of a lifetime." Unscrupulous talent agents, franchise sellers, and others with money-making schemes that *sound* plausible deftly convert their victims' hopes for success into quick profits for themselves. A few of the most common schemes are described below. But keep in mind that new schemes, like hope, spring up eternally.

DISTRIBUTORSHIPS

The appeal of owning one's own business is well known to those who work for other people for a living. Instead of a servant, you are master; instead of punching a time clock, you own one. Only those who have tried it know the immense difficulties which go with ownership, including back-breaking hours, substantial debts, long "dry spells" when no money comes in, and a million and one "little problems" that crop up each and every day. Statistics show that new ventures are almost always disasters: some 91 percent of small businesses fail during their first year. Despite this gloomy reality, dozens of promoters offer the public a rosy future of security, money, and happiness in their own businesses.

A few years ago, members of the public were offered the opportunity of paying $5,000 apiece to become distributors in a venture called "Koscot Interplanetary, Inc." The company claimed it would establish all investors in their own retail businesses selling cosmetics. But more important, Koscot offered to pay the investors $3,000 for each new investor they brought in. Finding just six new investors meant a quick $18,000—without having to sell a single jar of face cream. People persuaded friends, relatives, pets, business associates, and anyone else they could find to invest.

The company helped in the recruiting by holding "opportunity meetings" at which speakers urged the audience members to invest, promising huge incomes and little work. People struggling to make ends meet were exhorted to "get out of the rut" and to "take a chance on yourselves." To excite the crowd, the speakers would pass around thousand-dollar bills and ask the audience to chant "money, money, money!" The gatherings "took on the charged atmosphere of an old-fashioned revival meeting, except that the god was mammon," to quote an FTC hearing officer. One participant said of a typical meeting: "When I got back home I didn't sleep for five nights . . . neither did my wife. The guy got us so jacked up, in thousands, I was ready to sell the Brooklyn Bridge to Eisenhower."

Countless individuals put their money into these schemes, known as pyramid frauds. Mathematically, such schemes are doomed to failure. As more and more investors come in, finding new recruits becomes increasingly difficult. In fact, the number of new recruits needed to keep the scheme going quickly rises to astronomical levels. Assume, for example, that six persons begin a pyramid scheme on Day 1. On Day 2 each recruits six others, each of whom in turn recruits six more on Day 3. How many days could this scheme last before there were no more possible new recruits? The following progression helps reveal the answer.

DAY	PARTICIPANTS
1	6
2	36
3	216
4	1,296
5	7,776
6	46,656
7	279,936
8	1,679,616
9	10,071,696
10	60,466,176
11	362,797,056 (1½ times the U.S. population)

Depending on the size of the community and the gullibility of its members, the scheme might last four or five days at most. The handful of people involved in the early stages of the scheme make large profits. They do so, however, at the expense of the thousands of persons recruited at the end, who are unable to find new recruits and lose all their money. This was the fate of a huge number of citizens in cities all across the country. A few of the schemes even found victims in Europe and South America before they collapsed. Some perpetrators of these massive swindles have been prosecuted under state and federal anti-fraud and larceny statutes, but most often the cash has disappeared and the company is bankrupt. If you are approached by someone to invest in a pyramid scheme, decline politely and notify the state attorney general at once.

WORK-AT-HOME SCHEMES

Many elderly people, those confined to their homes, and numerous others fall prey to phony work-at-home schemes. Advertisements typically proclaim: "Earn money in your spare time—$100, $200, $300 a week and more—while you work in the comfort of your own home!" Unfortunately, these work-at-home "opportunities" usually cost their victims money, instead of helping them earn it. One company told Alaska residents they could earn $50 for every 100 envelopes they addressed and mailed for the company. Those who read the offer carefully found they had to buy the envelopes, advertising inserts, address labels, mailing list, and reply envelopes. They would be paid out of the profits (if any) from the mailing. The company stood to lose nothing if the mailing produced nothing; in fact, it profited from the sale of the envelopes themselves.

Some promoters offer to set you up in your own mail order business. For $4 or $10, you will receive a book explaining the "secret" of mail order success, revealed by a character who claims his fortune is so large that it bores him. He's willing to amuse himself by passing the secret on to you, for a small price. Those paying for the book are then requested to send more money for merchandise, sales aids, and the like. Once victims buy all the advice and assorted supplies the promoter has to unload, they discover how difficult the mail order business really is. Before long, the fledgling at-home businesses take a quick nose dive and disappear without a trace.

Other work-at-home schemes are even simpler. One company offered to pay people for giving their opinions on new products sent to them by the company—a flattering offer, as it implies that there's value to your reactions. Prospects were promised a $1 payment for each opinion they gave. To show good faith, however, everyone had to pay a $10 "registration fee" to join the program. Hundreds of people lost their $10, without being asked their opinion about anything. A similar ruse was used by a man who advertised that he would pay $25 a week for addressing envelopes at home. He asked for $1 from each victim as a registration fee, and 13,000 persons sent in their money. No one ever heard from him again.

Work-at-home gyps can be spotted by these characteristics:

◆ They ask you to buy something (raw materials, envelopes, mailing lists, etc.) first.

Check the stability of any scheme before you join it.

- They impose no risk on the company.
- They promise large earnings for little work.
- They seek a "registration fee" or other initial payment from you.

Most work-at-home schemes operate through the mails. If you spot one of them, contact the nearest Postal Inspector (for the address, check the telephone directory under United States Government—Post Office) and your local consumer protection agency. For a description of some of the other frauds that come to you in the mail, see chapter 14.

MODELING, ACTING, RADIO AND TELEVISION ANNOUNCERS

Nightly, we are the stars of our own dreams. If this is not enough for you, you may be tempted to seek your fortune in radio, television, movies, or modeling.

But it is not easy to break into these fields. All professionals know this. Some unethical agents, and a handful of training and modeling schools, however, encourage any and all interested persons in order to sell them lessons, photographs, and personal services. It is vital that young newcomers be aware of the tricks used to put them into the first role of their careers— that of patsy.

First, the phony talent agent. This operator may advertise in the classified section of newspapers, seeking "fresh faces" for jobs in TV, radio, or films. The office is covered with photos of famous stars (none of whom are clients). The young hopeful may be auditioned, judiciously appraised, and finally taken on, having met the agent's "exacting" standards. At some point, the agent will ask for a "registration fee," or will suggest a training school "to sharpen your skills" or a photo studio to buy photographs. The agent gets a kickback on these referrals, unbeknown to the victims.

Child talent and modeling agencies may similarly take advantage of parents' natural pride in and hopes for their children. One Hollywood agency sent letters to all parents whose names appeared in newspaper birth announcements, hospital birth records, and commercial mailing lists. The letters stated: "We have received information indicating that your child may have the necessary qualifications for the commercial advertising media. . . . If the information we have is correct, we could be very interested in your child." The happy parents responding to the solicitation were advised of the excellent chances for placement and big earnings for their children. All that the agency required was a $65 fee for its services, plus the purchase of photographs from a specified studio each year. In fact, 98 percent of the children never obtained a single offer to appear in a commercial, and the principals of the talent agency owned a piece of the photo studio.

Modeling schools may also lead the aspiring adult model down the primrose path, with visions of the glamorous life in the world of high fashion. The truth, of course, with all of these fields—modeling, acting, and broadcasting—is that jobs are difficult to come by, trained professionals are out of work, and the competition is intense. For any would-be performer, it is wise to:

◆ Discuss the qualifications, job opportunities, and price of training with someone already working in the field.
◆ Stay clear of anyone who makes success sound too easy.
◆ Avoid any agent who demands a fee before finding you a job (legitimate agents work on a commission basis).
◆ Contact the performers' unions concerning questions about the field and offers that seem "fishy." Direct your inquiries to the local affiliate, if any, of these unions (write to the main office given below if there's no local in your area):

AFTRA (American Federation of
Television and Radio Artists)
1350 Avenue of the Americas
New York, N.Y. 10019

AEA (Actors Equity Association)
1500 Broadway
New York, N.Y. 10036

SAG (Screen Actors Guild)
551 Fifth Avenue
New York, N.Y. 10017

AGMA (American Guild of Musical
Artists)
1841 Broadway
New York, N.Y. 10023.

Report complaints to your state attorney general's office and to any local consumer affairs bureau.

FRANCHISES

If you receive a brochure touting "the most phenomenal money-making opportunity in your lifetime," chances are you're about to be introduced to the franchising game, one of the fastest and riskiest around. You may be urged to buy a franchise in any one of a dozen businesses, from fast-food chicken to a high-fashion beauty salon (be especially alert to the slick promoter selling high-fashion chicken or a fast-food beauty shop).

Legitimate franchisors have a good product to sell and need franchisees to sell it. The *franchisee* buys his or her own sales outlet and becomes an independent dealer selling the franchisor's merchandise. Under the terms of a *franchise agreement,* the franchisee receives the right to use the franchisor's trade name and to market its goods in a particular territory.

The franchising field has been infiltrated by swindlers who try to sell franchises in nonexistent or failing businesses to people with limited business experience. They adopt the trappings of the successful franchisor: handsome leather-bound marketing books, reports indicating the company's past growth and expected sales figures, and a confident, optimistic view of the company's potential. In reality, they may have no assets, no potential, and no hope for making money except by selling franchises and pocketing the proceeds. A few years ago, the New York State Attorney General's Office discovered one company selling franchises while it was in bankruptcy; another projected returns of 150 to 300 percent on investments, even though it

(© Paul Sequeira. From Rapho / Photo Researchers, Inc.)

was running at a deficit and three of its franchisees had just gone out of business.

It is not always easy to distinguish the legitimate franchisors from the impostors. Sometimes the latter use a company name deceptively similar to that of a well-known franchisor. Others pay nationally known sports figures and Hollywood stars to lend their famous names to businesses which the stars know nothing about. The poor schnook who invests several thousand dollars in a franchise because of the glamour of these celebrities may find that the star has no interest in the business and will not participate in advertising or other promotions in the future.

At times, criminal elements are involved in the franchise business. Ex-convicts or persons under felony indictments have had controlling interests in such franchised businesses as vending machines, mobile homes, and restaurants, among others.

For the individual looking to start a new business, a franchise may well be the answer. A responsible franchisor can provide a marketable product, advertising, and training in operating techniques. But it is important to follow these steps before making any substantial investment:

◆ Know whom you are dealing with. Is the franchisor willing to furnish financial references, is the business successful, has the product been well advertised?

◆ Talk to current franchise owners, after obtaining a list from the franchisor. Have they made a profit? Are they satisfied with the assistance and training given by the franchisor?

◆ Consult a lawyer before signing the franchise agreement. Some of these contracts are very one-sided, giving the franchisor unreasonable fees, royalties on all sales, and other rights which make it difficult or impossible for franchisees to operate at a profit.

◆ Analyze the company's financial reports carefully. If you do not have the business experience to do this, hire someone who does, or else stay away from franchising. Too many people have lost their life savings in franchising disasters, relying on the franchisor's general claims of large "projected earnings" and on easy assurances that every franchisee is "making a fortune."

Because of the widespread abuses in this field, the Federal Trade Commission recently enacted a rule designed to help prospective franchisees. It requires the franchise seller to prepare a written statement containing information on twenty subjects of vital interest to any franchise buyer. For example, the statement must reveal:

◆ All fees and costs which the buyer must pay;

◆ Business background of the franchisor and its key management personnel;

◆ Financial data about the franchisor, including a current balance sheet and income statement;

◆ How franchises are renewed, terminated, or canceled;

◆ Training, if any, offered new franchise owners;

◆ Number of franchises terminated during the previous year, and the reasons why;

◆ All business limitations imposed on franchisees, including restrictions on the geographical area in which they may operate;

◆ Names, addresses, and telephone numbers of at least ten current franchisees operating in the area nearest to the prospective franchisee's intended location.

Look for this information before you invest in any franchise opportunity, and study it carefully. Report any franchisor who fails to provide you with the required disclosure statement to the Bureau of Consumer Protection, Federal Trade Commission, 6th and Pennsylvania Avenue, N.W., Washington, D.C. 20580.

For those caught by a smooth-talking franchise hustler, a private lawsuit may be the only answer. The franchise seller will blame the franchisee's poor business skill for the losses suffered, and the judge will have to decide if fraud or just the ordinary risk of doing business is involved.

16

When you need a fix: repairs

Things fall apart, the center cannot hold . . . —w. b. yeats, "The Second Coming"

It is questionable if all the mechanical inventions yet made have lightened the day's toil of any human being. — john stuart mill

Men have become the tools of their tools. — henry david thoreau

No problem is too small to baffle our experts. — Current expression

What do you do when your blender won't blend, your mixer won't mix, and your percolator won't perk? Or worse, when your television conks out, leaving you alone with your thoughts?

Machines, of course, are our labor-saving friends, and they deserve all the idolatry, worship, and enthusiasm that they receive in our society. But when they run down and slip their mechanical disks, we become their slaves, and sometimes their repairer's victims. More and more gadgets are put on the market every year, and each new item increases our dependency on the repair industry—one whose record for honesty and good service is not the best.

TELEVISION AND APPLIANCE REPAIRS

The proliferation of small appliances has complicated the repair problem considerably. Many are cheaply made, using plastics instead of metal. Some cannot withstand even ordinary wear and tear, but their low prices attract buyers. The glut of new gadgets also strains the resources of repair shops, which can't stock all of the parts and components needed to service them. As labor costs go up, more and more consumers are hearing the grim verdict of the repair expert: "It's not worth fixing."

While we can resign ourselves to the disposal of a malfunctioning pencil sharpener, it is a different matter when a prized color television or a 21-cubic-foot refrigerator breaks down. It is in the repair of large appliances and televisions that the most serious frauds occur. Unscrupulous fixers grossly exaggerate the repairs needed, inflating bills to whatever they think the traffic will bear. Some cheats use the lure of low-cost house calls and free estimates to snare unsuspecting customers. Once these characters gain possession of the customers' expensive property, they disregard previous estimates and present a huge bill, refusing to return the item until they are paid. This practice, which amounts to holding the customer's property for ransom, usually enables sharp operators to collect disputed bills without any trouble.

The extent of fraud in this field is impossible to measure accurately, but repeated investigations around the nation have turned up striking evidence of unconscionable conduct. Surveys conducted by New York's Consumer Affairs Department officials, for example, using municipal inspectors posing as repair customers, yielded these shocking results:

◆ Seven of eight television repairers, asked to fix a broken set with a single burned-out tube, charged for additional repairs or for work not in fact done. Bills averaged between $40 and $50. One shop sloppily put in the wrong type of resistor, a mistake which could have caused shock or fire when the set was turned on. All seven repairers claimed, falsely, that the television could not be fixed in the home.

◆ Three and a half years later, a random survey of 21 television repair shops uncovered 15 who gave estimates for unnecessary repairs. One shop demanded $73.95 to repair a set whose only problem was an unplugged cable (the cable had merely to be reinserted into the plug). Four shops returned the test television in worse condition than when they got it.

◆ Eight of 11 air-conditioner repair shops misdiagnosed a simple disconnected wire and charged exorbitant fees for unneeded and unperformed repairs. The biggest bill was for $98. One of the shops destroyed a test machine by miswiring it, causing a short circuit. The eight dishonest servicers said the test machine needed the following: a new compressor, a new fan motor, a new thermostat, repair of a refrigerant leak, replacement of cracked tubing, addition of Freon coolant, recharging a new overload protector, and a steam cleaning. The three honest shops just reconnected the loose wire.

◆ Fourteen washing-machine repair companies advertising in the Yellow Pages were asked to fix a test machine with an interior wire disconnected. Half made the correct diagnosis; the others claimed the motor, clutch, pump, and timer were defective, and insisted the machine couldn't be fixed in the home. The highest charge was $107, from a repairer who charged for three new parts but actually left the original parts in the machine.

No doubt there are thousands of capable, ethical men and women in the repair field who are just as distressed as consumers about the swindlers in their midst. But until the substantial number of unscrupulous operators are rooted out of the industry, it is incumbent upon consumers to take special care when dealing with repair problems. The initial precaution to take is: buy a well-built appliance in the first place. Cheaply made goods, even if attractive on the surface, quickly deteriorate into inoperable junk. In selecting merchandise, especially major items like refrigerators, freezers, washers, and dryers, look for reputable brands, and compare warranties for duration and coverage of essential parts. Electrical appliances should bear the seal of the

Where are the artisans of yesteryear?

Underwriters Laboratories (UL) and gas appliances the seal of the American Gas Association Laboratories (AGA). These seals indicate that at least minimal safety standards have been met. Avoid machines with fancy extras you can easily do without, like refrigerators with built-in drink dispensers and crushed-ice makers. They often break down and cost more to repair than they're worth.

No matter how formidable your shopping skill, however, only a miracle will prevent the need for repair services at some point. When that sad day comes, keep in mind these tips:

◆ Before you call the repair shop, make sure the appliance is plugged in. (Why pay a repairer $20 to plug in your TV?) Try two different electrical outlets, to ensure that the problem is with the machine and not in an outlet connection.

◆ Check the Owner's Manual. Some contain simple instructions for remedying minor dysfunctions.

◆ Deal with neighborhood repair shops that depend on repeat business and their own good reputation. Ask for recommendations from friends and neighbors.

◆ Don't depend on ads in the telephone company's Yellow Pages. A number of shady characters take out huge display ads, cheat their customers blind, and wait for the next victim to call. One crooked washing-machine repairman, later indicted, advertised under three different company names in one telephone directory. His first ad proclaimed "Service only on Kenmore"; the second said "Service only on Whirlpool"; the third offered service on nine other brands of washers. This repairer thus appeared to be both a specialist and a generalist at the same time.

◆ Call the local consumer bureau or Better Business Bureau office to see if there are complaints pending against repairers you're considering (particularly if the shops are unknown to you and the repair job is a big one).

Once you locate a shop, here are some pointers on how best to deal with it:

◆ Ask the price of a home service call. If possible, take portable products to the shop to save this fee.

◆ Request a written estimate. If it seems high, get estimates from other shops. If it's reasonable, write on it: "If cost is higher, do not go ahead without getting O.K. from me" (and include a phone number where you can be reached).

◆ Observe any work done in your home, and ask to be shown what's wrong.

◆ Ask that old parts removed from the TV or appliance be returned to you. If the part is hazardous (e.g., a picture tube) just ask to see it.

◆ Get an itemized final bill, stating exactly what has been done. It should also indicate the length of the servicer's guarantee on parts and workmanship.

If you have a complaint against a repairer which cannot be amicably resolved, contact your local consumer affairs bureau and the state attorney general's office. If the repair shop is a factory-authorized outlet, contact the manufacturer conferring the authorization also. Another place to turn to is an industry-backed mediation service called MACAP (Major Appliance Consumer Action Panel), which tries to find a mutually satisfactory compromise of consumer complaints (write to MACAP, 20 North Wacker Drive, Chicago, Ill. 60606, or call collect 312-236-3165). If all else fails, try suing in small claims court. Be prepared to show that the repair shop never did the work you paid for or so botched the job that it should be required to give you a refund.

AUTO REPAIRS

Your car may not take you for a ride, but many auto repairers will. The auto repair industry generates more consumer complaints than any other in the nation. Some estimates of the amount lost annually by consumers to fraudulent repairers, garages, and body shops run as high as $20 billion.

The way in which a trained mechanic can trick an unskilled customer are almost infinite. Most consumers probably feel about their cars the way Winston Churchill felt about Russia. "It is," he said, "a riddle wrapped in a mystery inside an enigma." The inexperience and lack of expertise of consumers make the field of automobile repair work particularly hospitable to consumer abuse.

There are two key elements in the auto repair problem: fraud and incompetence. Fraud has been documented many times, in tests run by consumer agencies, investigative journalists, and others. The New York *Times* cooperating with a suburban county consumer affairs department, tested 24 repair shops by sending them a car in perfect working order, except for a minor disconnection under the hood, easily visible and repairable. Honest shops charged a small fee or no fee at all for the quick repair. But over half

*"Tony asked me to ask you, Mr. Bates—do you know offhand
the whereabouts of your service manual?"*

(*The New Yorker*)

of the repairers charged unreasonable sums and did unneeded work. One
shop demanded a whopping $345 to do extensive work which it claimed was
absolutely necessary.

A test of transmission specialists in Minnesota turned up similar results.
State investigators drove cars needing minor adjustments to several outlets
of a well-known chain of transmission repair shops. The shops all demanded
unjustifiably high fees; some even stole good parts from the states' cars (the

parts were marked before the cars were taken to the shop). In one government car, half the transmission was stolen, with junk parts substituted for the original ones. Similarly, in South Carolina, a transmission shop falsely told undercover officials that their car's transmission was "burned up" and needed extensive work and new parts. The bill for $190 named the new parts supposedly installed, but the state's expert mechanics found the same old parts.

Numerous instances of bill padding, charging for work never performed, doing unnecessary work, installation of used instead of new parts, and other clearly fraudulent acts plague automobile drivers across the nation. It is commonplace for repairers to shock or scare motorists in order to induce them to buy spark plugs, tires, transmissions, engine parts, and any one of the other 15,000 parts that go into today's cars. In one common trick, the mechanic sprays oil on shock absorbers and claims they're "leaking." An itinerant mechanic in Georgia, who takes odd jobs in gas stations in the state, is known to spray barbecue sauce into car alternators and to surreptitiously slash the tires of people coming in to buy gas. He then splits the profits from the sale of new tires and parts with the station owners.

Another routine ploy is to hoist the car up, turn the front wheels to one side, and shake them in front of the customer. The ball joints rattle, and the mechanic gravely reports the need for replacements. Inexpert drivers are unaware that there is always some play in the ball joints, which rarely need replacement. Countless garages, however, sell them as if they're going of style.

If fraud thrives in the repair shop business, so does general incompetence. This may be the most pervasive problem of all. The pay of auto mechanics, as compared to that of carpenters, plumbers, electricians, and similarly skilled technicians, is generally low. Similarly, mechanics must supply their own tools, a $3,000 investment. Because of these monetary considerations, many talented young technicians look elsewhere for careers, avoiding the automotive trade entirely. A shortage of qualified mechanics is the result, making it difficult for consumers to find top-grade technicians to care for their cars. Many mechanics lack good diagnostic skills, and their poor guesswork can cost people money. Incompetent tinkerers tend to replace many parts, because they don't know which one is faulty. When they hit the right one, they stop—and the motorist pays for them all.

Compounding the problem is the fact that repair shops tend to skimp on repairs made under warranty, because auto manufacturers pay less for this work than the public pays for non-warranty work. The car under warranty may be given hasty attention, or no attention at all (in the trade slang, a "wall job" is a car parked by the wall waiting interminably for repair; a "sunbath" is the same car parked in the sun).

Auto manufacturers also bear their share of the blame for the auto repair mess. The poorer the quality-control systems in the factory, the more repair work will be needed later. Too often the manufacturers leave their mistakes for the repair industry to worry about, providing little help in solving the problems they have created.

A final contributing factor in the low quality of repair work is the high cost of sophisticated diagnostic and repair equipment. Independent gas station owners and small repair shops may not be able to invest the large sums needed to purchase the best mechanical devices on the market. Without them, mechanics are at a real disadvantage in trying to bring sputtering autos back to life.

What can the average individual do to avoid the twin evils of fraud and incompetence? The best thing to do would be to go into training and become a class-A mechanic yourself. Short of that, there are some things you can do to reduce the likelihood of victimization. None of these suggestions are fully guaranteed. They simply give you a fighting chance in the rough auto repair pit:

1. Get repairs done at the same shop each time (if you find it trustworthy) and, if possible, by the same mechanic. If you are known as a regular customer, the shop has more incentive to serve you well. The mechanic who knows you may take better care of your car, and benefit from being familiar with its past problems and peculiarities. But beware of the practice of some skilled mechanics who take on more work than they can do and farm out the excess to less able people. If you go to a mechanic with a good reputation, be sure to ask who will actually do the work on your car.

2. Ask for a written estimate before any work is done. If you simply say "Fix whatever's wrong," you're courting disaster. You may be handed the kind of bill that causes migraines and breaks up families. If the repairer says no estimate can be given without a careful inspection or disassembly, ask the price for this work and insist that no repairs be undertaken until you are told the estimated cost. When you get a written estimate, note on it, "If cost is higher, do not go ahead without O.K. from me."

3. Don't put your ignorance on parade. If you don't have the faintest idea what's going on under the hood, there's no need to say so. Do ask commonsense questions, and take time to think over (or corroborate) the explanations given you.

4. Have minor problems with the car attended to before you go on a long trip. Some gas stations feel it is always "open season" on cars with out-of-state license plates. You don't want some minor problem developing into a major one when you're in a strange place and pressed for time.

5. Beware of transmission shops that offer big savings. Not all jobs require dismantling the transmission, but too many of these specialty shops tear down every transmission that comes their way.

6. Ask that all replaced parts be returned to you. Some larcenous repairers will claim to have put in new parts when they in fact did nothing. Requesting the return to you of old parts may discourage this, although it is possible to simply give you some junk parts lying around the shop.

7. Get a second opinion if one shop gives you a high estimate. Another repairer might do the work for less, or indicate that so much work isn't even necessary. In at least two cities, St. Louis and Kansas City, there are diagnostic centers to turn to. The centers do not perform repairs and thus have no incentive to exaggerate the work needed.

8. Beware of great bargains. Low prices on brake repairs, for example, are advertised to lure customers into the shop, where they can be persuaded that they really need new brakes. Bargains can be traps for the unwary motorist. Good repair shops are always busy and don't need big giveaways to attract business.

9. Look for evidence of inefficiency. Are old heaps taking up valuable space in the shop? Good repairers are eager to get cars fixed and out. Poor ones are disorganized and keep customers waiting a long time for their cars.

10. Ask for an itemized bill, detailing the work done and parts replaced. This may be important later if the same trouble crops up after a week or two. Make sure you get a guarantee on parts and workmanship. The common ones last for 90 days or 4,000 miles, but insist on a longer period (e.g., one year or 12,000 miles) for major repairs.

11. Try to learn what you can about your car. Look at the Owner's Manual, ask mechanics about the repairs they perform, learn from observation and experience what recurrent car problems you have and how they're handled.

REFORMING THIS MESS

Several states have attempted to meet the auto repair crisis by licensing repair shops or repair personnel. These efforts have met with only limited success so far. One of the first states to try licensing, Louisiana, showed exactly how *not* to do it right. The license law gave control over administration and enforcement to the industry itself. The governor was given power to appoint board officials, but only from a list of names submitted by industry trade associations. With the legal machinery dominated by those supposedly subject to its sanctions, the result was inevitable: the power to revoke or suspend licenses was rarely invoked, penalties for fraud were extremely mild, and business went on as usual. But the licensing system was not merely ineffective; it actually cost the state's consumers money. The board created a system of apprenticeship which made it difficult for young mechanics to come into the field, thus creating a shortage of new mechanics, preserving the market for existing industry members, and driving up prices.

Even if the regulatory agency is not controlled by the repair industry, licensing still is not a complete answer to the abuses present in the auto repair field. Checking on fraud requires an agency with a large enough budget to regularly send test cars to repair shops for routine work. (California's Bureau of Automotive Repair is one of the few state agencies with this capability.) This sort of investigation is essential, because proof of fraud usually requires expert knowledge of the car's condition before repair, as well as analysis of its condition after repair. Consumer complaints alone rarely provide conclusive evidence of fraud, although they identify likely suspects. An enforcement bureau must be prepared to gather corroborating evidence, or it will not be able to lift licenses and penalize fraudulent operators.

If the problem of fraud is difficult to attack, the problem of incompetence is an even knottier one. Few licensing statutes provide penalties for incompetent work or attempt to define what level of competence is minimally acceptable. Some states, like Hawaii, have devised competency exams. to be given to all new mechanics. But there are hitches in this approach too. First, under so-called "grandfather clauses" all mechanics with one or two years' experience in the field are exempt from the exams. Obviously this takes in the vast majority of mechanics. Second, proper testing is a difficult task and can backfire if not done correctly. If an exam is too difficult, it will have the effect of limiting the number of new mechanics. When the supply of mechanics goes down, the price of repairs goes up. If, on the other hand, the test is too simple, the most inept candidates not only will pass but will possess a state certificate attesting to their competence for the rest of their inept careers.

A private organization known as the National Institute for Automotive Service Excellence (NIASE) administers voluntary exams in eight different repair specialties. Those mechanics passing the exam may wear a shoulder patch to display their NIASE certification. The organization advises motorists of the location of NIASE-certified mechanics in a booklet entitled *Where to Find a Certified Mechanic* (available from NIASE, 1825 K Street, N.W., Washington D.C. 20006). The certificate, of course, cannot guarantee honesty, and the organization does not attempt to resolve disputes involving those it has certified. A NIASE patch means only that the wearer has passed a written exam in the specialty indicated.

A new program which holds much promise is the American Automobile Association's experimental plan to inspect repair shops and recommend those which meet its criteria of honesty and quality. To gain AAA approval, a service facility would have to employ certified mechanics, own the equipment deemed essential for basic repair work, have a good service record (the AAA checks with local consumer agencies and makes random customer surveys), and provide a fair guarantee on work performed. If the repair shop further agrees to resolve promptly any complaints against it received by the AAA from its members, it is awarded AAA approval and may advertise its approved status to the public. This innovative program began in 1975, and now exists in Washington, D.C.; Orlando, Florida; Houston, Texas; Rochester, Minnesota; and Orange County, California. Other Triple A affiliates may join the program in the future. To find out more, contact the AAA in your area, or write to the American Automobile Association, 8111 Gatehouse Road, Falls Church, Va. 22042.

COMPLAINING

Complaints against repair shops should be directed to the state licensing agency, if one exists in your state. The licensing bureau may be part of the state motor vehicle department, department of consumer affairs, or professional licensing agency. It is wise to send a copy of any complaint to the state attorney general and your local consumer affairs bureau. Give details of your experience and include copies (not originals) of written estimates, final bills, and other documents.

If a complaint involves inadequately performed warranty work, you might also contact the car manufacturer. Most auto companies have customer service representatives to help solve disputes between dealers and customers. Check the Owner's Manual or the official warranty for the nearest company office.

If the complaint concerns repairs performed at a gas station, send a copy of your letter to the oil company. If it is a company-owned station, the corporate headquarters may take action. Finally, an industry-sponsored effort at complaint mediation, known as AUTOCAP (Automotive Consumer Action Panels), exists in some localities. To determine if one is available in your area, contact the National Automobile Dealers Association, 8400 Westpark Drive, McLean, Va. Keep in mind, though, that this group has no power to force a settlement on either you or the repair shop.

SELECTED BIBLIOGRAPHY

Car Care and Service, a 13-page booklet prepared by the U.S. government, available from Consumer Information, Pueblo, Colo. 81009 (other car booklets are listed in the free *Index to Consumer Publications,* at the same address).

HABEEB, VIRGINIA. *MACAP's Handbook for the Informed Consumer,* available from MACAP, 20 North Wacker Drive, Chicago, Ill. 60606.

KLAMKIN, CHARLES. *If It Doesn't Work, Read the Instructions.* New York: Stein & Day, 1970.

17

Up, up, and away: travel and vacations

When the horses gagged at going farther up the steep hill, the driver shouted: "First class passengers, keep your seats. Second class passengers, get out and walk. Third class passengers, get out and shove." —CARL SANDBURG, *The People, Yes*

A traveler must have a falcon's eye, an ass's ears, an ape's face, a merchant's words, a camel's back, a hog's mouth, and a stag's legs.   — English proverb

When I was at home, I was in a better place. —SHAKESPEARE, *As You Like It*

If an ass goes travelling, he will not come home a horse. —THOMAS FULLER

TOURS AND VACATION PACKAGES

"You look like you need a vacation." It's bad enough to hear this about yourself *before* your vacation. But what about *after* it? More and more, travelers are coming home angered, annoyed, frustrated, and outraged.

Columbus' ship (inset) was beset with problems: so are many modern voyages. (Courtesy the American Museum of Natural History)

What has happened to turn these smiling, happy-go-lucky vacationers into purple-faced, wild-eyed, vengeance-seeking fanatics? For an answer, put yourself in any one of these situations:

◆ A couple arriving at their new, "first-class" hotel find it a little too new: the swimming pool isn't built, the tennis courts aren't ready, the lobby is under construction. Sleeping isn't easy either—the room lights won't turn off.

◆ An Italian ocean liner, billed as a luxurious "Fun Ship," is scheduled to cross the Atlantic and stop at seven Mediterranean ports, terminating in Trieste. Before reaching its first stop, the Fun Ship collides with another vessel. After docking for several days for repairs, the ship hobbles into Naples. One hundred and fifty passengers are herded into a small hotel lobby where they wait for eleven hours while the shipping line arranges transportation to Trieste. The vacationers are then taken to the railroad station, where they are installed in tiny compartments in the most inferior overnight train accommodations in Italy. Each compartment contains six narrow shelves, without mattresses, for sleeping. There are no ladders or footholds to reach the higher shelves. At Trieste, they begin their journey home.

◆ Vacationers anticipating a fabulous time in a "tropical paradise" in Jamaica find their "deluxe" accommodations are actually thatched huts infested with insects and rats. Pieces of foam rubber serve as mattresses; there are no working toilets. The "adjoining private beach" is a twenty-minute bus ride away. Once there, swimmers risk laceration on the sharp underwater coral.

◆ In the course of a month's vacation in South America, two Americans fly from São Paulo to Rio de Janeiro. They arrive, disembark, and wait for their baggage. While the plane is on the runway, an airline employee informs the couple that it would be too time-consuming and expensive to remove their luggage from the plane, which is going on. The couple watch in amazement as their luggage takes off for New York. They have eighteen more days to spend in South America, without their clothing.

◆ A honeymoon couple arrive in Hawaii to find that their overbooked hotel will not give them a room, despite confirmed reservations. They are asked to share a room—with another honeymoon couple.

◆ Travelers promised superior accommodations at a posh hotel in a Caribbean island find the "championship tennis courts" closed during the day and the "swinging discotheque" closed at night. Torrential rains fall for six out of the seven tour days.

The travel industry is a complex one. Its many components—travel agents, tour organizers, air carriers, hotelkeepers, bus and shipping lines, railways, and all their employees—must work together harmoniously in order to guarantee successful vacations. With all this teamwork required to serve the crush of travelers every year, it's a wonder that anyone ever gets where they're going without incident. Yet most people do, and the mishaps that occur are the exception rather than the rule. This is small comfort, of course, to the traveler whose vacation is ruined by the errors and miscalculations of industry personnel. Knowing a little about the industry and maintaining a healthy skepticism can help you minimize the chances of your holiday turning into a harrowing ordeal.

You may be promised this . . .

. . . and end up with this. (Photos by Byron, the Byron Collection, Museum of the City of New York)

The central figure in many people's vacation planning is the travel agent who acts as a link between the traveler and the rest of the industry. A poor agent can put you on a disorganized tour, lodge you at grimy hotels, or send you on a disastrously overbooked cruise. In other words, it's crucial to choose a travel agent carefully. Personal recommendations from people whose word you trust help the most. Keep in mind, too, that some agents specialize in certain areas of the world, and your destination may not be familiar to the particular agent recommended. The only way to tell is to see for yourself if the agent seems knowledgeable about the places you want to visit. Ask questions about local weather conditions, cultural events, currency, and accessibility of beaches or sports facilities you're interested in. You should be able to tell if the agent is talking from experience or just pulling phrases out of promotional literature. As a further check, you can call the Better Business Bureau and your local consumer affairs agency, to see if they have complaints against that agent on file. The American Society of Travel Agents (711 Fifth Avenue, New York, N.Y. 10022; phone: 212-486-0700) will also inform you if it has received complaints against the agent and if they've been resolved. (But, since most disgruntled travelers don't register their complaints, their absence is no guarantee of competence and trustworthiness.)

The most popular sources of travel ideas and information are those handsomely illustrated multicolor travel brochures. In them, everywhere is paradise (except, of course, where you live). If the world were as splendid as these brochures claim, we'd all be dancing in the streets and laughing hysterically at our good fortune. Of course, there are magnificent spots to visit, but don't accept brochure ballyhoo at face value. What, for example, do you think is a "first class" hotel? The best and most luxurious available, you might say. But the term actually means nothing, any dive can use it.

Another pitfall to watch out for is the description of the length of your trip. An "eight-day tour" often means two days of traveling (the first day to get there and the last to get home) and six days of touring. If there are several stops on the tour, a major portion of your vacation may be devoted to the arduous task of traveling. Rarely do the brochures indicate distances between stopovers. If your "exciting day in Brussels" includes getting to it by bus from Paris, you may find yourself arriving spent and exhausted after the seven-and-a-half-hour ride. Further bad omens may be contained in the small print—for instance, the substitution of different (usually inferior) hotels, changes in itinerary without notice, and other undesirable departures from the large-print promises. Be sure you understand all the conditions and limitations on attractive travel offers. Some reduced-rate packages require double, triple, or even quadruple occupancy of hotel rooms, inconvenient departure times, minimum stays, and other restrictions which may make them completely unappetizing.

In considering any vacation offering, look carefully before you leap into a tour promoter's arms. Don't deal with those who are strangers to you and your travel agent. There are hundreds of wholesalers who sell travel packages, including some incompetent, undercapitalized types who will take your money and disappear, or spend it quickly and head for bankruptcy court. If your travel agent can't vouch for a promoter's integrity, look elsewhere. Consider the various packages offered by the airlines and railroads. With the multitude of travel plans on the market today, you should have little trouble finding several enjoyable and reliable ones to choose from.

Of course, even the best-laid plans of travelers manage to go awry some of the time. You arrive at a hotel with confirmed reservations, and the desk clerk never heard of you. The nearest hotel with a vacancy sports weeds sprouting from the cracks between the floorboards, creaky furniture, and a funny odor in the air. What can you do when things go wrong?

Despite its size and the significant problems that sometimes arise, the travel industry is subject to very little government regulation. Most states do not have special laws requiring licensing, proof of financial responsibility, or evidence of competence in the field. There is little that one can do when in a fix far from home. Loud and persistent complaining at the scene of trouble sometimes helps. When it doesn't, the next-best thing is to carefully document what happened. If you are lodged in a run-down boardinghouse instead of the Ritz, take photographs of the inferior accommodations. Keep a written record of the unreasonable delays and abusive treatment you suffer.

When you get back home, confront the travel agent or tour organizer with your complaint, and if your tribulations stemmed from a failure to honor promises made to you, insist on whatever refund seems appropriate (include some reimbursement for the annoyance and inconvenience caused). Follow this up with complaints to consumer bureaus and the American Society of Travel Agents. Finally, if you still receive no satisfaction, consider suing. While lawyer's fees may make it impossible to hire counsel, a number of people have been successful in small claims courts. Others have banded together to bring class-action lawsuits (suitable when many people on the same tour, for example, are all victimized in the same way). Lawyers may be found to take these cases, on a contingency basis, since the sums involved are, collectively, usually substantial.

AIR TRAVEL

Problems associated with air travel are unique, because of the federal regulation of interstate airlines exercised by the Civil Aeronautics Board (CAB). While the companies are supposed to be regulated in the public interest, some of the rules are very protective of the industry, not the public. Many of the rules, technically known as "tariffs," are actually written by the airlines themselves and adopted by the Board. These tariffs contain the fares, routes, and all responsibilities the airline assumes for passengers and their baggage. You have the right to see the tariff rules at the airport or at any airline ticket counter. While the rules are not easy to read (fine print legalese never is), with persistence and determination they can be mastered. Airline reservation clerks and other employees do not always correctly un-

"We don't ski, we don't play golf, we hate the beach and tennis, we don't gamble, drink or dance. We're not gregarious and dislike games of any sort. What can you suggest?" (© 1978. Reprinted by permission of New York *Times* and Joseph Farris)

derstand the tariffs. If they give you incorrect information about fares, baggage liability limits, or similar matters, however, the airline is not responsible for their mistakes; the written tariff will be enforced.

Consumer anger with air travel usually takes off at three points: (1) failure to honor reservations; (2) lost baggage; and (3) botched charter flights. Here are your rights in those situations.

1. FAILURE TO HONOR RESERVATIONS

The scene: an airport in Washington, D.C. A man in a rumpled suit with a plain brown briefcase shows an Allegheny Airlines gate attendant his confirmed, reserved ticket for a morning flight to Hartford, Connecticut. The attendant refuses to permit him to board the plane, because the airline has sold more tickets than the plane has seats. The man's protests that he is to deliver an important speech in Hartford in two hours are ignored, and his guaranteed reservation is brushed aside. In the industry vernacular, he has been "bumped."

The traveler to Hartford misses his speech. The airline offers him $32 to compensate him for any damage caused. He refuses this paltry sum and, instead, sues. After a long court fight that takes the case to the Supreme Court, the persistent consumer is vindicated. The airline is ordered to pay him $25,000 for its deliberate refusal to honor his reservation. Maybe next time, Allegheny will think twice before it "bumps" Ralph Nader.

Or maybe it won't. Nader won his lawsuit because the court found that Allegheny had misrepresented itself when it "confirmed" his reservation without disclosing that it might not honor it. Soon after, the CAB issued a rule requiring airlines to notify passengers that they might be bumped, thereby freeing them from the kind of misrepresentation claim made by Nader.

In 1978, the CAB enacted a new rule on airline bumping. It permits the airlines to exclude people from their reserved flights, but requires that they pay them for this inconvenience. The practice of deliberate overbooking of flights which results in the need to bump passengers is defensible, say industry and CAB spokespeople, because consumers too often make a reservation and fail to appear for the flight. To compensate for this, the airlines oversell their seats. Only occasionally will too many people with reservations show up, forcing the airline to leave a few unlucky "extras" behind. But last year some 150,000 passengers were unceremoniously left at the boarding gate, mournfully watching their flights take off without them.

What are the bumped passenger's rights? Under CAB rules, passengers who are involuntarily bumped are divided into two categories. Those who reach their destination within two hours of their original schedule (four hours for international flights) must be offered the full amount of the ticket price, up to a maximum of $200 (the minimum is $37.50). Those suffering longer delays must be offered *twice* the value of the fare, including the price of connecting flights, up to a maximum of $400 (the minimum is $75). But there is an unusual twist to the rule. The airline gate attendant may ask passengers with confirmed reservations if they will *volunteer* to be bumped, in return for some negotiated amount of money (which can be less than the amounts specified in the rule).

Thus if you are not in danger of being bumped (you can tell by asking to see the airline's rules on passenger priorities for oversold flights) you may be asked if you would like to take a later flight and be paid cash for the delay and inconvenience caused. The amount of money offered will vary from airline to airline, and if you're interested, you may haggle for more. By this means, it is the CAB's hope, those travelers not in a rush will accept the offered payment and fly a few hours later, thereby permitting those in a hurry to leave on time.

This rule does not apply when the entire flight is canceled or delayed for any reason. It only applies when some passengers are left behind while others are permitted to board. For international flights, denied-boarding compensation is given only when the flight originates or ends in the United States and the reservation has been made in the United States. Further, the passenger must comply with any reconfirmation requirement of the airline (many carriers require reconfirmation of international flights at least 72 hours in advance of scheduled departure). The CAB advises international travelers to obtain a written reconfirmation at the ticket office, or to note the name of the agent and the date and time of the call when reconfirming by telephone.

Any passenger may reject the offer of denied-boarding compensation and sue the airline in civil court for actual damages sustained.

2. LOST BAGGAGE

You're jetting to Jamaica, but your bags are shuffled off to Buffalo. What if they're lost in the shuffle?

When baggage is lost, it is imperative that you report the loss immediately to the airline, before you leave the airport. Ask to fill out a "Property Irregularity Report," describing the luggage and its contents. The airline will then attempt to trace the baggage. If it is not found within three days, you should receive soon thereafter a *claim form* from the airline. If you haven't received this form within two weeks of the loss, write to the airline for it. Otherwise, you will lose your right to compensation.

The claim form asks for details of the loss, including full description of lost articles, their cost and date of purchase. You will be expected to produce the baggage claim check and your ticket receipt (as proof that you were on the plane and that you in fact checked luggage).

Do not exaggerate the value of your lost articles. The airlines are aware of fraudulent claims, and they examine all requests for reimbursement with great care. The major carriers even have a computer programmed to show them whether you have made prior claims of lost or stolen baggage. If your claim is supicious in any way, it may be denied entirely, or the airline may offer a much lower compensation than you requested. Airline claims departments deduct depreciation on all items which are not new and estimate the value of lost clothing based on standard tables prepared for this purpose. You may be requested to provide sales slips as proof of the existence and value of items claimed to be new.

If your baggage was damaged, you should also report that right away. Claim forms here too must be completed quickly and accurately. Airline liability for loss or damage is limited to a maximum of $750 per passenger. If you wish to increase the airline's potential liability, you should purchase "excess value" coverage at the ticket counter where you check in your baggage. The fee is 10 cents for each additional $100 in coverage.

On international flights, the airline's maximum liability is $9.07 per *pound* for checked baggage and $400 per *passenger* for carry-on baggage. This was established by the Warsaw Convention—an international treaty on air travel. It is important to note that the liability coverage is not the same as insurance—that is, you will not receive the maximum upon baggage loss or damage. You will only be offered an amount to cover your actual loss, which may be considerably less than the maximum. Further, the airline's estimate of your loss may be much lower than your own estimate. If you are unsatisfied with the offer, all you can do is pursue your claim in court. The CAB has no power to adjust individual claims or to direct the airline to make larger settlement offers.

Fragile items present a special problem in damage claims. It is safest to carry delicate items with you on board the aircraft, to minimize the chances of breakage. Airlines are not responsible for damage to such items as antique clocks and glassware sustained during normal baggage handling. Under CAB rules, however, they are responsible for damage to fragile items which are (1) commonly packed in suitcases (e.g., eyeglasses, one camera per passenger, toiletries) or (2) damaged due to negligent mishandling of baggage (provable, perhaps, by evidence of external bruises, cuts, or punctures).

In filing a claim for lost, delayed, or damaged luggage, include all "consequential damages"—i.e., the cost of telephone calls made to resolve the matter, the price of necessary interim purchases, the cost of obtaining estimates or other documents required by the airline.

The CAB is considering changes in the rules governing lost baggage. To check on the current status of these rules, write to the CAB, Washington, D.C. 20428, or call 202-673-5526.

CHARTER FLIGHTS

Everyone is familiar with stories of charter flights which never get off the ground or which deliver passengers to European countries and then leave them stranded there. Here the airlines are not at fault. The responsibility for charter flights rests entirely with the charterer—the person or business which organizes the trip. The charterer makes a contract with an airline to hire a plane; if the airline doesn't get paid in time, it doesn't fly the plane. In that event, your complaint is with the charterer, not with the airline.

When charters are organized by responsible individuals, they usually go well. Charters are desirable when they offer significantly cheaper fares than are available ordinarily (which is becoming less true with the increased appearance of cut-rate fares on regularly scheduled airlines). When you fly on a charter, you will be asked to sign a contract which commits you to pay the charterer for that flight and which spells out your rights with respect to baggage allowances, refunds if you must cancel, limits on liability for loss of your luggage or other mishaps, and all the other details of your trip. Read this document carefully before signing it.

Every charter organizer must file its plans with the CAB. The agency will look them over but does not have the time or the resources to fully investigate them. If you see an advertisement which says a charter is "CAB approved," this is no guarantee of honesty or reliability. It merely means that, on paper, the plan seems reasonable.

In the past, you had to be a member of some social, business, or professional group in order to qualify for a charter flight. The group itself served as the flight sponsor, and only its members of at least six months' standing could sign up. This type of arrangement, known as an "affinity charter," still exists, but it is not alone any more. Other charters, which do not require affiliation with any outside groups, are available to the public. If you are offered a place on an affinity group charter, make sure that you honestly qualify as a group member. Do not accept a phony membership card or one which has been specially backdated. This jeopardizes your entire vacation, and since other charters are readily accessible (in addition to reduced-rate deals on non-charters) it is foolhardy to violate government charter rules.

The wide variety of non-affinity group charter plans now available are known as "public charters." In August 1978, the CAB removed the restrictions it had previously placed on these plans. Now the public charter operator need not (unless it so chooses) include mandatory minimum stays, minimum group sizes, ground accommodations, or advance bookings as part of its offering. Limits on charter arrangements will be dictated more by the marketplace and less by government regulation.

There are some disadvantages to charters, which you should be aware of before you purchase your ticket. The important ones are these:

1. If enough seats aren't sold, the entire flight may be canceled. Charters can offer low fares only if their planes are full. Most charterers reserve the right to call off the trip if a certain minimum enrollment isn't reached.

2. You may be asked to make your travel plans far in advance. Once you agree to a charter flight, you are committed to that arrangement. You won't be able to change your flight times or dates, as are travelers on ordinary scheduled airlines. Furthermore, if you must unexpectedly cancel your trip, you will usually have to pay a substantial penalty fee (as specified in your contract). See if the contract offers to sell you insurance to protect you in case you must cancel. This can be a good investment where the penalty is high and the premium is low.

3. The price you pay for some charters may be increased prior to departure because of increases in fuel costs or for other economic reasons. This will also be part of your charter contract.

4. Airport delays are all too common. Don't be surprised if the plane leaves four or five hours late. (The CAB is now considering a rule which would require charterers to provide overnight accommodations or alternate transportation if the delays exceed six hours.)

5. Charter planes are always packed. A plane that normally seats 200 may be redesigned to seat 261, by reducing the space between seats and eliminating lounges and carry-on luggage racks. Don't expect too much elbow room.

6. If the charter flight is part of a package offering accommodations, look for a clause in the contract which permits the charterer to change hotels and to revise the itinerary without notice. This is a common provision, but one which can be used by an unscrupulous organizer to justify substantial alterations in your trip. This is a good reason to be certain that you are dealing with a reputable charter firm. If you're unsure of its reliability, ask your travel agent about its past record and reputation. Don't base your decision solely on a brochure.

COMPLAINTS ABOUT AIRLINES AND CHARTERS

If an airline or a chartering company will not resolve a consumer complaint, you can write to the Bureau of Consumer Protection, Civil Aeronautics Board, Washington, D.C. 20428. This office will review the complaint to determine if applicable CAB rules have been violated and advise you about your rights. Where the volume of complaints in a particular area is significant, the CAB may propose new regulations or revise old ones. Bear in mind, however, that many disputes will have to be settled in court; the CAB does not have formal authority to adjudicate individual cases.

You can also send a copy of your complaint to the Aviation Consumer Action Project (ACAP), P.O. Box 19029, Washington, D.C. 20036, a private consumer organization set up by Ralph Nader which monitors the performance of the airline industry. ACAP does not resolve individual complaints, but it can provide useful information concerning your rights and support you in your effort to obtain satisfaction. Your experience will also be used as a guide for future ACAP challenges to unfair airline rules and practices.

A SPECIAL NOTE ON BUSES, TRAINS, AND SHIPS

Travel by bus, train, or ship is slower but, to many people, more pleasurable than air travel. These people movers will rarely lose your baggage (since you take it aboard yourself) and generally don't cause as many headaches as the airlines, but they are hardly immune from customer complaints.

Buses traveling interstate are regulated by the Interstate Commerce Commission. Complaints ignored by the bus company may be forwarded to the ICC, Washington, D.C. 20423, which also maintains a toll-free number for consumer inquiries—800-424-9312. State transportation departments generally handle local service complaints.

The national network of railroads run by Amtrak has a consumer complaint department for all rail service problems. Write to the Adequacy of Service Bureau, Amtrak, 955 L'Enfant Plaza North, S.W., Washington, D.C. 20024.

Ships pose a special problem, namely, they can make you nauseous. You can't blame the captain for high seas and rowdy weather, of course, but don't be too quick to assume your stomach agitation is seasickness. The U. S. Public Health Service, which inspects ships for unsanitary conditions, frequently finds that passenger illness can be traced to poor cleanliness on board. Of the 73 ships examined between December 1976 and November 1977, only five passed all inspections. To get a free summary of recent ship inspections, write to: Chief, Sanitation Vector Control Activity, Public Health Service, 1015 North America Way, Room 107, Miami, Fla. 33132. (If a ship you're interested in failed its last test, you can also obtain a copy of the specific report on it, containing all the revolting particulars.)

BON VOYAGE!

EARLY VOYAGES TO THE MOON

An exhibition in honor of the conference sponsored by President Eisenhower's Committee on Scientists and Engineers and the William Benton Foundation, on "America's Human Resources to Meet the Scientific Challenge," from the collections of Colonel Richard Gimbel, Yale 1920, and the Yale University Library, February, 1958.

A. VOYAGES

1.	c. 135A. D.	Lucian	A True Story	(1496)
2.	c. 135A. D.	Lucian	Illustration of Lucian's ship	(1551)
3.	c. 140A. D.	Lucian	Icaromennipus	(1551)
4.	c. 350A. D.		Historia Alexandri Magni	(1489)
5.	c. 350A. D.		Illustration of Flight of Alexander	(1517)
6.	1516	Lodovico Ariosto	Orlando Furioso	(1547)
7.	1593-95		Satyre Menipee	(1612)
8.	1620	Ben Jonson	News from New World Discovered in Moon	(1816)
9.	1634	John Kepler	Somnium	(1858-71)
10.	1638	Francis Godwin	The Man in the Moone	(1638)
11.	1638	Francis Godwin	Voyage and Adventures of Domingo Gonsales	(1765)
12.	1638	John Wilkins	Discovery of a World in the Moon	(1638)
13.	1638	John Wilkins	Discovery of a New World	(1640)
14.	1650	Cyrano de Bergerac	Histoire Comique (vials of dew)	(1650)
15.	1650	Cyrano de Bergerac	Histoire Comique (rockets)	(1699)
16.	1650	Cyrano de Bergerac	Comical History of the Sun	(1687)
17.	1660	Grimmelshausen	Journey to the Moon	(1660)
18.	1686	Fontenelle	A Plurality of Worlds	(1686)
19.	1690	Gabriel Daniel	Voyage to World of Cartesius	(1692)
20.	1698	Huygens	Celestial Worlds	(1698)
21.	1705	Daniel Defoe	The Consolidator	(1705)
22.	1705	Daniel Defoe	Journey to World in the Moon	(1705)
23.	1727	Samuel Brunt	Voyage to Cacklogallinia	(1727)
24.	1751	Ralph Morris	Life and Adventures of John Daniel	(1770)
25.	1751	Ralph Morris	Daniel's Flying Machine (print)	
26.	1760?	Filippo Morghen	Raccolta Della Cose...	(1760?)
27.	1764-65	Francis Gentleman	A Trip to the Moon	(1764)
28.	1784		Count D'Artois...Passage to the Moon*	(1784)
29.	c. 1785		Monde Lunare (print)	(c. 1785)
30.	1786		Voyage a Ching-y-ang	(1786)
31.	1813	George Fowler	Flight to the Moon	(1813)
32.	1827	Joseph Atterly	Voyage to the Moon	(1827)
33.	1835	Edgar A. Poe	Hans Phaall	(1835)
34.	1835	Edgar A. Poe	Hans Phaall (Illustration)	(1944)

35.	1835	Richard A. Locke	Great Astronomical Discoveries	(1835)
36.	1835		Inhabitants of the Moon (print)	(1835)
37.	1835		Denison Olmsted (portrait)	(1835)
38.	1835		Elias Loomis (portrait)	(1835)
39.	1835	Richard A. Locke	The Moon Hoax	(1859)
40.	1836		Partenza di Pulcinella la Luna (print)	(1836)
41.	1836		Arrivo di Pulcinella Nella Luna (print)	(1836)
42.	1836		Scoverte di Sir John Herschel (print)	(1836)
43.	1836		Diligenza di Ritorno Dalla Luna (print)	(1836)
44.	1895	L. P. Senaren	Lost in the Mountains of the Moon	(1895)
45.	1899	Allyn Draper	The Rocket	(1899)
46.	1863-65	Jules Verne	From the Earth to the Moon	(1874)
47.	1894	John Jacob Astor	Journey in Other Worlds	(1894)
48.	1900	H. G. Wells	First Men in the Moon (presentation)	(1900)
49.	1901	H. G. Wells	First Men in the Moon (frontispiece)	(1901)

B. CREATION, SPECULATION, AND MAPS

50.			The Bible (Gutenberg)	(c. 1455)
51.		Petrus Comestor	Historiaux de la Bible	(c. 1460)
52.	c. 340B. C.	Plato	Phaedo **	(1450A. D.)
53.	c. 51B. C.	Cicero	Somnium Scipionis **	(1450A. D.)
54.	c. 70A. D.	Plutarch	Face in the Roundle of the Moon	(1509A. D.)
55.	c. 70A. D.	Plutarch	Face in the Roundle of the Moon	(1603A. D.)
56.	1610	Galileo	Siderius Nuncius	(1610)
57.	1634-35	Claude Mellan	Maps of the Moon	(1634-35)
58.	1649		Man in the Moon (poem)	(1649)
59.	1742	Rousseau	Le Nouveau Dedale	(1801)
60.	1742	J. Doppelmayer	Atlas Novus Coelestis (map)	(1742)
61.	1651	Riccioli	Tabula Selenographica (map)	(1651)
62.	1752	Voltaire	Micromegas	(1753)
63.	1775	Tobias Mayer	Monds Charte (map)	(1837)
64.	1837	Beer and Maedler	Mappa Selenographica (map)	(1834)
65.	1924		Map of the Moon	(1924)
66.	1953	Cornelius Ryan (ed.)	Conquest of the Moon	(1953)
67.	1953	Patrick Moore	Guide to the Moon	(1953)
68.	1937-38	Lick Observatory	Composite Photograph of the Moon	(1937-38)

Order of columns: exhibit number; date originally written; author; abbreviated
title; and date of copy shown (in parenthesis).
        * Courtesy of Robert L. Fisher, Yale 1920
      ** Courtesy of Thomas E. Marston, Yale 1927

The Great Hall of the Sterling Memorial Library
Yale University, New Haven, Connecticut

(Courtesy the American Museum of Natural History)

SELECTED BIBLIOGRAPHY

Civil Aeronautics Board booklets available from the Consumer Information Center,
    Pueblo, Colo. 81009:
    Air Travelers' Fly Rights
    Consumer Guide to International Air Travel
Civil Aeronautics Board booklet available from the Publications Services Division,
    CAB, Washington, D.C. 20428: *Consumer Facts on Air Fares.*
"A Guide to Discount Air Fares." *Consumer Reports,* March 1978, p. 161.
U. S. Customs Service pamphlet available from any District Director of Customs (or
    write to U. S. Customs Service, Washington, D.C. 20229): *Customs Hints for Re-
    turning U.S. Residents—Know Before You Go.*

18

School daze:
vocational and correspondence courses

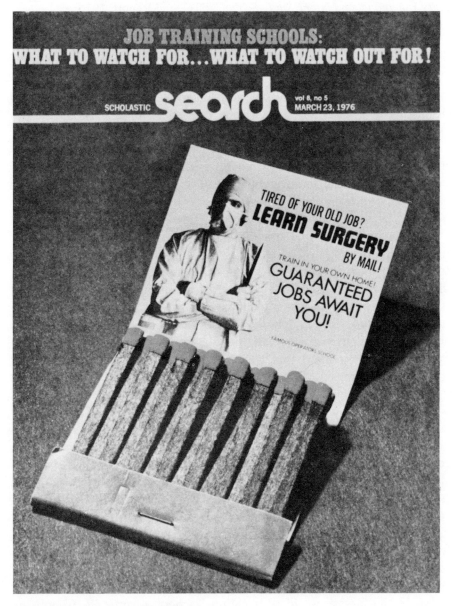

(*Scholastic;* photo by Hollis Officer)

The following question was asked by a relatively green, unseasoned representative at a state sales seminar at which were present over 40 sales representatives. "What should be done if I feel a particular prospect lacks the ability or mental stamina to handle a course in electronics?" This answer came from the department director officiating at the seminar who had designed and was responsible for extensive sales and training procedures for the particular institution and who was responsible for nearly 100 representatives in his department. "Well, there is absolutely nothing in this course that could harm him and possibly if he shows interest, it could prove to be valuable therapy . . . Gentlemen, money is the name of this game." — H. HOLLEY, *Fact or Fallacy: The Pro's and Con's of Home Study and Correspondence* (Hol-Cot Enterprises, Inc., 1972), quoted on p. 138 of *Proprietary Vocational and Home Study Schools,* FTC Staff Report, 1976

You may pay more for your schooling than your learning is worth.
— Proverb

Vocational training in America is largely left to a multitude of independent profit-making institutions. Their ads appear all over—on television, in buses and subways, and even on matchbook covers.

Few businesses, however, are conducted with the cynical hypocrisy characterizing the private trade school industry. Many schools' financial success depends more upon the large number of fee-paying dropouts than on the small number of students who graduate. Schools often hold out the promise of high-paying jobs in fields where jobs of any sort are nonexistent. And they sell education with brochures and ads which are themselves textbook lessons in fraud and deceit.

Vocational training was not always in this sorry state. Trade schools first developed to meet the need for specialized training in a variety of occupations, particularly those in which technological advances made new skills essential. The most striking example is the computer industry, created entirely by new technology. In its early years, the field experienced an acute shortage of trained workers. In time, jobs were filled, and the excessive demand for new workers leveled off. Computer training schools, however, could not afford to cut back on enrollment. To turn a profit they had to fill classes even when jobs in the industry were no longer available.

Faced with the need to survive, schools for truck driving, fashion modeling, computer programming, airline personnel, and many other occupations aggressively recruit new students, although the need for trained workers subsided long ago. As the Federal Trade Commission warns· "In some fields, vocational schools may . . . be turning out several times more graduates in one vocational skill than there are jobs available throughout the United States.'"

How do trade schools prosper even when the industries they serve are depressed? The answer is found in the school's advertisements and sales techniques. Misleading promotional brochures proclaim that jobs are always plentiful. In the fantasy world of vocational school advertising the job opportunities are "limitless," the times are "booming," the need is "urgent," the employers are "desperate." As one school puts it: "You won't have to do any job hunting; they'll be hunting for you!"

To bolster their credibility, representatives of the schools call themselves "career counselors" or "admissions officers," never sales agents. This has the advantage of placing the consumer in the dependent role of advisee or applicant. Those seeking vocational training are often embarrassed about their previous education, or feel their present salary or job is inferior—vulnerabilities which the school salespeople exploit. Some sales agents will actually demean the prospective student in front of other members of the family. ("You really support your family on that salary? Frankly, I don't see how.") The goal is to make the prospect feel desperate for help; then the seller offers the course as the only path to financial security and personal self-respect. (When done properly, this ploy leaves the victim feeling grateful to the seller.)

In another version of this technique (called the "negative sell") the school representative hands the prospect a questionnaire, supposedly to determine the applicant's suitability for training. The questionnaire begins:

> Does your wife work?
> Do you want her to?
> What can you do about having her stop working?

This is a blatant (and sexist) appeal to male pride, used no doubt to make the prospect feel inadequate and ashamed that his own salary must be supplemented by his wife's.

The "counselors" are, of course, anxious to sign up anyone who can pay the admission fee. Schools minimize the amount of study involved and the need for any aptitude for the training. One pamphlet for a school says: "Only an hour or two of study a night for a few short weeks qualifies you to step immediately into an exciting, well-paid position." Another predicts: "You will be surprised by how quickly and easily you learn even if you never did well in school." Some schools administer easy "aptitude tests" which are used to convince prospects that their success is assured.

While salespeople attempt to create the impression that admission to the school is selective, in most cases anybody can enroll. A former district manager for a major trade school told the FTC: "In all of the hundreds of students I have enrolled, I have never had one rejected. In fact, I had a letter from an attorney—La Salle had a letter from the Attorney General of North Dakota wanting to know why I enrolled a moron in a computer programming course." (FTC Staff Report, p. 138, n. 84.)

Many vocational schools devote substantial resources to recruiting students, but meager resources to actually teaching them. One nursing school hired unlicensed nurses as teachers, and put them in classes in which twenty or more students had to share one thermometer. Some computer schools train students on obsolete equipment, which the students will never use again. This sort of training is worse than no training at all: it costs the student a good deal of money, but no employer will consider it worthwhile.

Many schools capitalize on the fact that students can obtain veterans' benefits or low-cost government loans. In their sales pitches sellers regularly claim that their courses have "government approval," misrepresenting what is merely federal loan and benefit qualification as government endorsement of the quality and integrity of the school.

CORRESPONDENCE SCHOOLS

Correspondence schools offer to teach everything from taxidermy to law, by mail. The overwhelming majority of students never finish these courses. One estimate puts the number of students who drop out at 75 to 90 percent of all who enroll. This is partly the fault of the schools: the courses are often of poor quality and the time spent per student is insufficient. But many consumers are at fault here too, letting themselves think that home study will not require the same kind of time, effort, and, especially, discipline that all serious study demands. The schools, of course, encourage this self-deception, with ads that portray instant success. One common advertising trick is to present the "testimonial" (usually solicited by the school) of a previous graduate who has succeeded (no matter that success came ten years later, or that the course played no role in it).

Learning by correspondence is even more difficult than learning in a classroom. Home distractions can keep the most well-intentioned student from completing lessons. Like it or not, most people need the discipline of a regular class schedule and the personal attention of a responsive teacher. If you do not have the time to take a course in the community once or twice a week, then you probably don't have the time for a home study course either. Statistically, the odds are against your ever finishing a correspondence school course. Learning in this fashion should not be attempted unless no other alternatives exist and you have a substantial amount of time available for study. Otherwise, you'll be one of the thousands of non-students who pay lots of money for uncompleted lessons.

ACCREDITING AGENCIES

Schools frequently boast of their accredited status in advertising and sales literature. Unfortunately, these are empty claims, because the accrediting agencies' standards are abysmally low. In fact, they rarely deny accreditation to any school, no matter how many consumer complaints or findings of fraud have been made against it. This is not surprising, because the accrediting organizations are trade associations, composed of and controlled entirely by members of the industry. Some accrediting bodies do not even monitor sales activities or regularly review the schools' advertising and promotional literature for misrepresentations. In short, accreditation provides *no* guarantee of the honesty, reliability, or quality of the school in question.

LICENSING AGENCIES

Forty-six states require private schools to be licensed. (The four which do not are Iowa, Missouri, Utah, and Vermont.) Theoretically, this is done to ensure quality instruction, financial responsibility, and honesty in sales efforts. In reality, state regulation has been a monumental failure, giving the appearance of responsible state supervision without the substance. The FTC Staff Report on the industry concluded that state oversight of private schools "is inadequate, confusing, contradictory, and often inept."

This sorry performance of state agencies can be traced to a number of causes. In some states, the "division" in charge of vocational school licensing consists of a single individual, who must inspect dozens, if not hundreds, of schools annually, enforce all licensing rules and regulations, and investigate all consumer complaints. The lack of resources causes many states to issue "temporary" licenses to schools without any inspection whatsoever. These temporary licenses may last for years. An unscrupulous operator can open a school, operate fraudulently, and go out of business before the state even looks at the license application. A lawyer in the California Attorney General's office stated, "Al Capone could start a school for gangsters and the state would have to let him do it."

In many states, the licensing procedure is automatic, and no genuine scrutiny of applicants' backgrounds, financial stability, or educational qualifications takes place. Any operator with the required fee and the minimal intelligence needed to fill out government forms can get a license and start a school. Add a second-rate curriculum, a third-rate faculty, and some obsolete equipment, and you're in business—with full state approval.

Frequently state supervisory boards are made up of members of the industry. Consequently, license revocations are virtually unheard-of in many states, despite the widespread fraud in the field repeatedly documented by federal investigators, investigative journalists, and consumer groups.

Even the federal agencies which annually pay out over $500 million to subsidize vocational training do not take measures to assure that the schools receiving federal money are minimally adequate.

Because existing laws have been so ineffectual, the FTC finally enacted a new rule to protect consumers. The rule, effective January 1, 1980, requires that vocational and correspondence schools:

1. disclose their student drop-out rate;
2. provide a fourteen-day "cooling off" period following the signing of the contract, during which buyers may cancel their contracts without obligation; and
3. create a pro rata refund policy, under which a student who drops out of the course pays only for the lessons actually taken plus a reasonable registration fee. Any amount paid above this must be refunded.

If the school makes any claim about job placement or earnings available after graduation, it must provide specific figures which show the number of recent graduates who obtained jobs and their approximate starting salaries.

With this information, consumers can avoid those schools with high drop-out rates and low job-placement rates. If schools refuse to provide this data, report them to the Bureau of Consumer Protection, Federal Trade Commission, 6th and Pennsylvania Avenue, Washington, D.C. 20580.

COMPLAINTS

Complaints against private schools should be resolved by licensing departments (usually located in the state education department), but, as noted above, these agencies are notoriously ineffective. We suggest sending complaints to the state attorney general's office, with a copy to any local consumer office and to the state education department (some agencies may be functioning properly, after all). At the same time, write to the Federal Trade Commission. There's always the chance that one of these agencies will act, but if none of them responds adequately, you can sue in small claims court (see chapter 28) or look for other students who would be willing to hire a lawyer with you to bring a class action suit against the school (in a class action, a few individuals can sue for all others similarly situated; the potential for a substantial recovery makes it economical for a lawyer to take the case).

HOW TO FIND GOOD VOCATIONAL TRAINING

1. **Find out if there is a program offered by the local school system, community college, or a community group offering adult education courses. Do not accept the first school whose advertisement you see. Many excellent courses are offered by nonprofit institutions which do not have advertising budgets.**

2. **Find out if the industry in which you wish to work offers on-the-job training. In many fields, such as airlines, employers prefer to do their own training.**

3. **Contact people who know the field. Ask their opinion about the best training; whether there are jobs available; and the usual starting salary. Find out what additional qualifications you may need (some computer firms will hire only college graduates as programmers; most trucking firms will hire only union members with special licenses and experience). Good people to contact are personnel directors for companies in the field, and union officers if workers are unionized.**

4. **Visit the school before you sign up for training. Sit in on a class, talk with students, and find out what the school is really like. Never believe all you read about the school in its brochures.**

5. **Insist on obtaining the following information: the number of graduates who obtained employment in the last year; their average starting salary; the number and percentage of students who dropped out of the course before its completion. Since the school salespeople often lie about this information, ask for it in writing. Also, ask for the names of some graduates, and talk to them.**

6. Comparison-shop for the best training at the lowest price. Some nonprofit organizations and employers offer free training; private schools often charge thousands of dollars for training courses.

7. If there is an enrollment charge, find out what the refund policy is. Many consumers do not finish the courses they start, forfeiting large sums of money when they drop out. Look for a reasonable refund policy, in which a small sum is forfeited if you drop out early in the training.

For information on obtaining copies of "The Door-to-Door Career Con," write to: Consumer Law Training Center, New York Law School, 57 Worth Street, New York, N.Y. 10013.

DON'T GET CAUGHT IN THE DOOR-TO-DOOR HUSTLE!

BEWARE OF BUYING FROM ANY DOOR-TO-DOOR SALESPERSON

✳ **FRAUD** AND UNFAIR DEALING **ARE COMMON.**

✳ DOOR-TO-DOOR BUYING USUALLY IS **MORE EXPENSIVE** THAN STORE BUYING.

✳ RESIST **"PRESSURE TACTICS"** — IF YOU ARE PRESSURED TO "SIGN IMMEDIATELY," INSTRUCT THE SELLER TO LEAVE.

✳ NEVER DECIDE IMMEDIATELY: ALWAYS TELL THE SALESPERSON YOU NEED A FEW DAYS TO **"THINK IT OVER."** IF THE OFFER IS VALID, IT WILL BE THERE TOMORROW.

✳ IF YOU DO SIGN A CONTRACT IN YOUR HOME OR OFFICE, YOU HAVE THE LEGAL RIGHT TO CANCEL THE SALE WITHIN 3 DAYS. YOU MUST **CANCEL IN WRITING!**

BEWARE OF SIGNING EXPENSIVE CONTRACTS FOR VOCATIONAL SCHOOL TRAINING.

✳ MANY SCHOOLS GIVE **LOW-QUALITY** JOB TRAINING, AND **CANNOT** PLACE THEIR STUDENTS IN **GOOD JOBS.**

✳ BEFORE SIGNING UP FOR VOCATIONAL TRAINING:
  ● ASK HOW MANY OF LAST YEAR'S GRADUATES GOT JOBS IN THE FIELD.
  ● FIND OUT WHAT THE DROP OUT RATE IS. IN MANY SCHOOLS MORE STUDENTS DROP OUT OF THE COURSE THAN FINISH IT!
  ● CALL POTENTIAL EMPLOYERS AND ASK THEM WHETHER THEY WOULD HIRE YOU IF YOU GRADUATED FROM THIS SCHOOL EMPLOYERS KNOW BEST WHICH SCHOOLS ARE NO GOOD.
  ● VISIT A CLASS AND TALK WITH THE STUDENTS.
  ● ASK WHAT FEE YOU MUST PAY IF YOU CANCEL YOUR CONTRACT.

SELECTED BIBLIOGRAPHY

Consumer Bulletin No. 13, Consumer Education, available from the Superintendent of Documents, U. S. Government Printing Office, Washington, D.C. 20402.

FTC Packet ⌗1 on Vocational School Program, available from the Federal Trade Commission, Washington, D.C. 20580.

Proprietary Vocational and Home Study Schools, published by the FTC Bureau of Consumer Protection; available from Superintendent of Documents, U. S. Government Printing Office, Washington, D.C. 20402.

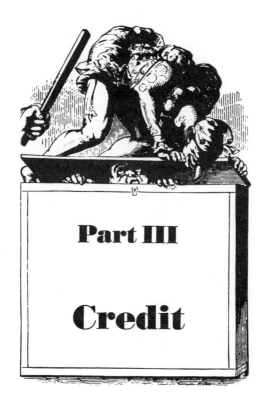

Part III

Credit

19

Are you getting all you deserve?

A pig bought on credit is forever grunting.   — Spanish proverb

Say nothing of my debts, unless you mean to pay them.   — Proverb

Creditors have better memories than debtors.   — Chinese fortune cookie

Take the Cash and let the Credit go.   — The *Rubáiyát* of OMAR KHAYYÁM

In 1733, *Poor Richard's Almanack* counseled Americans against borrowing ("Neither a borrower nor a lender be"); high living ("Early to bed and early to rise makes a man healthy, wealthy and wise"); free spending ("A penny saved is a penny earned"); and sleeping late ("The early bird catches the worm"). Thrift, prudence, and austerity were the highest virtues. To our colonial ancestors, moneylending seemed a dubious occupation, on the respectability scale falling somewhere between witchcraft and highway robbery.

Disapproving attitudes toward debt persisted throughout the nineteenth century. While lenders obtained the legal right to exist, their activities were strictly confined by law. By the end of World War I borrowing had become slightly more respectable, and consumer credit reached the $1 billion threshold. It climbed, slowly, over the next thirty years. Then, without warning, consumer credit shot up through the roof.

It was as if the entire nation had gone debt crazy. Americans went on a deficit-spending spree the likes of which had never been seen before. By 1960, consumers owed $56 billion to lenders; by 1978, they owed a staggering $227 billion—or $1,000 for every man, woman, and child in the United States. Credit cards appeared on the national scene in 1946; by 1978 there were over 580 million in circulation. A citizenry weaned on self-denial and frugality suddenly was up to its ears in debt, and in all the goods and services that a debt-fueled economy could provide. Factories strained to turn out their cars, televisions, and food freezers fast enough. Without the phenomenal growth in credit, the unprecedented expansion of the consumer goods market would have been impossible.

Today, the largest share of installment credit goes toward the purchase of cars. Ironically, auto industry executives at first were adamantly opposed to selling cars on credit. William Wilson, author of *Full Faith and Credit* (New York: Random House, 1976), quotes auto executive Charles Nash as saying in 1919: "I will see this company in receivership before I permit one of my automobiles to be sold on installment credit." Not long after, Nash and his auto industry cronies jumped aboard the credit bandwagon, where their corporate descendants have been ever since.

WHO'S SELLING MONEY?

Borrowing money, like buying a mule, costs money. But the similarity doesn't end there. If you were in the market for a good stubborn mule, would you buy the first beast you saw? Of course not. You'd go around to several mule owners and get the best buy you could find. It's the same with money—it is foolish just to accept the first deal on money you're offered. Even though one lender's dollar is exactly the same as another's, the prices they charge vary tremendously. On a small loan, you might pay anywhere from under 8 percent interest to over 30 percent. The lesson for consumers seeking credit couldn't be more clear: shop around for credit, as you would for any other commodity.

"I'll be straight with you. I don't want a car or anything. I just want some money

(© Punch—ROTHCO)

In 1968, Congress passed the Truth-in-Lending Law,* designed to make the cost of credit readily apparent to consumers. The law requires everyone who gives credit to consumers to reveal the price charged for it in two ways. First, it must be disclosed as an interest rate identified by the term "annual percentage rate." Second, the total cost must be disclosed in dollars and cents, identified by the term "finance charge." Thus, for any kind of consumer credit, to compare the price of borrowing money you simply look for the "annual percentage rate" and the "finance charge."

What are the choices facing the consumer who wants to buy now and pay later? Probably more than you think. Here is a rundown of the various sources of credit available and what interest rates you may expect to pay with each. Since rates vary from state to state, a general range will be given. The cheapest sources of credit are listed first.

1. Passbook loan. If you have a bank savings account, you can borrow against your savings while your account continues to earn interest. Thus, if the bank's annual percentage rate is 7½ percent for the loan, and your savings account earns 5½ percent, the effective charge to you for the loan is 2 percent. Keep in mind that the savings account is frozen, with withdrawals not permitted while the loan is outstanding. (Some banks do permit partial withdrawals as the loan is paid off.)

2. Life insurance. You can borrow against the cash value of your life insurance policy, paying an annual percentage rate of 5 to 8 percent. If you die before the loan is paid back, your insurance coverage is reduced to cover the debt. To maintain full coverage, repay the loan promptly.

3. Credit unions. Various employers, labor unions, and other organizations operate credit unions offering relatively low-cost (9 to 13 percent) loans to their members. (See chapter 31 for details on credit unions.)

4. Banks. Savings and commercial banks offer loans to finance the purchase of cars, home improvements, vacations, etc. Rates vary around the nation, depending on state banking laws, but fall within the 10 to 15 percent range. Some banks also permit depositors to borrow money by writing checks larger than the balance in their accounts; this plan, however, may cost more than a simple loan.

5. Retail store charge accounts and installment contracts. Retailers offer charge accounts and installment plans to encourage the purchase of their goods. The annual percentage rate is high (12 to 18 percent). On charge accounts, however, many stores give customers a 30-day "grace period" during which no interest charges are imposed. To take advantage of this interest-free time, you must pay the full amount due within the first 20 or 30 days after purchase.

6. Credit cards. Credit cards are also expensive financers (annual percentage rate is 12 to 18 percent). But most card issuers give customers a 30-day interest-free period, a valuable opportunity to avoid the high costs to follow.

7. Finance companies. Finance companies (also known as small-loan

* 15 U.S.C. 1601.

companies) advertise heavily and actively solicit customers, but are the worst places to go for money. Interest rates are very high, exceeding 30 percent in some instances. They are very likely to employ aggressive debt collectors and to pursue overextended debtors with a vengeance. The high interest rates they charge will drain your paycheck with alarming speed. Dealing with finance companies may hurt your chances to get credit in the future from other lenders, who sometimes view loans from these companies as a negative characteristic in your credit profile. In short, finance companies are to be avoided. Consider them only if emergencies arise and other lenders refuse to extend credit.

INTEREST RATES IN HISTORY

Permissible rates of interest according to:

Laws of Manu in India	**24%**
24th Century B.C.	
Code of Hammurabi	**33⅓%**
1900–732 B.C.	
Temple of Delos in Greece	**10%**
4th Century B.C.	
Ancient Rome	**8⅓%**
443 B.C.	
The Bible	**0%**
Charlemagne	**0%**
A.D. 800	
Pope Alexander III	**0%**
1159–81	
Massachusetts Bay Colony	**8%**
1641	

— **Source: National Commission on Consumer Finance.**

CASH VS. CREDIT

Everyone knows the temptations of buying on credit. "Cash or charge?" displaced "I love you" as the most popular three-word phrase in the language during the credit boom of the sixties. While Credit enjoys all the attention, Cash, like a shy girl at a wild party, receives less than it truly deserves. To help right this wrong, we list here the many tempting attractions of Cash.

1. Using cash increases your total purchasing power. The more you use credit, the more your income goes to paying off interest charges—not buying goods.

2. There are no repayment anxieties with cash. No brutish characters call to ask where your payment is; no one threatens to repossess your furniture.

3. Cash preserves your privacy. You don't have to reveal your name, address, income, occupation, rent bill, bank accounts, etc., etc., etc. You need not submit yourself to credit checks or appraising glances from skeptical credit managers.

4. You sometimes get lower prices for paying for things with cash. Department stores and other retailers may take up to 5 percent off their prices for cash customers, to save the cost of processing credit card transactions.

5. Cash is real. You can see it in your hand, feel it in your fingers, and watch it as it goes. If the spirit moves you, you can even kiss it goodbye. Credit deceives the senses. You can spend more than you have, but your wallet stays full. The plastic cards and other emblems of credit give you no tangible sign that you've reached (or exceeded) your limit.

HOW TO ESTABLISH CREDIT

Despite the advantages of using cash, credit has become a vital part of our economy, and many people, lacking any credit history, find themselves in a bind when it comes to establishing credit. Divorced, separated, and widowed women may also need to establish credit, because while they were married their own credit histories ceased. (Before the Equal Credit Opportunity Act, virtually all credit transactions of married couples were attributed to the husband and recorded as part of his credit history.)

Listed here are some suggestions for establishing or re-establishing credit. Any one of them could be used to initiate a good credit profile:

1. Apply for a charge account at a retail store. These are usually easier to obtain than other types of credit, and you can pay bills early to avoid heavy finance charges. The same goes for bank credit cards, such as Master Charge and Visa. If you drive, gasoline company credit cards are also a way to get started.

2. Keep savings and checking accounts. Some banks will grant a line of credit as part of your checking account. Advertised as "overdraft checking," it is simply a loan activated by writing a check for more than the balance in the account. The ceiling on these checkbook loans generally ranges from $500 to $2,000.

3. If you have accumulated savings in an account, and want to build up a credit history quickly, you can apply for a passbook loan. This requires you to pay interest charges, but is a relatively inexpensive way to borrow. Make regular payments for at least six months to establish a good repayment pattern, and then pay the balance before it is due.

HOW CREDITWORTHY ARE YOU?

Are you a good credit risk? This is the $64,000 question any credit grantor—be it a bank, a retail store, or your brother-in-law—will ask when you apply for a loan. Credit grantors are essentially gamblers. They take chances, not on rolls of the dice, but on people. They bet on which ones will repay their debts and which ones won't.

To decide whether you are a good credit risk, lenders consider a variety of factors, arrived at through a combination of common sense, past experi-

A woman who has successfully solved her credit problems. (Wide World Photos)

ence, assumptions about human behavior, and guesswork. Listed below are the most commonly used yardsticks of creditworthiness. Keep in mind, however, that not all creditors think alike: some consider all of the factors listed below, others consider only a selected few. Since there is no scientifically accurate way to evaluate a credit applicant, there are as many credit evaluation techniques as there are creditors in the United States.

Income. Most borrowers expect to repay loans out of their income, so lenders are interested in knowing how large, steady, and dependable your source of income is. Also important in their calculations are the demands on your income—the number of dependents who must live on it, the size of outstanding debts which you must pay out of it.

Be aware that income alone does not satisfactorily predict the risk of debtor nonpayment. Put another way, experience has shown that there are bad risks in every income category. For this reason, creditors do not base their decisions solely (or even, in some instances, primarily) on the applicant's income. Many give heavy weight to the other factors.

Occupation. Creditors favor regularly employed people over those only seasonally employed or self-employed. A civil servant will be viewed more favorably than a playwright earning the same income, since the former's job is more steady and secure. Other occupations may be favored simply because statistics show that their members, for whatever reason, regularly pay back their debts. For some credit grantors, however, the length of time on the job is more important than what the job is.

Stability. Creditors have concluded that the best debtors are those who display signs of stability in their lives. Great significance may be placed on the length of time you have lived at your current residence, the number of years you have been at your present job, and whether you own your own home. The more established you are in home and job, the more attractive you'll be to credit grantors. Many creditors also assume that married persons are more stable and therefore better risks than single or divorced individuals, but federal law now prohibits creditors from considering an applicant's marital status (more on this later).

Credit history. An important consideration for most creditors is the applicant's credit history, revealed in a "credit report" provided by a credit bureau (for a look at how these bureaus work, see chapter 21). The report describes which credit cards you own, where you have opened charge accounts or taken out loans, and what your repayment record has been (i.e., do you pay your bills on time, chronically late, or never?). While it is an advantage to have a good credit history, it may be a disadvantage to have done too much borrowing or to have too many credit cards and charge plates. A loan officer might interpret this as evidence of an addiction to debt. Too many credit cards also may be thought to pose a continuing danger of overextension.

Keep in mind that the creditor will check your application form against the credit bureau report, to see if you recorded your outstanding obligations accurately.

Age. Creditors who have researched the correlation between age and creditworthiness have found that older persons are the best credit risk, and young people (ages 18 to 24) the worst. Nevertheless, many credit card companies and others automatically turned down citizens over 65 applying for credit. New provisions of the federal Equal Credit Opportunity Act† forbid creditors from rejecting older applicants on the basis of age alone (although they may consider the fact that an individual will soon reach retirement). As long as a statistical correlation between youth and poor repayment rates exists, young people will find their age counted against them in the credit application.

Assets. Bank accounts, investments, and other property of value are considered positive attributes, especially if you are willing to pledge them as security or collateral. Merely keeping savings and checking accounts, no matter how modest the balances, is a positive factor to some creditors.

Once the creditor has the information supplied by you and by the credit bureau, the difficult task of evaluation begins. Each credit institution uses its own system. Some lenders place major emphasis on occupation and salary, while others favor stability of residence and a sober (if not somber) life style. Some lenders are willing to take big risks, others are cautious and conservative. Some demand extensive documentation from the applicant, and others offer credit to practically anyone.

More and more, banks and other major lending institutions are experi-

† 15 U.S.C. 1691.

menting with scoring systems to help them evaluate credit applications. A scoring system assigns numerical values to the various factors the lender believes important. For each applicant, the numbers are added up, and a final figure computed. A scoring system used by a bank, for example, may allocate 0–30 points for income, with "high" incomes (as defined by the bank) receiving 30 points and very low incomes receiving none. Number of years on the job may be worth up to 40 points, length of time at your present address 50 points, a good credit history 25 points, etc. The bank adds up your point total, and if it exceeds the bank's minimum qualifying score, gives you the loan.

The best predictor for one creditor is not the best for another. A bank in a particular community may find, for example, that of all the young lawyers earning $18,000 a year who apply for loans, 99 percent repay them promptly. A credit card company, however, may find that these same lawyers are not so reliable or prompt in paying their outstanding credit balances. So, if both the bank and the credit card issuer devised scoring systems, the bank's would give the lawyers a high score, the credit card's system would give them a low one.

Creditors concede that the scoring systems now in use are far from infallible. It is impossible to identify with certainty exactly what makes some people good risks and others not. If scoring systems are not perfect, how close to it do they come? This is a very difficult question to answer. Most credit extenders are very tight-lipped about their systems, and do not publicly report on how well they are working. Evidence of the skepticism with which scoring systems are viewed, even by their users, is the fact that few creditors follow these systems 100 percent. Lenders routinely authorize their officers to "override" the system, i.e., to grant credit to someone who has not met the point requirement (or deny it to one who has). Within a single credit department, some loan officers may be given more latitude than others in substituting their own judgment for the result dictated by the system.

IF YOU ARE TURNED DOWN FOR CREDIT

If a bank turns down your loan application, a department store refuses your request for a charge account, or any other credit grantor denies you credit, you have a right to learn the specific reason why. The rejection letter you receive may advise you that you "constitute too great a risk for our current lending policies" or that "you belong to a risk classification for which it may not be to your advantage, nor to ours, to establish a credit account." This is generalizing at its worst. Make a written request for a more specific reason. Under federal law‡ you have the right to receive a specific explanation for a credit denial, if you ask for it. It is to your advantage to know what your credit problem is, so that you can correct it if possible. You will incur no penalty by making the request.

What sort of reasons might creditors give? The Federal Reserve Board,

‡ 15 U.S.C. 1691.

which administers this federal credit law, has issued a suggested form for creditors to use in notifying consumers of credit denials. It reads:

PRINCIPAL REASON(S) FOR ADVERSE ACTION CONCERNING CREDIT

———— Credit application incomplete
———— Insufficient credit references
———— Unable to verify credit references
———— Temporary or irregular employment
———— Unable to verify employment
———— Length of employment
———— Insufficient income
———— Excessive obligations
———— Unable to verify income
———— Inadequate collateral
———— Too short a period of residence
———— Temporary residence
———— Unable to verify residence
———— No credit file
———— Insufficient credit file
———— Delinquent credit obligations
———— Garnishment, attachment, foreclosure, repossession, or suit
———— Bankruptcy
———— We do not grant credit to any applicant on the terms and conditions you request.
———— Other, specify:————————————————

Once you find out the reason for the denial, you can, if you wish, ask the creditor to reconsider. Many consumers don't realize that all credit managers, even those operating under rigid scoring systems, have some discretionary power to reverse an initial decision. If a bank turns you down for a loan, for example, you can visit the bank, find an official with the power to alter the decision (don't waste your time with someone who can't do anything), and make a personal appeal for reconsideration. Present yourself as a reliable individual, emphasizing your integrity and your strongest creditworthy qualities. Remember that you must persuade the lender that (1) you have the financial ability to repay the debt and (2) you are the kind of person who will repay and who takes the obligation to do so seriously. It may be that despite one weak element in your credit credentials, your application will be granted.

If you are denied credit because of negative information in your credit history, make sure to ask the lender for the name and address of the credit bureau which supplied the information about you. This will enable you to write to the credit bureau to find out what is in your credit file. (See chapter 21 for details on how to do this.)

SEX DISCRIMINATION

Creditors have long discriminated against women in granting credit. In the past, many lenders commonly refused to consider applications from single or divorced women (while readily accepting them from single or divorced men) and forced married women to apply for credit in their husbands' names. This meant that their own creditworthiness was ignored, *and* they were unable to establish credit records for themselves. The stories of unfair treatment are legion. Here are just a random few:

> A woman who worked full time was married to a student. When she applied for credit she was told she had to apply in his name. She followed this instruction and was denied credit—because he had no income.

> A bank refused to grant a mortgage to a qualified working woman who supported herself and three children, until she got her 70-year-old father, retired and living on a pension, to co-sign the application.

> A widow moved to a new city and attempted to obtain new charge accounts in her own name. All her applications were denied because of an insufficient credit history. The charge accounts she had had all her life were recorded under her husband's name. Finally, in desperation, she reported her own income and savings, but applied under her dead husband's name—and got the credit.

> A husband and wife who were both employed full time applied for a mortgage. The bank officer asked whether the wife took birth control pills. He said that her income could not be considered as part of the application unless she had a hysterectomy or some other form of permanent sterilization. The officer also stated that the bank would not be satisfied if the husband had a vasectomy, because the wife would still be able to bear children!

The indignities suffered by women led to cries for reform of the consumer credit system. Responding to the outrage generated by blatant sex discrimination, Congress enacted the Equal Credit Opportunity Act. The Act expressly prohibits discrimination on the basis of sex or marital status by any consumer credit grantor. Under the law, a creditor may not:

- Use sex or marital status in any credit scoring system.
- Inquire into birth control methods or childbearing intentions.
- Treat a woman's income differently from a man's, or assume that a woman of childbearing age will stop work to have children.
- Ask information about the applicant's spouse, *unless* the spouse's income will be used to support the application; the spouse will be allowed to use the account; or the applicant lives in a community property state (Arizona, California, Idaho, Louisiana, Nevada, New Mexico, Texas, Washington).
- Request information about the receipt of alimony, *unless* the applicant

desires alimony payments to be counted as income (in which case the applicant must be prepared to prove that the alimony payments are dependable).

The Act also directs those who send information to credit bureaus to report joint accounts in both husband's and wife's names. This allows married women to compile good credit histories (an impossibility when creditors regarded all joint accounts as only the husband's).

Any woman who believes she is the victim of unlawful sex discrimination should complain to the creditor and to the relevant government agency listed below. Also, the law permits private lawsuits in which the guilty creditor is liable for your actual damages, plus a penalty of up to $10,000, plus your attorney's fees. For more information on women's credit rights, write for copies of the pamphlets entitled *Equal Credit Opportunity Act* and *Women and Credit Histories,* available from the Federal Trade Commission, Washington, D.C. 20580.

OTHER KINDS OF DISCRIMINATION

The Equal Credit Opportunity Act also prohibits discrimination on the basis of race, religion, national origin, or the receipt of public assistance. A limited restriction is placed on age discrimination. Creditors may consider your age if:

1. You are over 62 years old and the creditor views this age as a favorable factor.

2. The creditor employs a scoring system which (a) is statistically sound and (b) does not assign a negative value to anyone over the age of 62.

3. The creditor uses age to determine the amount and probable continuance of income levels (thus the creditor can take into account the fact that an individual is approaching retirement age to evaluate the applicant's future earnings potential).

Any consumer complaints about these forms of discrimination should be directed to the federal agencies specified in the chart below. State and city human rights commissions also handle such complaints.

TYPE OF CREDITOR	WHERE TO COMPLAIN
Retail Store, Small-Loan and Finance Company, Gasoline Credit Card, Travel and Expense Credit Card, State-Chartered Credit Union, Government Lending Program	Federal Trade Commission, Equal Credit Opportunity, Washington, D.C. 20580
Bank—nationally chartered ("National" or "N.A." will appear in the bank's name)	Comptroller of the Currency, Consumer Affairs Division, Washington, D.C. 20219

TYPE OF CREDITOR	WHERE TO COMPLAIN
Bank—state-chartered and member of Federal Reserve System	Board of Governors of the Federal Reserve System, Director, Division of Consumer Affairs, Washington, D.C. 20551
Bank—state-chartered and insured by FDIC, but not a member of Federal Reserve System	Federal Deposit Insurance Corporation, Office of Bank Customers Affairs, Washington, D.C. 20429
Savings and Loan Association— federally chartered or insured	Federal Home Loan Bank Board, Equal Credit Opportunity, Washington, D.C. 20552
Credit Union—federally chartered	Federal Credit Union Administration, Division of Consumer Affairs, Washington, D.C. 20456

20

Dealing with the problems

A hundred cartloads of anxiety will not pay an ounce of debt.
— Italian proverb

Debt is like fire: manage it wisely and it will serve you well; let it out of control, and it will consume you. Every year, hundreds of thousands of Americans lose their homes, cars, and other vital possessions, sacrifice their wages, and sink into bankruptcy, overcome by their overgrown debts. Countless others endure intense periods of anxiety as they struggle with a constant stream of bills, dunning letters, and threats of legal action. Studies show that debt problems interfere with harmonious family relationships, disrupt mental concentration, and affect performance at work.

Debts get the better of debtors for several reasons. For many, a sudden illness, a job layoff, or any other emergency brings with it financial ruin. A number of debtors, however, are forced to admit that their troubles are of their own making. The most common attitudes leading to debt disaster are:

1. "I never realized I owed so much!" An uncounted, but probably huge number of people haven't the faintest idea of what their debts really are. They don't keep track of car and mortgage payments, credit card purchases, and charge account transactions. For some, there comes a point (no one can say exactly when) at which spending overtakes income, and troubles begin. Initially, bills that can't be paid just get put off a month or two (while spending goes on as usual). But finally, when creditors demand payment and there's no money available, these consumers look at their finances for the first time and wonder, "What happened?"

2. "If it isn't cash, it isn't really money." Millions march under this banner. The substitution of anything—plastic cards, checks, merchandise scrip, installment coupons—for cold hard cash works a psychological transformation in almost all of us. Non-cash methods of payment permit shoppers to leave stores with the same number of dollars in their pockets as when they went in, creating an illusion of financial well-being. Even though we really know what's happening there is a lingering feeling (perhaps inspired by Monopoly games) that anything not cash is "funny money" and not to be taken seriously. Many professional debt counselors, recognizing this phenomenon, rip up their clients' credit cards before their eyes and put them on a strict cash diet. This usually results in an immediate reduction in unwanted budget fat.

3. "We must maintain an appropriate life style, you know." This is the downfall of all those in the middle and upper income brackets who feel pressured to live in an expensive home and to own the luxurious (and unaffordable) cars, clothing, and country club memberships necessary to their desired status in life. Hopeful young executives and middle managers striving to be top managers sometimes fall into this trap, promoting their standard of living long before their bosses promote them.

Having said this, it must be added that creditors share the blame for much of the overextension that occurs in society. Unethical loan companies and other lenders urge credit upon people even when repayment problems can be expected, because they know they will be able to seize all or part of the debtor's wages by "wage garnishment." This collection remedy, lawful in all states except Connecticut, Delaware, Florida, Pennsylvania, and Texas, authorizes the regular payment of a portion of the debtor's paycheck directly to the creditor, until the debt is satisfied. Wage garnishment guarantees repayment for such creditors, but often inflicts great hardship upon those dependent upon the debtor's salary for the necessities of life.

"Our problem is that whereas money doesn't grow on trees, credit cards do." (*Pearson-Knickerbocker News,* Albany, N.Y.—ROTHCO.)

AVOIDING DEBT DISASTER

If money seems to be flowing out at a disquieting rate, if you are nervously contemplating a new, large purchase, or if you can't seem to save a dime, the best way to decide what to do (and to secure peace of mind) is to construct a family budget. Although the budget won't give you any more money, it will help you to get your financial life in order. A simple format might look like this:

_____ *MONTH BUDGET*

INCOME			EXPENSES	
Salary and tips	$_____		**I. FIXED**	
Savings bank			Rent	$_____
interest	_____		Utilities	_____
Alimony and child			Telephone	_____
support	_____		Installment pay-	
Social Security			ments (car,	
received	_____		furniture, etc.)	_____
Earnings on			Loan repayments	_____
investments	_____		Insurance	_____
Insurance, veterans or			Car	_____
other benefits	_____		Life	_____
Other	_____		Other	_____
TOTAL			Car upkeep (gas,	
INCOME	$_____		oil, etc.)	_____
			Taxes	_____
			Transportation	_____
			Dues (union,	
			other)	_____
			Education	
			(tuition)	_____
			II. FLEXIBLE	
			Food	_____
			Clothing	_____
			Entertainment	_____
			Household supplies	_____
			Medical bills, drugs	_____
			Laundry, dry	
			cleaning	_____
			Liquor and	
			cigarettes	_____
			Non-installment	
			major purchases	
			(appliances,	
			furniture, car,	
			etc.)	_____
			Gifts and donations	_____
			Haircuts, beauty	
			parlor	_____
			Newspapers, maga-	
			zines and books	_____
			Toys and sports	
			equipment	_____
Total Income	$_____		Other	_____
Total Expenses	$_____			_____
Amount left				_____
for saving or				_____
new spending	$_____			_____
OR			TOTAL	
Amount overspent	$_____		EXPENSES	$_____

Computing budget figures requires careful work. Accuracy is critical. Refer to sales slips, canceled checks, or records whenever possible. If records don't exist, make estimates which are realistic. You may have to interview family members to see what their spending patterns are. If you're budgeting to determine future spending power, make allowances for the inevitable inflation that will occur. To be safe, be liberal in estimating future expenses and conservative in estimating future income.

Expenses are classified as fixed or flexible as an aid in budget analysis. Flexible expenses are more subject to change in the short run; if you are pressed for money, look to them first to decide what items of expenditure to slash. It is not as easy to reduce fixed expenses, such as rent and loan payments, which are usually established at a set rate for a year or more.

A budget can be done for any time period. An average one-month budget or an annual budget is usually easiest to prepare. Of course, everything in the budget must be based on the same time period. For expenses which vary over the year, like clothes or vacations, calculate what is spent annually and divide by twelve to arrive at an average monthly expense.

Once you have prepared the budget, take a good look at it. The size of your expenditures may come as a shock (as may the mere pittance that separates total income and total expenses).

Plan to save some of the excess of income over expenses. If modest savings aren't possible, you are walking too fine a line between solvency and financial collapse. And if expenses already outrun income, you need to act quickly. Read on.

RESOLVING DEBT PROBLEMS

The first step in extricating yourself from a mountain of debt is to assess the dimensions of the problem. Write down every item of expense you have each month apart from your creditors' bills. Include everything—minor expenses as well as major: rent, transportation, telephone, laundry, household supplies, haircuts, etc. Examine the list carefully and cut down any expenses you can. Next, subtract the total of expenses from your monthly income. This is the amount you have left to pay the outstanding bills.

List the bills you have to pay, and you'll see at a glance how far your bills exceed your ability to pay them. However bad the situation, most people can climb out of debt if they are truly determined to do so. It is essential, however, to resist the impulse to hide from creditors and hope they won't find you. The best course is to contact each creditor and explain why you can't make the usual payments. Offer to make some payment, however small, to everyone. This will show that, despite your difficulties, you are determined to pay off your debts in full. Most creditors will accept diminished payments if they know that the debtor honestly can't afford to pay any more. If any threaten to sue, explain that your only alternative to smaller payments is bankruptcy. (Creditors hate bankruptcy more than anything else, since they get very little, if anything, from the debtor in most bankruptcy proceedings.

Face your creditors—don't hide your head in the sand. (Photo by Robert Davidson)

They'd rather receive full payment, even if they must wait longer for it, than see you declare bankruptcy.)

If you need help in doing all this, there are various organizations which offer assistance to those deep in debt.

In many cities throughout the country, there are free or low-cost debt counseling services, affiliated with community groups or religious institutions. There are also some 200 nonprofit counseling centers which are loosely affiliated with the National Foundation for Consumer Credit. To obtain a list of the names and addresses of these centers, write to the Foundation at the Federal Bar Building West, 1819 H Street, N.W., Washington, D.C. 20006. Generally, these centers will make the necessary contacts with creditors, arrange extended payment periods, and see to it that the client does not use credit cards (usually by destroying any the debtor owns). These business-funded centers have been criticized, however, for failing to recommend bankruptcy when that course would be best for the debtor.

Professional debt counselors generally frown on "consolidation loans" from banks or finance companies. The purpose of such a loan is to replace all debts with one long-term loan, requiring smaller monthly payments the debtor can afford. This loan costs the debtor more in interest payments, however (the longer the loan period, the more the finance charge), and so may work to keep the debtor in financial straits for an extended period of time. Also to be avoided are the profit-making "debt adjustors" or "debt consolidators" who charge a hefty fee (usually a substantial percentage of your total debts) for their debt counseling services. They see to it that their bills are paid first, and sometimes this added payment makes bankruptcy inevitable. No matter what the situation, stay away from these characters.

IF IT REALLY ISN'T YOUR FAULT: CORRECTING BILLING ERRORS

Computers have taken over the job of sending out bills for large companies, and their speed and accuracy are genuinely remarkable. But occasionally they go haywire, and the mass confusion they can cause is equally remarkable. Long-running battles between consumers and computers used to be commonplace. The supremely confident mechanical brains would never listen to complaints, and would certainly never admit that a mere human (ugh!) could be right. Desperate consumers dreamed up all sorts of strategies for getting the computer's attention, such as folding, spindling, and mutilating the computer's delicate cards.

Finally, Congress stepped in to give some relief to the frustrated bill payer. Under the Fair Credit Billing Act,* credit card companies, retailers offering charge accounts, and others who send out bills on a regular basis must now pay attention when you spot a billing error. Specifically, the Act provides that if you, the consumer, inform the creditor *in writing* about a mistake on a bill, the creditor must investigate the problem and, within 90 days, notify you of its findings. Your original letter must refer to your account number (if any) and indicate exactly why you believe the bill is wrong. Send it as soon as you notice the problem, and pay only the portion of the bill that you know to be correct. The place to address your inquiry must be given to you on the bill itself.

If the creditor discovers you are correct, it must adjust the bill (make sure both the incorrect charges and the finance charges on them are eliminated). If the creditor concludes that the bill is correct, it must tell you why. You may not agree with this result; if you don't, send a letter within 10 days telling the creditor you still believe you are correct. This will not stop the creditor from informing credit bureaus of your delinquency, but under the law the report will have to disclose that you dispute the bill, and the creditor will have to tell you to whom the reports were sent.

A special provision of the Fair Credit Billing Act covers the situation in which you receive faulty or misrepresented goods or services paid for by credit card. If the transaction took place in your home state (or within 100 miles of your residence) and if the purchase price exceeds $50, you can inform the credit card company of the problem and refuse to pay its bill. Furthermore, the $50 minimum and the in-state (or 100 miles) criteria need not be met if the card company owns, operates, or just mailed you the advertisements for the goods or services in question. You must, under the law, try to return the goods to the merchant or else give the seller a chance to correct the problem, before you advise the card issuer of your refusal to pay.

The Fair Credit Billing Act does not guarantee that you will get your problem resolved to your satisfaction. It merely compels your creditors to read your complaint, investigate, and respond with an explanation of the

* 15 U.S.C. 1681.

bill. While it is investigating, no lawsuit may be instituted and no attempts to collect the disputed amount from you may be made. If the bill issuer fails to follow these rules, the law entitles you to $50 off your bill (even if the bill turns out to be right), and you can sue for an additional penalty of $100 plus reimbursement for your attorney's fees.

BANKRUPTCY

Bankruptcy is a federal court proceeding which wipes out debts for those who are unable to pay them. In the last five years, almost a million Americans (or one out of every 200) officially declared bankruptcy. The great majority of these persons are salaried employees.

Although bankruptcy is a legally recognized proceeding, many people see it as unethical or immoral. The purpose of bankruptcy, however, is a humanitarian one: to rescue individuals from overwhelming financial troubles. It is a right important enough to be written into the Constitution, and one which businesses readily take advantage of when the need arises. For indi-

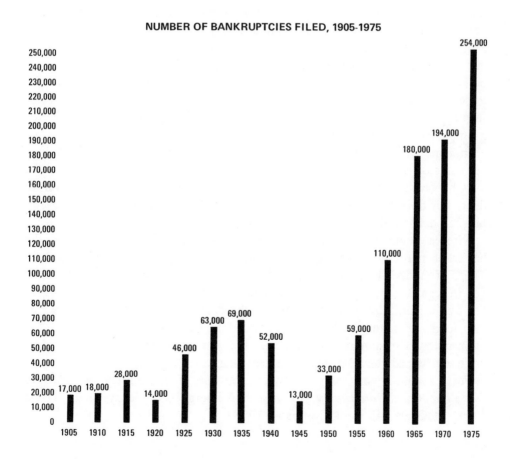

NUMBER OF BANKRUPTCIES FILED, 1905-1975

Source of data: Administrative Office of the United States Courts

viduals, it serves as a financial life preserver, providing relief from destitution and the despair which comes with hopeless indebtedness.

A bankruptcy proceeding generally takes place in three steps. First, the individual applies to the clerk of the local federal court. The clerk asks the debtor to fill out forms listing all assets owned and all debts owing. This is followed by a hearing before a judge which all creditors are invited to attend (very often none show up). The hearing is held in order to determine if the forms are in order; if there is property which the debtor should turn over to the court for distribution to creditors; and if any fraudulent or dishonest statements have been made by the debtor. Finally, if all goes well, the court issues an "order of discharge," which wipes out the individual's debts.

Bankrupts are never stripped of all their property by the court. Under laws which vary from state to state, the debtor is permitted to keep a number of items (usually necessities such as furniture, clothing, and household goods) up to a specified dollar value. Items which are not subject to seizure are known as "exempt property." Many debtors own only exempt property and so lose none of their belongings when they go bankrupt.

Although it is possible to do your own bankruptcy without a lawyer, it is not a good idea. There are many complications in the law which can cost the do-it-yourselfer money and property. A lawyer can help you to protect personal property from seizure, can advise you on which debts the bankruptcy will not erase (e.g., alimony and child support payments), and can inform you how the bankruptcy will affect your spouse (in some instances both husband and wife should declare bankruptcy). It is absolutely essential to see an attorney if you own your own home, since it might be subject to seizure in the proceeding. Low-cost legal clinics charge as little as $150 for a simple personal bankruptcy.

In some cases a debtor is well-advised not to declare bankruptcy. A lawyer can suggest other alternatives, such as the Wage-Earner Plan (known as a "Chapter 13" proceeding), which does not involve the elimination of debts but does provide a mechanism for reducing some of the salaried employee's debt burdens.

After a bankruptcy, a debtor's credit standing suffers. Nonetheless, the bankrupt may soon receive calls from finance companies offering credit. These "friendly" loan companies really want the debtor to agree to repay (or in legal terms, "reaffirm") the debts owned to them which were wiped out by the bankruptcy. If they can get the debtor to volunteer to repay former loans, then they will have succeeded in overcoming the effect of the bankruptcy. Consumers should never reaffirm such debts—once the slate has been "wiped clean" it should be kept clean.

For a readable and comprehensive discussion of bankruptcy, see *How to Do Your Own Bankruptcy,* by Aaron Milberg, and Henry Shain (New York: McGraw-Hill Book Company, 1978).

21

Compiling credit report cards:
the work of credit bureaus

> His pen had slid voluptuously over the smooth paper, printing in large neat capitals—
>
> > DOWN WITH BIG BROTHER
> > DOWN WITH BIG BROTHER
> > DOWN WITH BIG BROTHER
> > DOWN WITH BIG BROTHER
> > DOWN WITH BIG BROTHER
>
> over and over again, filling half a page. . . .
>
> Whether he wrote DOWN WITH BIG BROTHER, or whether he refrained from writing it, made no difference. Whether he went on with the diary, or whether he did not go on with it, made no difference. The Thought Police would get him just the same.   — GEORGE ORWELL, *1984*

If you've ever leafed idly through the help-wanted section of a large metropolitan newspaper, you know that there are a variety of businesses which employ hundreds of thousands of people but which you never hear about (unless your nephew lands a job there). One such "invisible" business has a profound effect on your life—it determines whether you get the house, the insurance policy, and even the job you want. It is the credit-reporting industry, and it affects every one of us.

People have pointed out that this country runs on credit, but it's less often realized that the credit business depends on the credit-rating business in order to function. Credit bureaus or credit "data" or "information" or "reporting" companies are in the business of compiling and maintaining information about people, which they sell to potential creditors, insurers, and employers. They are information brokers—the bureaus do not grant credit themselves, but collect and then sell the data which department stores, banks, finance companies, and insurance companies use to decide whether to extend credit or insurance to an applicant.

There are more than 1,900 credit bureaus across the country, some operating nationwide and others confining themselves to one city or geographic area. Most of them (all but about 100) are members of Associated Credit

Bureaus, Inc., a trade association located in Houston. The ACB estimates that its members generate about 100 million reports on individuals annually.

If you have ever taken out a loan, opened a charge account, or applied for life insurance, it is fairly certain that information about you and your finances is neatly stored in the archives of one or more credit bureaus.

There are two kinds of reports compiled by credit bureaus—*credit reports* and *investigative reports*. They differ in a number of ways, as shown in the following table:

	CREDIT REPORT	INVESTIGATIVE REPORT
contents	objective information on: salary employment bank accounts charge accounts loans—history of repayment, list of outstanding ones.	subjective information on: character reputation life style personal habits
source of data collected	consumer applications for credit, insurance, or employment court dockets and other public records (county clerk's, Department of Motor Vehicles, etc.)	interviews (personal and telephone) with neighbors, associates, co-workers, etc.
usual uses	credit applications insurance applications	life insurance employment

One recurring problem stems from the way credit bureaus gather information from banks and merchants and from searching records. They are programmed to look for problems and routinely pick up negative credit information. However, they do not routinely note when cases are settled or dismissed or debts paid (things which look good on a consumer's credit record).

The greatest source of trouble is hearsay or secondhand information. This information is gathered hastily, since credit bureau investigators have large case loads and neither the time nor the training to do serious in-depth spadework. Some bureaus demand that their investigators come up with negative data, and may even impose quotas on them to do so. Inaccuracies or malicious untruths reported to the investigators find their way into the files, and can haunt the subject of the gossip for many years to come.

TRW *CREDIT DATA*   **UPDATED CREDIT PROFILE**   **CONFIDENTIAL**

INQUIRY INFORMATION

TCA1

RTS 3123456XXX CONSUMER JOH QS..10655 B 91502.
P-11283 G 92708.165 A 86024,S-548603388.Y-1944.T-18010005.
E-AJAX HARDWARE/2035 BROADWAY/LOS ANGELES 90019

PAGE 1	DATE 2-28-79	TIME 1:23:42	PORT AB32	H/V A19	CONSUMER

JOHN Q CONSUMER 10655 BIRCH ST BURBANK CA 91502	2-79 AJAX HARDWARE 2035 BROADWAY LOS ANGELES 90019	SS# 548603388

ACCOUNT PROFILE		SUBSCRIBER NAME			SUBSCRIBER	ASSN. CODE					PAYMENT PROFILE NUMBER OF MONTHS PRIOR TO BALANCE DATE
POS	NON NEG	STATUS COMMENT	DATE REPORTED	DATE OPENED	TYPE	TERMS	AMOUNT	BALANCE	BALANCE DATE	AMOUNT PAST DUE	1 2 3 4 5 6 7 8 9 10 11 12
	A	MOUNTAIN BK 30-2NC 32	8-78	8-76	3131035 SEC	0 36	$4200	$933	3562401973 2-1-79		CCCCCC1CC1CC
A		HILLSIDE BK CURR ACCT	2-79	7-78	3140018 AUT	1 48	$5300	$4748	29144508119 2-15-79		CCCCCCC
	A	HEMLOCKS DL 90 NWCR	7-78	6-75	3306601 CHG	2 REV	$600	$437	986543184026 2-12-79		CCCCCCC321CC
	A	BAY CO DL 60 NWCR	10-78	10-Y	3319232 CHG	1 REV	$300	$206	46812391013 2-11-79		CCCC2CCCCCCC
A		BOWERS CURR ACCT	9-75	8-75	3365771 CHG	0 REV	-$100		212250		
M		WISTERIA FIN PAID SATIS	7-75	6-74	8542240 SEC	0 12	$500		5238610		
	A	HILLSIDE BK INQUIRY	7-18-78		3140018 AUT	1 48	$5300				
	M	REVOLVING CREDIT CORP INQUIRY	2-27-79		3600829 ISC	0 24	$800				
	A	GROVE CREDIT UNION INQUIRY	10-15-78		378434 H/I	1 12	$500				
	M	JUDGMENT JONES	9-19-77		3011207		$300		07505853		

ATTN FILE VARIATION: SPOUSE INIT IS W

JOHN Q CONSUMER
10655 BIRCH ST
BURBANK CA 91502

	A	GARDEN FIN DELINQ 90	2-79	12-77	3500132 UNS	1 12	$590	$49	241870 2-15-79	$49	21CCCCCCCCCC

TRW CREDIT DATA WILL ACCOMMODATE UP TO A 100 WORD CONSUMER STATEMENT
IN ACCORDANCE WITH THE FAIR CREDIT REPORTING ACT

END

(Courtesy TRW, Inc.)

© **TRW** *INC.* 1971, 1978

A CLASSIC HORROR STORY

One such victim who fought back was a journalist named James Mill-stone. He worked for the St. Louis *Post-Dispatch* and had been its Washington correspondent when he was called back to St. Louis to accept an editorial position. When Millstone, who thought of himself as a stable, sober citizen, tried to change his auto insurance to a local company, his application was denied. He was puzzled by this denial and traced it to one "investigative" credit report full of lies. It spoke of his "hippie" orientation and history of drug use, described his "uncontrollable children," and concluded that he had a bad attitude, exercised "poor" judgment, and was thoroughly loathed by his acquaintances.

The source of these "data" was probably a single hostile neighbor interviewed by the credit bureau's investigator. After a one-man legal battle by Mr. Millstone (he received his insurance early on, but thought the issue deserved pursuing) which went up to the federal appeals court, he won a judgment for $40,000. The court found that the credit bureau's investigator "devoted at most 30 minutes in preparing this report [which was] . . . ripe with innuendo, misstatement, and slander."

Millstone resurrected his reputation and won his case because of a fairly recent federal law—the Fair Credit Reporting Act.*

HISTORY OF THE FAIR CREDIT REPORTING ACT

Credit bureaus serve a legitimate business need. They make it possible for credit to be granted as quickly and freely as Americans take for granted it will be. They also screen applicants for insurance and for employment—retrieving information already stored in their files and compiling reports more quickly and more cheaply than if prospective insurers and employers were compelled to do it themselves.

As credit bureaus became larger and more numerous, reflecting the country's conversion to a credit-based economy, more and more complaints were registered. The bureaus were criticized for the mistakes they made; for methods of operating which did not minimize errors or ferret them out; and for the invasions of privacy which often accompanied their "investigative" work.

In response to this concern, in 1970 Congress passed the Fair Credit Reporting Act. The Act was the result of much lobbying and negotiating and is not as clear and strong as consumer advocates wished. However, it is the core of the consumer's rights in this area. A number of states have added their own credit-reporting statutes to expand its provisions. To see if a state law gives you broader rights, check with your state or local consumer agency or with the state attorney general.

* 15 U.S.C. 1681.

CONSUMER RIGHTS UNDER THE FAIR CREDIT REPORTING ACT

This Act regulates all interstate credit bureaus, which includes just about all of them, according to the Federal Trade Commission. The most important provisions of the law are:

1. **Access by others to your file.**
    A credit bureau is allowed to sell a credit report on you *only* to someone who intends to use it:
    ◆ to decide whether to extend credit to you;
    ◆ to decide whether to hire you;
    ◆ for insurance purposes;
    ◆ for another "legitimate business need for the information in connection with a business transaction involving" you. (This fuzzy phrase enables a broad range of people to obtain the information, unfortunately.)
2. **Your right to inspect any credit file kept on you.**
    If you are simply interested in seeing what a particular credit bureau has in your file, you have the right to be told:
    ◆ the "nature and substance" of that information (*except* for any medical information), and

A credit bureau is not a happy place. ("Government Bureau," by George Tooker. Courtesy the Metropolitan Museum of Art, George A. Hearn Fund, 1956)

◆ who has received the report during the past six months (two years
   if it was for employment purposes).

The law does not give you the right to see the file, but many credit bureaus will give it to you.
   The credit bureau can charge you a "reasonable" fee (the major bureaus charge $3 to $5). But if you have been denied credit within the past
30 days, no fee is allowed.

3. Right to know why credit was denied.
Any store or other lender which denies you credit must tell you the reason
it turned you down. If the reason is connected with negative information
in a credit report, you are entitled to know the name, address, and telephone number of the bureau that furnished the report.

4. Rights regarding investigative reports.
The credit bureau must notify you immediately if someone has asked for
an investigative report on you, *unless* it is requested by an employer who
is considering you for a job for which you have *not* applied. Any investigative report becomes part of your credit file, and you may find out its nature and substance.

5. Rights to have errors corrected.
The files kept by credit bureaus often contain mistakes. If you learn of
any mistake in your file, you should notify the credit bureau immediately,
in writing. The law requires the credit bureau to investigate the disputed
information within a "reasonable period of time," unless it has reason to
believe your dispute is "frivolous or irrelevant." (But there are problems
in interpreting both those phrases.)
   If the credit bureau refuses to delete or change the information, you
have the right to add a statement (of 100 words) telling your side of the
story. This statement must then be included in all credit reports given out
by the credit bureau. You should also request that the statement be sent
to all those who have already received credit reports containing the
disputed information. If a credit bureau does make the correction, it can
charge you a reasonable fee, *unless* your request was made within 30 days
of the denial of credit.

6. Updating information.
By law, the credit bureau must delete all negative information about you
that is more than seven years old, with two exceptions. First, the fact that
you filed for bankruptcy may be kept on file for 10 years. Second, if the
credit sought is for $50,000 or more, or if the potential employment is for
a salary of $20,000 or more, all information, no matter how old, can be
reported.

7. Penalties.
A bureau which does not obey the Act can be sued by anyone who has
been harmed by its actions. If a consumer proves the case, the bureau can
wind up paying for whatever damage it has caused (including damage to
reputation), the consumer's court and lawyer costs, and additional "puni-
tive" damages if the court chooses. Also, anyone who obtains information
from a bureau under false pretenses can pay a $5,000 fine or spend a year
in prison. The same penalties apply to a bureau employee who gives out
unauthorized information.

HOW TO EXAMINE YOUR CREDIT FILE

Here are the steps to take in order to see what's in your file.

First, call or write to the credit bureau which you know or suspect has a file on you. (Any large retail store or bank can tell you the major ones in your area. The largest one in the country is TRW Credit Data, with files on 50 million Americans and nationwide offices.)

The credit bureau will send you a form to sign and return. Send it back with the fee required (*unless* you've been denied credit within the last 30 days).

Most credit bureaus will simply mail a copy of your file or a summary of it to you. Some may arrange a time for you to visit the bureau to see it. If you visit, you may bring anyone you wish with you. Be ready to furnish identification when you visit.

NOTE: Never sign any form releasing the credit bureau from liability for giving out false or damaging information. It is illegal for the credit bureau to ask you to do this. If a credit bureau refuses to tell you about your file, report the bureau to:

> Division of Special Projects
> Bureau of Consumer Protection
> Federal Trade Commission
> Washington, D.C. 20580

22

The merchants of menace: debt collection

PROTECT YOUR GOOD NAME WITH STORES, BANKS, FRIENDS, YOUR JOB. PAY
YOUR BILL WITH_____
   According to the terms of the legally binding contract you signed with
_____, your past due account is $_____. We are notifying
. . . the stores from which you buy on credit, your family, your friends, your
neighbors, your landlord, your bank, your job, your employer, your church,
etc. . . . you will lose your precious good name and reputation, which is everything in your life.

MY ATTORNEY IS SUING YOU. HE HAS A CONTRACT SIGNED BY YOU. . . . You
will have to appear in court and lose time and money from your job. In
court the judge will declare you GUILTY. Do you want such a court record of
GUILTY to damage your reputation? You have only 5 days to still plead NOT
GUILTY and protect your good name and reputation by paying your past due
account. . . .

In November 1968, a Texas couple whom we shall call the Lawrences fell
behind in their monthly payments to a Houston loan company. When an
employee of the loan company telephoned them to ask for their payment,
Mrs. Lawrence explained that she had been ill and was temporarily unable
to continue her work as a nurse, but that she would be working again within
a month. Over the course of the next month, someone who identified himself
as the collection manager for the loan company telephoned the Lawrences
every day, yelling into the phone, demanding payment, and refusing to listen
to their explanations. When the Lawrences' 18-year-old daughter answered
the phone, the collection manager told her that her parents were a "bunch of
bums" who wouldn't pay their bills. Finally, one evening in February 1969,
he came to the Lawrences' home. A large burly character, the collector
stood over Mr. Lawrence and in a harsh, loud voice told him he was "a
damn deadbeat" and "a liar." He menacingly shouted down all of Mr.
Lawrence's explanations and continued his tirade of abuse. Lawrence was
ashen-faced and trembling, barely able to stay on his feet. His teen-age son
came to help him, and the collector turned on the boy, shouting and asking

him what kind of man his father was. Mrs. Lawrence, alarmed by the noise, entered the room. The collector bore down on her as well, at one point asking to use her phone so he could call for a truck to come and pick up the Lawrences' furniture, which he referred to as "junk." After an hour, the collection manager left, threatening to come back later with a truck for the furniture. That night, Mr. Lawrence, sick and exhausted, felt chest pains and was taken to the hospital. He had suffered a heart attack. Despite all this, over the next week the abusive telephone calls to the Lawrence household continued.

This story, though difficult to believe, is entirely true. Mr. Lawrence, ill and unable to work for a long time, sued the collector and won a court judgment for $138,000.

HOW PROFESSIONAL BILL COLLECTORS OPERATE: AN OVERVIEW

A "debt collector" may be anyone from a neighborhood dry cleaner asking a customer to pay a bill as soon as possible to a professional hired by a large business to do nothing but collect hundreds of overdue accounts.

Some debt collectors are unappealing individuals.

Collection efforts usually begin with a letter or notice from the seller asking for payment. If you don't pay within a reasonable time, or at least inform the seller why you refuse to pay, the seller may turn over the account to a *professional collection agency.*

These agencies are not known to the general public, and, unlike the stores they collect for, they are not concerned with maintaining a good public image. To the contrary, many professional debt collectors view their jobs as requiring an aggressive, frankly unpleasant manner, coupled with a fierce, bulldog-like tenacity. Inevitably, such a job attracts some individuals who would gladly make others' lives miserable even if they weren't paid to do it. The collector's usual first step is to send out dunning letters demanding payment. These letters can be quite unnerving. Sometimes even the envelopes are threatening. One company sent its communications in envelopes bearing the picture of a helpless figure about to be struck by lightning. The letters themselves, no more congenial, typically contain a variety of threats, such as those found in the two collection letters at the beginning of this chapter.

If these letters are ignored by the consumer, or if the collector refuses to accept the explanation offered by the consumer, the next step in the collection process is to turn the account over to a *collection attorney.* Debt collectors hate to do this, since they do not get paid for their unsuccessful collection efforts. Thus the incentive exists to make whatever threats they can invent (whether they intend to carry them out or not) to get the consumer to pay without a lawsuit.

Debt collectors know that many people are intimidated by the prospect of being sued. To take full advantage of this fear, one New York collector went so far as to send out dunning notices which actually duplicated the form of the court summons used in the state. His only change was to replace the word "Summons" with the words "Demand for Payment." Presumably the consumers thought they had been sued, although in fact the collector was not an attorney and his "Demand for Payment" was nothing more than a letter.

Although being sued over a debt is not a pleasant experience, it is not as frightful as debt collectors would have you believe. In fact, very few lawsuits for amounts under $100 are ever brought—it simply isn't worth the time. And if a lawsuit is brought and you have a legitimate reason for not paying, you will win the lawsuit. This is a point which is always glossed over in collection letters. Collectors act as if bringing a lawsuit means automatic victory for them and additional court costs for you. Don't believe it—losing is a foregone conclusion only if you fail to respond to a summons issued against you.

AVOIDING BILL COLLECTION PROBLEMS

Many people have definite reasons for not paying a particular debt. It has been estimated that up to 30 percent of unpaid consumer debts are "protest defaults"—situations where the consumer had received shoddy merchandise, or no merchandise, or had another gripe against the seller. In many other cases loss of income, unexpected medical expenses, or other pressing needs keep a consumer from paying back a debt on schedule, although the debtor fully intends to pay back the debt.

If you have reasons for not paying, or for not paying on time, you should communicate them to the seller promptly.

IF YOU ARE NOT PAYING A DEBT FOR A REASON, SET THE RECORD STRAIGHT!

1. If You Dispute the Debt: Write a clear, full letter with all the facts, including date, time, and place of purchase, and why you feel you don't owe the amount claimed. Attach photocopies of all relevant documents (e.g., receipts, warranties, etc.). Send the letter, preferably by certified mail, to the seller, with a copy to the collection agency if one is involved, and be sure to keep one copy for yourself. (Always keep the originals of all documents.)

2. If You Simply Can't Pay on Time: Contact the seller to explain the situation and try to arrange a new payment schedule. This will usually work if you do it early enough, as the seller prefers money late rather than never.

LEGITIMATE COLLECTION TACTICS

Naturally, someone to whom you owe money is perfectly justified in trying to collect the debt. The creditor has the clear right to contact you to urge you to pay. Reasonable efforts are legitimate, as is a certain amount of aggressiveness. In many instances the creditor has the right to repossess goods bought. And the creditor's ultimate recourse is a lawsuit to recover the amount owed.

If you have no reason for failing to pay a bill, a creditor has the right:

♦ to send you *dunning notices* (letters, often threatening, which notify you of the overdue bill and demand prompt payment).

♦ to inform a *credit-reporting agency* that you have not paid your bill, thus damaging your credit rating. (Your right to see your credit report and to correct errors in it are detailed in chapter 21.)

♦ to *sue* you or threaten to sue you for the amount owed. If the creditor wins, you could lose the amount owed plus reasonable interest (usually the interest rate is set by state law at 5 to 7 percent) and court costs ranging from $5 to $50.

♦ to *repossess* the goods you bought, if your contract contains a provision allowing the seller to retake possession upon your failure to pay. (Note: the seller may choose to proceed with a lawsuit as well, if the goods have been used and thereby lost their original value.)

Thus the law does provide significant assistance to the legitimate creditor who has not been paid what is properly due. Inability to pay a debt because of your own financial problems is not a legally valid excuse, and a creditor may take legal action against you to collect a bill. However, as noted previously, most sellers will arrange a new payment schedule if you are experiencing honest financial difficulties.

AGGRESSIVE COLLECTION TACTICS

The Lawrence case represents an extreme example of debt collection abuse. Yet numerous instances of coercive and intimidating debt collection tactics have been documented in court cases throughout the country and in testimony before government agencies.

The list of outrageous tactics used by debt collectors is lurid and lengthy. They usually fall into four categories: deception, harassment, threats, and humiliation.

1. Deception. The most common misrepresentations center on the collector's identity and what steps will be taken if the debt is not paid promptly. Collectors seeking information about debtors' whereabouts or assets may pretend to be innocent, even welcome strangers (such as givers of prizes, free gifts, even movie auditions). Sometimes they pretend to be court officers, government officials, county sheriffs, police officers, or attorneys.

2. Harassment. The classic varieties of harassment are midnight telegrams and special-delivery letters; repeated phone calling; and obscene, insulting, or degrading remarks. Tactics become harassing, rather than merely aggressive, because of their context or frequency. For example, it is appropriate to telephone a debtor at home or at work to discuss a debt—but not to telephone five times in one day, or to discuss the matter with the debtor's co-workers.

3. Threats. Threatening can be by explicit statements or by implication or innuendo. A favorite is the threat to have the debtor arrested, jailed, or criminally prosecuted; it is often successful since many people don't know that debtor's prisons were abolished long ago in this country. Debt collectors have been known to make such sinister comments as "I see your children walking to and from school every day." A less sinister but effective tactic is to threaten to contact the debtor's relatives or employer, in order to embarrass the debtor or to make him or her fearful about the possible effect of the debt on his job.

4. Humiliation. Humiliation tactics—like telling the debtor's friends, family, and fellow workers that the debtor is a fraud and a deadbeat—are now expressly outlawed. The need for this law was described by a Michigan judge, who said:

> It is true that we live in a credit economy. But when one of our people buys a refrigerator on time, he does not thereupon hang the vestments of his privacy in the creditor's closet, to stand naked and exposed to whatever measures the creditor chooses to employ to collect the debt. . . .
>
> [The creditor] may not invade his privacy for the purpose of coercing him into payment of the debt by the device of exposing his private affairs to

"Jail or Debtor's Prison, 1763" (The J. Clarence Davies Collection, Museum of the City of New York)

others. . . . He may not subject the debtor to the duress of purchasing a cessation of public humiliation, or employer pressure, by payment.

COLLECTION ABUSE: THE TELEPHONE AS WEAPON

If written notices don't do the job, professional collectors pursue their quarry over the telephone. Over the phone, collectors' threats, harassment, and humiliation tactics often know no bounds. One of the most shocking cases brought to light was that of a collector who, posing as a policeman, telephoned a woman and said, "Get down to the hospital. Your son has been in a car accident and has had both legs cut off." After rushing to the hospital she learned that the collector had used this false story to get a chance to meet her, in order to talk about an overdue bill.

An unethical but common ploy is to leave a phony message with the debtor's co-workers, friends, or relatives to the effect that a local constable is out with a truck and armed with a warrant to seize the debtor's furniture and personal belongings. This scare tactic has the advantage of involving the debtor's relatives and friends, adding humiliation and embarrassment to the debtor's woes. Such pressure may get the consumer to pay any bill, even one he or she disputes.

YOUR RIGHTS

Debt collector abuse had become so widespread that in 1977 Congress acted to curb it. The Fair Debt Collection Practices Act* is now in effect everywhere.†

The Act pertains only to people who are collecting debts for another as part of their business. Thus, it does *not* cover staff members working in the collection department of a store or hospital or lawyers collecting bills for their clients. Some state laws do cover those situations, so check yours. The federal act is administered by the Federal Trade Commission and prohibits debt collectors pursuing consumers from engaging in these activities:

◆ communicating with the consumer or anyone else once the collector has been notified that an attorney is representing the consumer.

◆ communicating with anyone other than the consumer or spouse, *except* if seeking the consumer's whereabouts or if a court has ruled against the consumer.

◆ indicating to friends, employers, or others, when seeking to learn the consumer's whereabouts, that it's about a debt.

◆ contacting the consumer before 8 A.M. or after 9 P.M.

◆ contacting the consumer more than twice a week.

◆ contacting the consumer at work more than three times a month; or contacting him or her there at all *if* the consumer tells the collector not to do so and gives another phone number.

◆ continuing to communicate after a consumer has told the collector, in writing, to cease further contact.

◆ harassing or intimidating or threatening a consumer. (This section of the Act is broadly defined and specifically includes using abusive or profane language; publishing a list of deadbeats; advertising the sale of debts in order to coerce payments; seeking the whereabouts of a consumer when the collector really knows them; and making repeated or constant phone calls or visits.)

◆ false or misleading representation about:

the *consumer* (e.g., as having committed a crime or willfully refused to pay a creditor);

the *collector* (e.g., as acting on behalf of the government; being an attorney; seeking information in connection with a survey; offering a gift);

the *debt* (e.g., as to its amount or legal status, its having been turned over to an attorney);

the *consequences of nonpayment* (e.g., arrest or imprisonment);

* 15 U.S.C. 1601 *et seq.*

† Except for states whose own laws were similar enough that they were specifically allowed to keep them instead of using the federal act. The Federal Trade Commission, which is charged with enforcing the Act, has the power to make such a decision and you can check with the FTC or with your state attorney general to see if that's the case in your state.

the *taking of any action* which the collector cannot or does not intend to take.

There are other prohibitions too, dealing with the collection of extra charges not due; the furnishing of deceptive legal forms; and improper notification if a suit is begun against the consumer.

The Act also requires collectors to send consumers, within five working days of their initial contact, a written notice stating:

> the amount of the debt;
> the name of the creditor;
> a statement that unless the consumer responds in 30 days the collector will assume that the debt is valid; and
> a notice that if the consumer writes within that period and says that the debt is disputed the collector will cease efforts to collect until it's validated by the creditor and a notice sent to the consumer.

If a debt collector violates any of these provisions, a consumer can sue within two years, and collect for any actual losses or harm suffered plus a sum of between $100 and $1,000. Class-action suits can also be brought against chronic offenders.

The Act is quite clear about what collectors cannot do. Therefore, if one of them violates your rights, consider going to small claims court (see chapter 28).

Whether or not you consider suing, be sure to alert the FTC (or your state agency) to any violation. They proceed against major offenders only and can use consumer complaints to determine who they are.

HOW TO HANDLE AGGRESSION

There are some general ways in which you can prevent potential abuses from aggressive collectors from escalating:

1. Refuse to discuss anything over the telephone and insist that all contacts be confined to written correspondence.

2. Always get the name of the person you are dealing with, and the name of the business or agency he or she is working for. Someone is less likely to abuse if there is no mask of anonymity to hide behind. Be aware, however, that bill collectors frequently use phony names, so you might want to verify the caller's identity before continuing your conversation.

3. Never give personal information about yourself (or about a friend or relative) to a stranger over the telephone. If the caller persists in seeking such information, hang up.

4. Refuse to meet any debt collector in your home. On rare occasions collectors will show up uninvited at your home or office. You do not have to grant them admittance, and you shouldn't. If they enter without permission, call the police.

5. Complain right away if a bill collector attempts to frighten, harass, or abuse you. Don't wait.

FIRST, complain to the seller, especially if that store (or person) is a generally reputable one concerned with its public image. Sometimes sellers send their accounts out for collection without knowing what tactics the collector will use. Such a seller may order an irresponsible collection agent to stop contacting you, or may even change collection agencies.

SECOND, contact the nearest office of the FTC (or the state attorney general).

THIRD, if you've received annoying, abusive telephone calls, complain to the telephone company. It can cut off telephone service to a collection agency that attempts to frighten, harass, or threaten people over the telephone. Notify the telephone company in writing, and send a copy of your complaint letter to the FTC (or state attorney general).

APPENDIX

The following is a script about debt collection practices developed by the Consumer Law Training Center.‡ It has been broadcast on radio and been used in consumer classes and workshops as a teaching device.

THE CASE OF THE DERANGED DEBT COLLECTOR!
A radio script

ANNOUNCER: One morning as Lydia Shrapnel was doing her wash, the telephone rang.

(Telephone rings.)

LYDIA: Hello?

VOICE: Mrs. Shrapnel, I presume?

LYDIA: Yes, who is this?

VOICE: This is the Federal Debt Bureau, and you're in debt to us, Mrs. Shrapnel. It's a little matter of $83. The Skunkly Design School . . . you remember now, Lydia?

LYDIA: Why yes, I remember that. A salesman came and offered me a chance to take an art course from them. He said I could sign the application, and decide later whether I wanted the course. The next day I called and told them I didn't want it.

VOICE: Lydia, skip the stories. This debt has to be paid, and I'm not about to take it out of my pocket; so you better start reaching into yours, sweetheart.

LYDIA: But I don't owe this!

VOICE: We've got your contract, and *it* says you do. You can be put in jail for this, Lydia. The marshal will come and pick you up, right out of your house, and cart you away; I don't know what will happen to your kids.

L: Oh no!

V: And this'll ruin your credit everywhere . . . when your landlord hears about this he'll evict you. You'll be out on the street, honey . . . where you started, I bet. (snickers)

‡ The CLTC was a consumer education project of the New York Law School, the New York Public Interest Research Group, Inc., and Brooklyn Legal Services Corp. B, funded by the U. S. Office of Education.

L: Now look here . . . I don't owe this money and even if I did, I don't have the money anyway. My husband has just been through major surgery.

V: Don't give me any sickly-boy stories, Lydia. Everyone's got problems. If you paid your bill, we'd both have one less problem.

L: I can't pay *any* bills right now. I'll have to go bankrupt the way they're piling up.

V (false friendly tone): Now listen, Lydia. I'm trying to help you, believe me. Ignoring a little bill like this can be bad. If we have to go to your employer, you lose your job, and then where are you? I'll tell you what. Pay me forty bucks now, and twenty bucks next week, and we'll call it even. O.K.?

L (withered): I can't. It's just not right. We need this money, and I don't owe it to you.

V (hardening again): All right, Lydia, I tried to be nice about this. We know how to deal with deadbeats. (sinister:) We have ways of getting our money. So long, honey. (click)

SCENE TWO

A: Three days later. Lydia's neighbor, Sally Rembrandt, visits Lydia at home.

SALLY: Hi, Lydia.

L: You look worried, Sally. Is that rotten Harvey of yours playing around again?

S: No, Lydia. Now listen. Someone just called my house who said he was a marshal, and he wanted to know if I knew where you were. He said he had a warrant to arrest you for defrauding creditors. I told him he must be mistaken. But he said he was sure. Said you owed him $83 and refused to pay, and he had a warrant.

L: Gee, Sal, I'm scared. Can they really arrest me?

SCENE THREE

A: One night later, at 3 A.M.
(Telephone rings.)

L (Drowsily): Hello?

V: Pay your bills, deadbeat! (click)

SCENE FOUR

A: Lydia goes to her job as a weekend night watchperson for the Zucchini Storage Company. Her boss is waiting for her.

L: Hi, boss.

BOSS: Hello, Lydia. (stern-voiced:) I want to talk to you.

L: What's up, boss?

B: A fella called up today about some money you owe to some school or something. Said they would have to get a garnishee on your wages if you didn't pay. We can't have people working for us who have their salaries garnisheed—understand? Get that bill straightened out—or we'll find a new watchperson.

L: Yes, sir, you won't be bothered any more. I promise.

B: Good.

(Footsteps and door closes; boss has left.)

L: I've really done it this time. I guess I'd better pay. (sighs) But it just isn't fair.

(organ music—fanfare that ends soap operas)

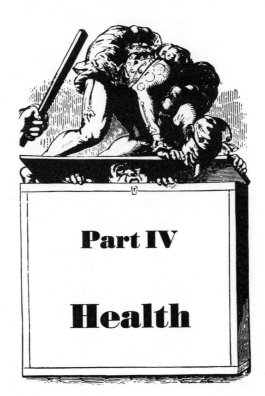

Part IV

Health

23

Doctor and patient: an ailing relationship

You medical people will have more lives to answer for in the other world than we generals. — NAPOLEON I, to a doctor at St. Helena, 1817

All idiots, priests, actors, monks, barbers and old women think they are physicians. — Latin proverb

There is no medicine against death. — Proverb

The unfortunate phrase "witch doctor" has frequently been employed in connection with African medicine, tending to suggest some kind of unholy alliance between witches and traditional doctors. In fact, one of the primary functions of the doctor in traditional society was always to protect its members from the dangerous activities of witches . . . It is still considered an important part of the herbalists' and the diviners' business to discover whether witches have had a part in causing an illness with a prolonged or puzzling course . . . — UNA MACLEAN, "Magic and Medicine," in *Frontiers of Healing: New Dimensions in Parapsychology,* edited by Nicholas M. Regush

The relationship between a primitive tribe member and a medicine man is not so different from the contemporary patient-doctor relationship as we'd like to believe. Fear, faith, and irrationality play major parts in both. The most sophisticated people today react to their doctors with a lifetime's accumulation of respect, fear, suspicion, and hopefulness—not very different from what tribe members brought to their medicine men. The fear of pain and the dread of death are probably worse in our society than in many more "primitive" cultures, where death is accepted as an integral part of life.

All this makes rational analysis of one's own health care very difficult indeed. To add to the difficulty, many Americans have been inculcated with a blind reverence for medical "science" and expect too much from their physicians. The truth is that medicine is a most inexact "science" which relies a great deal on educated guesswork and hunch following, and that its practitioners vary enormously in their capabilities—from the brilliant to the incompetent, with most falling somewhere in between.

Our need to believe uncritically in doctors has led to an unhealthy doctor-patient relationship. As one physician recently wrote:

> The relationship between doctor and patient is as serious a problem in medicine today as are disease and ignorance.
> Many patients either fear their doctors or hold them in such unrealistic high esteem that they can't communicate freely.*

Clearly all is not well in the $140 billion medical business. Complaints about our medical system are on the rise, and a new patient-consumer movement has begun making itself heard. Almost as if in reaction to the long tradition of viewing doctors as demigods, a spate of books and articles highly critical of the health establishment have appeared. Both extremes are dangerous: neither degrading or idealizing the medical profession is likely to lead anyone to a satisfactory patient-doctor relationship. The best that can come of the present controversy is for individuals to begin to think of themselves as purchasers of health services, and to ask questions and make demands for proper care. This chapter will talk about what you can do to become a more effective health consumer.

SELECTING A DOCTOR

Medical care is the most vital consumer service any of us will ever buy. Yet people usually spend much more time and effort in selecting a new car than in choosing a physician.

The medical mystique has been nurtured by the difficulty of obtaining any factual data on its practitioners. It has been easier to get objective information on the toasters sold in a department store or on local exterminators than on the medical professionals in whose hands you may be placing your life. Patients are still often unable to learn what is in their own medical records, are ignorant of the backgrounds and fee scales of the available doctors, and generally have no idea of how to find the physician most suitable for them. But the situation is improving.

ADVERTISING AND FEES

Doctors have long considered themselves "professionals" whose dignity would suffer from advertising or from frank discussion of fees. Patients respected the taboo on discussing cost, and state regulations backed up the advertising ban.

Fortunately, the last few years have seen a steady erosion of this professed distaste for such a mercantile matter. A 1977 U. S. Supreme Court decision ruled, in a case involving advertising by lawyers, that it was a violation of the right of free speech for a state to flatly prohibit the advertising of professional services and fees. This decision opened the way for advertising by doctors. While only a minority of doctors have advertised, the decision may have a far-reaching effect in opening up the area of fee information.

---

* Marvin S. Belsky, M.D., and Leonard Gross, *How to Choose and Use Your Doctor* (New York: Arbor House, 1975), p. 17.

CONSUMER DIRECTORIES

Another catalyst for change was the efforts of consumer groups to compile directories of local physicians. These booklets contained information on doctors' educational background; board certification or eligibility in a specialty; office location and hours; whether Medicaid and Medicare patients were accepted; and fee information.

The early directories faced a number of obstacles. Doctors often refused to answer questions or supply information, medical societies advised them not to cooperate, and state licensing agencies sought to stop publication.

Some of the groups whose efforts were being impeded filed lawsuits. The courts upheld their right to seek and publish information about doctors. Subsequently the professional societies and the state boards softened their opposition. The American Medical Association (AMA) began to see directories as inevitable. The American Dental Association (ADA) took a position supporting consumer directories in 1977 and has provided a model directory and guidelines to encourage local dental societies to work on them with consumer groups. Some states are even considering laws requiring doctors to furnish data about their practices which would be compiled and made available to the public.

FAMILY PRACTICE / FAMILY MEDICINE†

ALEXANDER, Steven K.   104 Jamesville Road.   446-6626

BISHOP, Thomas E.   245 Main St., Minoa   656-7031
  Graduated: (1945) Syracuse
  Affiliations: Chairman Advisory Board of Health, Onondaga County; Deputy Health Office, Onondaga County; Medical Consultant Sunnyside Skilled Nursing Facility; Company Surgeon Penn Central R.R. Co.
  Staff: Nurse clinician, x-ray technician
  Hours: Mon. Tues. Wed. Fri. 10:00–5:00. By appt. only. Day off-Thurs. and every other Sat.–Sun. Will accept house calls. Will accept new patients by referral only and will see some emergency unscheduled walk-in patients. Average time required for an appt. is variable.
  Fees: Payment preferred at appt. time.
  Hospitals used: Crouse-Irving Memorial, VAH, Upstate, Silverman, Community General, St. Mary's, St. Joseph's.

BROWN, Marvin   Lake St., Cleveland (Oswego County)   675-3619
  Graduated: (1935) Syracuse College of Medicine
  Certified: Charter Fellow American Academy of Family Physicians
  Affiliations: Ass't clinical professor, Dept. of Family Practice, Upstate.
  Hours: By appt. Mon. 1:00–3:00, 6:30–8:00. Tues. 10:00–12:00. Wed. and Fri. 10:00–12:00 and 1:00–5:00.
    Sat. 9:00–11:00. Day off-Thurs. Will make house calls. Will accept new patients and sees unscheduled walk-in patients. Same day appts. available.
  Fees: Payment required at appt. time. Routine office visit = $7.00 "Everything else is extra." Medicaid accepted but accepts no new Medicaid. Prescribes birth control.
  Hospitals used: Refer patients to other doctors in Syracuse.

CINCOTTA, Armand J.   7209 Buckley Rd., Liverpool   458-5027
  Graduated: (1967) University of Ottawa Faculty of Medicine, Ottawa
  Certified: Board qualified.
  Affiliations: Ass't attending St. Joseph's Hospital, Ass't Professor of Family Medicine at Upstate, Board of Directors-American Heart Assoc.
  Staff: Registered nurse
  Hours: Mon. Tues. Wed. mornings and afternoons. Fri.-afternoons. Day off-Thurs. Will rarely make house calls. Will accept new patients and will see emergency unscheduled walk-in patients. One month required for physicals, but time required for an appt. varies with complaint.
  Fees: Payment preferred at appt. time. Precribes birth control.
  Hospitals used: St. Mary's, St. Joseph's

---

† From the NYPIRG *Consumer's Guide to Onondaga Physicians.*

As a result, information about health professionals has become increasingly available. To find out if a directory exists in your area, contact any local consumer group or agency or the consumer reporter of your local newspaper. If you are interested in compiling a directory, contact the Health Research Group (2000 P Street, N.W., Washington, D.C. 20036), which has written a guide.

WHAT TO LOOK FOR

If you don't have a family doctor, or are dissatisfied with the one you have, there are ways of maximizing the chances of finding a competent doctor to meet your needs. Doctors are unevenly distributed in the United States, and many people have no choice of physicians. If you do have a choice, here's how to make a wise selection.

1. Choose a doctor when you are healthy, before you need one. This gives you both the time and the psychological ease to evaluate what you want *and* whether a particular doctor meets those criteria.

2. Choose a general practitioner or general internist (or pediatrician for small children) as a family doctor. Let that doctor recommend specialists as they are needed. Don't refer yourself to a surgeon or other specialist before selecting a family doctor. Specialists usually are not familiar with your total health picture and are often shortsighted about causes and effects outside their area of expertise.

But you should see a specialist, preferably one who is board-certified, whenever one is needed. They are more likely to have advanced, ongoing training than a general practitioner. In parts of the country where specialists are rare, family doctors often take on the functions of surgeons, gynecologists, and dermatologists. This saves patients travel and other expenses, but often results in second-rate medical care.

3. Compile a list of candidates. Ask for a recommendation from another health care professional whom you trust (such as a dentist or a family doctor from a previous neighborhood). Ask friends and relatives for recommendations, *if* you think that they have good judgment *and* would look for the same qualities in a doctor that you want. If neither of these sources exist, call the chief resident of a local hospital (a "teaching" one, if possible) or go to the outpatient department and ask for referrals. Only if you are armed with several choices will you be able to select the best doctor.

4. Check the doctor's credentials. Look into the doctor's educational background and, especially, hospital affiliation(s) before going further (the place where the doctor is affiliated is important, because that's where you'll go if you need hospitalization).

If there is more than one hospital in the area, you can compare them by using three criteria. First, the hospital should be accredited (by the Joint Commission on Accreditation of Hospitals). Second, it should be a "teaching" hospital—one with a formal program for training medical students or resident doctors or other medical personnel. Third, a voluntary (nonprofit) community or municipal hospital is usually preferable to a proprietary (profit-making) one.

There are directories available, in medical libraries and in many public libraries, which contain information on physicians. They include the reference book which doctors use, the *American Medical Directory,* put out every few years by the American Medical Association. Also, there are various state directories—your local medical society should be able to tell you if one exists for your area. Sometimes there is also a consumer group's directory, offering more extensive information, particularly about fees.

It is a good idea to select a family physician who has received special training in family medicine or internal medicine and is either "board-certified" (i.e., has passed the qualifying requirements and the examination given by the specialty board) or "board-eligible" (has taken the training but not the examination).

5. Check on particular factors which are important to you, by telephone, before making an appointment. Here are some to consider:

- Is the office in a convenient location?
- Are the office hours ones you can make?
- Does the doctor or staff speak another language (if someone in your family is more comfortable with one)?
- Does the doctor practice alone or in a group? (Group practice means that if your doctor is away, you can usually be seen by one of his or her colleagues.)
- What is the charge for a routine visit?

6. Recognize your personal feelings about what you want in a doctor. Communication is at the heart of a successful patient-doctor relationship, so it is essential that you feel comfortable with your doctor. Therefore, honor your own prejudices in this area. You may prefer a female or a male doctor or one whose race, religion, or background is similar to yours. The doctor's attitude toward such matters as drinking, birth control, and abortion may be important to you.

7. Visit the doctor. Only after a personal visit will you be able to evaluate whether a physician is the right one for you. A routine checkup is probably the best situation in which to evaluate a new doctor, although it doesn't show you how he or she reacts to more stressful situations. You need not view it as a waste of time and money if you go through an appointment and then decide not to go back to that doctor—it's an investment which could save you untold grief later on. Look and listen carefully on your initial visit. Ask yourself these questions:

a. Is the office reasonably neat, clean, and well-running? Are appointments scheduled so that patients are given enough time and so that delays are minimal? Emergencies occur, of course, but be wary of a doctor who chronically keeps patients waiting hours or rushes them through.

b. Did the doctor ask for a complete medical history (including information about family) and do a thorough exam? The history should include questions about your eating and drinking habits, exercising, sex life, and employment. These data enable the doctor to treat you as a whole person, rather than dealing in isolation with any symptoms that arise. Did he or she seem relaxed?

c. Did the doctor take notes on what you related and what the physical examination revealed? If not, the information can't be used in later treatment by this doctor or by any subsequent ones.

d. Was the doctor prevention-oriented? Did he or she discuss health care matters in general?

e. Were your questions answered fully by the doctor and were you treated courteously by the staff?

PROBLEMS IN DOCTOR-PATIENT COMMUNICATION

One doctor has estimated that 70 to 75 percent of his diagnoses are based on the history which patients give (with 15 to 20 percent based on the physical signs obtained from examination, 5 to 10 percent from laboratory findings, and 5 percent on the clinical developments). Therefore it is essential that you observe, remember, and communicate all the details about your health. If you think that you may forget some of the data which you ought to relay, make a list of symptoms and questions and bring it to the doctor's office. Apparent trivialities may be important for diagnostic purposes. And remember, it is self-destructive to color information about symptoms, or drinking, eating, or drug-taking habits, in order to "please" the doctor or spare yourself embarrassment.

Another common, but counterproductive trait is caused by fear of being thought a hypochondriac. This leads people to put off making a call or an appointment and to "forget" to give the doctor all the information.

Just as important as communicating information is discussing your questions and fears. Ask what the doctor has found, what treatment alternatives exist, and what risks are involved. Many doctors do not spontaneously give full explanations. The classic rationale for not explaining diagnoses and choices of treatment is that medical issues are too difficult for laypeople to grasp. That argument has been overstated. Most people are capable of understanding and dealing with an explanation of what is wrong with them, if it is put into understandable English. This requires the doctor to have an interest in communicating with the patient and to take the time and effort to give the appropriate explanation.

If a doctor keeps putting off questions or insisting that you won't understand, change doctors. Your health is too important a matter to be ignorant about.

Nor can you afford to suspend all critical evaluation once you've chosen a physician. Doctors are as capable of error and weakness as other people. In fact, the AMA itself has estimated that 5 percent of all U.S. physicians are mentally ill, alcoholic, or drug abusers—the true figure may well be much higher.

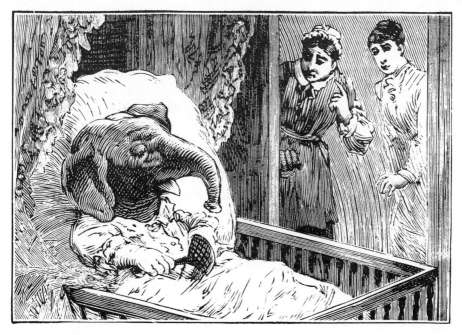

Patients, particularly if they are seriously ill, want to believe that their doctor has the situation thoroughly in control. So they fail to see danger signs that they would notice in other situations. The best antidote is to ask all the questions you need to understand the doctor's diagnosis and course of treatment, and trust the instincts that you use in judging the competence and conduct of other people.

A PITFALL TO AVOID: UNNECESSARY SURGERY

Boggling though the thought may be, several studies have shown conclusively that much of the surgery done in America is unnecessary. Estimates vary, but all agree that for at least one out of ten operations performed, a more conservative course of treatment would have suited the patient as well. Some of the most commonly overprescribed operations are hysterectomies, tonsillectomies, and gall bladder surgery.

The physical and psychic cost to the victims of the unnecessary operations is inestimable. Since surgery always involves some risk, a substantial number of people die from operations which could safely have been avoided. (It has been determined by the National Center for Health Statistics that one of every 72 patients dies from surgery or its complications.) Sidney Wolfe, the physician who heads the Health Research Group in Washington, D.C., estimates that there are 16,000 fatalities each year from unnecessary operations (based on his projection that 17 percent of all surgery is superfluous). The financial cost, too, is considerable. Wolfe estimates it to be $4.8 billion annually.

What can you do to make certain that you don't become an unnecessary surgery statistic? Three things. First, be sure you understand from the doctor recommending surgery exactly why the operation is needed; what it can be expected to accomplish; and what the risks and possible side effects are. Second, don't immediately agree to elective (non-emergency) surgery. Even if time is of the essence, you can take a day or so to think about it and talk it over with your family or friends. And third, get another medical opinion, from someone who is not recommended by the doctor who has decided that you need surgery. This step is well recognized as the prudent course of action. In fact, an increasing number of health insurance plans will pay for a second opinion. Blue Cross and Blue Shield of Greater New York discovered, after a two-year study, that in 27 percent of the cases a second opinion found no need for the non-emergency surgery originally recommended.

MEDICAL RECORDS: ANOTHER SORE SPOT

There are various reasons why a patient may want to see his or her personal medical records compiled by a doctor or hospital. They include a desire to change doctors or hospitals, a belief that one may have been mistreated, a concern that something damaging (and perhaps untrue) in that record is being conveyed to third parties, such as potential employers, and simple curiosity.

Some doctors and some hospitals will provide this information routinely. Others won't, and in many states the patient does not have a legal right to see these records (although they are readily made available to other doctors and government agencies).

Those states which do grant a right of access to medical records often limit the right. For example, Connecticut law gives access to hospital records only; New York regulations require a doctor to let a patient see his or her own record, *unless* the doctor believes it "would adversely affect the patient's health." Other states allow access only if and when a lawsuit is started (usually by the patient).

A publication that should be of help in gaining access is *Getting Yours: A Consumer's Guide to Obtaining Your Medical Record,* put out by the Health Research Group, 2000 P Street, N.W., Washington, D.C. 20036.

IF YOU'VE BEEN MISTREATED BY A DOCTOR

> What is astonishing about malpractice is not how many suits may have been filed in recent years, but how late the concept of public accountability has been in coming to medicine.‡

There may be times when a doctor's behavior strikes you as thoroughly inappropriate or outrageous. When he recommends a drastic medical procedure which you later learn was unnecessary. When she bills you at a rate

---

‡ Senator Abraham Ribicoff, with Paul Danaceau, *The American Medical Machine* (New York: Harrow Books, Harper & Row, 1972), p. 121.

several times higher than what others charge. When he or she refuses to turn your medical records over to a subsequent doctor.

People who have been mistreated by a doctor and have suffered as a result often consider suing for malpractice. In fact, malpractice suits are difficult to win and should be undertaken rarely. To win, it must be reasonably clear that the doctor acted negligently (not just mistakenly) *and* that such action (or inaction) had demonstrable negative effects on the patient. *Only* in those cases do patients sometimes succeed and win substantial judgments. A lawyer, especially one who has handled malpractice cases before, can advise you as to whether you have a possible case.

Everyone is familiar with malpractice lawsuits, but many people do not realize that there is another way to take action against an incompetent or unethical doctor. Registering a complaint will not result in a money award, but it can serve a number of useful purposes.

(Drawing by Richter, © 1977 *The New Yorker* Magazine, Inc.)

Doctors (as well as dentists and other health professionals) are licensed to practice medicine by the state. Commonly, it is the state health department, but not always (in New York, for example, it is the Education Department).

To find out who licenses doctors and handles disciplinary matters, call or write to your state health department or consumer agency or attorney general. File your complaint with the state licensing agency rather than with the local medical society. A medical society is a voluntary membership organization—a professional trade union, in effect. It does not have the legal duty to protect the public (although the state regulatory agency can delegate part of that duty to it) or the necessary impartiality. Medical societies can refer cases to the state authorities, but physicians have been loath to tell tales on each other and have generally failed to monitor each other's behavior effectively.

It is usually best to register a complaint by letter. Be certain that the letter sets out all the facts, in chronological order, and that it includes *copies* of any necessary papers or photos. Send copies to the doctor involved, to the medical society, and if a hospital or clinic was involved, to its director or board chairperson.

After sending the letter, wait a couple of weeks and then begin following it up if there's no reply. (See chapter 3 for follow-up techniques.)

In only a very few cases will the letter result in the doctor losing his or her license to practice, and even then it will happen only after an involved proceeding. Agencies don't like to deprive a person of a license without being very certain that the action is justified. They often require overwhelming evidence before taking such a step.

However, filing a complaint letter can have several positive side effects. First, it alerts the doctor to the seriousness of your complaint (which, naturally, should be voiced first to the doctor) and may make him or her think seriously about continuing that behavior with other patients. Second, if anyone else complains about the same doctor, your letter becomes part of the type of cumulative evidence that does prompt agency investigation and proceedings. And, of course, it usually makes you feel better to try to right a wrong.

24

Drugs: prescription and over-the-counter

The desire to take medicine is perhaps the greatest feature which distinguishes man from animals. — SIR WILLIAM OSLER, quoted in Stephen Barrett, M.D., and Gilda Knight, eds., *The Health Robbers: How to Protect Your Money and Your Life*

She went over to the medicine cabinet . . . Before her, in overly luxuriant rows, was a host, so to speak, of golden pharmaceuticals . . . The shelves bore iodine, Mercurochrome, vitamin capsules, dental floss, aspirin, Anacin, Bufferin, Argyrol, Musterole, Ex-Lax, Milk of Magnesia, Sal Hepatica, Aspergum, two Gillette razors, one Schick Injector razor, two tubes of shaving cream . . . a bottle of Wildroot hair ointment, a bottle of Fitch Dandruff Remover, a small, unlabelled box of glycerine suppositories, Vicks Nose Drops, Vicks VapoRub, six bars of castile soap . . . a tube of depilatory cream, a box of Kleenex, two seashells, an assortment of used-looking emery boards, two jars of cleansing cream, three pairs of scissors, a nail file, an unclouded blue marble. . . . — J. D. SALINGER, *Franny & Zooey* (Boston: Little, Brown Company, 1961, p. 75)

Prescription, n. A physician's guess at what will best prolong the situation with least harm to the patient. — AMBROSE BIERCE, *The Devil's Dictionary*

He's the best physician that knows the worthlessness of most medicines. — BENJAMIN FRANKLIN, *Poor Richard's Almanack* (1773)

Most Americans have a drug problem. Not with heroin, but with analgesics, antibiotics, vitamin pills, tranquilizers, sleep aids, foot powders, and the thousand and one other potions on the market. We tend to believe in medicine as the answer to all bodily ills, from aching feet to "the blahs." Many of us expect a prescription each time we visit the doctor. And we like to think that any drug that a doctor prescribes or that is sold over the counter will, in the advertiser's phrase, "work wonders."

The uncertainties and dangers associated with the taking of medication are unpleasant, perhaps frightening, to contemplate. We want easy cures for our woes (and taking medication is much simpler than eating better, drinking less, or exercising regularly) and we want someone to tell us what that cure is and to promise us that it will work. But the consequences of being a careless consumer of medicine can be drastic. They are particularly tragic when they could have been easily avoided.

Medicine or medication falls into one of two categories—*prescription drugs,* which are recommended specifically for you and can be bought only with a doctor's written order, and *over-the-counter* (OTC) drugs, which can be bought by anyone. In general, prescription drugs are stronger and thus have greater potential to cure and to cause harm.

Any substance that can help can also hurt; all drugs are, by their nature, double-edged swords. If a preparation has qualities capable of bringing about a positive bodily change, it has negative potential too. In considering whether a new drug should be marketed, the government weighs, at least theoretically, its potential for helping against its potential for causing harm.

And a doctor's decision whether to prescribe a particular drug is also the result of weighing the probable good to be gained against the possible harmful side effects. As can be imagined, this is no easy task. Your participation in the process can increase the chances of the right choice for you being made.

The harm done by prescription drugs which backfire is considerable. It has been estimated that almost 100 Americans die each day as a result of taking medication prescribed for them, and ten times that number suffer life-threatening and often permanent side effects. Another staggering statistic: one out of three hospital patients is affected adversely by medication prescribed for the condition that led to the hospitalization.

A WARNING FROM A TOP DOCTOR

A Harvard professor of medicine and pharmacology has written a useful book for laypeople on the prescription drug industry and prescribing problems. It includes a lengthy description of and price list for the most common drugs. He says:

. . . far too often a patient takes a drug when he may need none at all. Or he takes a drug with dangerous side effects when a safer drug is available. Or he takes a drug of unproved clinical value, or one which carries important risks and therefore never should be given for minor conditions. In each of these situations—and even in the happy instance when the prescription is both justified and safe—the patient is far too likely to pay much more than is necessary.*

AVOID BECOMING A STATISTIC

Some drug-related mishaps are caused by unpredictable results; some result from pharmaceutical or medical errors. Negative side effects will always occur. But you can lessen the chance of becoming a victim by taking certain simple precautions.

1. First, inform the prescribing doctor of any bad reactions that you've ever had to medication. A doctor often has a choice of drugs to use to treat your problem and can steer clear of the kind that has been troublesome.

2. Tell or remind your doctor of everything that you are currently taking. This includes vitamins, birth control pills, and over-the-counter drugs. A medication can drastically change the effect of others if taken in combination. For example, plain aspirin can increase the blood-thinning effects of certain drugs prescribed for heart conditions. So a heart patient could be risking hemorrhages by taking aspirin for headaches.

3. Be certain that you understand what the medicine is supposed to do and when and how it should be taken. Doctors don't always remember to tell patients, for example, that antibiotics will not be fully effective if they

* Richard Burack, M.D., with Fred J. Fox, M.D., *The New Handbook of Prescription Drugs* (New York: Ballantine Books, 1976), p. 12.

are taken with food. And some medicines have negative interactions with ordinary wholesome foods. A case in point: the tetracyclines, which are rendered largely useless if the patient drinks or eats dairy products, because calcium in the food inhibits the absorption of the medicine.

4. So find out whether you should avoid any particular foods or booze while you are on the medication. Alcohol interacts negatively with certain drugs, sometimes creating real danger to you. In an ideal world the prescribing doctor would always remember to tell you this and the dispensing pharmacist would verify it. But don't count on them—ask before you take the drugs. Ask, too, whether it will be necessary to restrict your activities. There are drugs (like certain antihistamines) which induce drowsiness, making it unsafe to drive or operate machinery. Knowing beforehand what the effects of medication are likely to be can help you plan your schedule to accommodate necessary interruptions.

5. Be sure to alert the prescribing doctor if *there is any chance* that you are pregnant. Any number of preparations can harm a fetus, which is most vulnerable in its earliest weeks (when you are not even certain that you are pregnant). Because of the sensitivity of unborn babies to medication (and nicotine and alcohol), prudent physicians will prescribe as little medication as possible to sustain the mother's health. However, it is essential to anticipate any possible pregnancy and alert the doctor.

ANTIBIOTICS

> We seem to have a national belief that there is a drug for every affliction. Physicians as well as patients are too often victimized by a kind of chemical ceremony in which no visit to a physician is complete without ending in a written prescription.†

Americans have an unhealthy fondness for antibiotics, spending the amazing sum of $1 billion a year on them. Antibiotics are antimicrobial agents, that is, they effectively kill certain kinds of bacteria. For that purpose they are an important and effective medication; countless lives have been saved thanks to them. But their reputation and their usage far exceed that legitimate function and constitute a health problem. The danger stems from the risk of adverse reactions. Side effects are fairly common and sometimes serious. In addition, antibiotics can be expensive (especially the brand-name versions).

A study published in the respected *Journal of the American Medical Association* showed that, in a single year, one out of four people in the United States was given a prescription for penicillin. Ninety percent of the time the drug was unnecessary (and therefore possibly harmful). Various other surveys conducted by the medical profession have demonstrated that doctors overprescribe and misprescribe antibiotics for a variety of non-bacterial ailments. As a result, perhaps, patients have gotten into the habit of asking for

† Donald Kennedy, U. S. Commissioner of Food and Drugs, speech delivered before the Consumer Federation of America, Washington, D.C., January 19, 1978: "Turtles & Other Chronic Hazards—Consumer Influence on Decisions," reprinted in *Vital Speeches of the Day,* Vol. XLIV, No. 10, March 1, 1978.

them to treat colds, sore throats, and flus—caused by viruses, which won't respond to such treatment. Doctors sometimes give in to such requests even when they know better.

Once you've learned all you can about the medication which has been prescribed for you, monitor your own reactions. If you believe that you are experiencing a side effect, get in touch with the doctor who prescribed the drug at once.

HOW TO CUT THE COST OF PRESCRIPTION DRUGS

For many people medication is a major expense—especially for those with chronic illnesses and for the elderly, who spend more than three times as much on prescription drugs as those under 65.

There are two ways to whittle down drugstore bills—first by buying generic drugs, and second by comparison shopping. The generic versus brand name distinction is often misunderstood. Every new prescription drug is assigned an official, generic name, even before being marketed, by the U. S. Adopted Names Council. That is usually multisyllabic and scientific-sounding—for examples try Propoxyphene Hydrochloride and Sulfamethoxazole. When a drug is first approved, the company which developed it is given exclusive right to market it over the next seventeen years. So for that period

(*The New Yorker*)

there is only one version of the drug available, for which the company usually coins a snappier unofficial brand name, like Darvon (Propoxyphene Hydrochloride) or Gantanol (Sulfamethoxazole). After that patent expires, anyone can market the drug under either its generic name or the marketer's own brand name. If the drug is a popular one, there will be several manufacturers selling it under different names and at different prices.

A brand-name version of any drug is frequently five or ten times more expensive and sometimes up to thirty times more costly than the least expensive generic version. Pharmaceutical catalogues show how much more some brand-name versions cost. In 1975, for example, druggists had to pay $26.75 for 1,000 standard capsules of Benadryl (a Parke-Davis brand name), but only $5.40 for the same medication put out as a generic (named Diphenhydramine Hydrochloride) by Veratex. That's a difference of almost 500 percent, which would be reflected in the retail price. Similarly, druggists paid $93 for 1,000 capsules of Pentids, Squibb's formulation of Potassium Penicillin G, but *under $13* to buy the identical tablets from one of four other manufacturers—a difference of more than 700 percent.

It's not surprising, then, that a survey of 60 pharmacies in New York City conducted by Consumers Union found the same quantity of the same drug (tetracycline) costing from $0.79 to $7.45! There are few, if any, other markets that tolerate such enormous price disparities between identical commodities. Why does it exist in prescription drugs? The answer can be found in the U.S. pharmaceutical industry, which for the past twenty years has been one of the top two profit-making businesses in the country. The big pharmaceutical companies have worked hard to perpetuate the myth that generic drugs are not as "safe" or as "good" as their brand-name versions. This *is* a myth and has been denounced as such by any number of impartial task forces, government agency heads, and academicians. Brand-name versions of drugs may cost more, but the cheaper generic versions are often made by the same manufacturer. A study by the nonprofit Council on Economic Priorities showed that a significant number of manufacturers sell a single batch of a drug to several distributors. They, in turn market it under different names, at different prices.

Generic drugs are purchased by most big buyers—all military medical facilities, major hospital pharmacies, and many state and municipal health centers. In addition, a growing number of states are repealing the industry-sponsored "anti-substitution" laws which prohibit pharmacists from substituting generic equivalents for the expensive brand name scribbled on the prescription.

Therein lies the problem—most physicians are familiar only with the brand-name versions and prescribe them without thinking. This is to be expected, because the big pharmaceutical firms annually spend about $5,000 per physician to familiarize doctors with their high-priced products. The companies advertise in medical journals; they write to all medical students and doctors; they send free gifts (the first stethoscope and doctor's bag a medical student receives is just such a gift); and they employ a battalion of salespeople ("detail men") who visit doctors and leave them ample literature and free samples. Further, most of what doctors (and the public) hear about pharmacology comes to them through symposia, lectures, and articles paid for by the drug companies. Private physicians, overwhelmed by this data about drugs, rarely have the time, training, or inclination to look much further.

Unless they are prodded to do so. Once you've explained your interest in having a generic prescription it's a simple matter for the physician to look up the generic name (in the standard *Physicians Desk Reference* or any of several other books). In fact, in most states the doctor needn't bother—he or she can write the brand name and simply indicate that the pharmacist may substitute a generic.

But it's not enough to request "a generic" version: the price variation among the generics can be great. You've got to go a step further and ask for the least expensive version. Some pharmacists won't automatically give you the least expensive one, especially if they charge a percentage markup rather than a flat dispensing fee. Also, pharmacists can't stock all versions of all drugs, and some may have gotten into the practice of stocking the more expensive versions.

So, once again, it pays to comparison-shop, particularly for a medication which you will be taking regularly. Consumer studies have shown a great variation in price for the same brand-name drug among drugstores in the same neighborhood (even on the same block). And they're not always consistent—one pharmacy may be high-priced on some drugs and quite low on others. Telephone calls can sometimes elicit the information you need, if you've made sure to get a legible prescription. Some druggists are reluctant to give such information over the phone, but many will.

Pharmacists had a long-standing tradition of not advertising prices and of not giving price information over the telephone. A U. S. Supreme Court case led the way in the early 1970s to a change in that policy, and states and trade associations have been amending their old notions. As of this writing, the FTC is considering a nationwide rule designed to foster greater disclosure of prescription drug prices.

A final point about cutting costs: be sure that the quantity you buy is appropriate. Buying more than you'll need or buying too much of a highly perishable drug is a mistake, of course. But if you'll be taking the drug for a while, *and* if it is one that keeps well (which a pharmacist should be able to tell you), buying in quantity can save money. If you are over 55, you might consider joining the American Association of Retired Persons (1909 K Street, N.W., Washington, D.C. 20049) to take advantage of its nonprofit mail order pharmacy service.

THE GOVERNMENT'S ROLE

The federal government is responsible for all drugs that are sold (prescription and over-the-counter), while states are responsible for the conduct of pharmacists. You may know that the U. S. Food and Drug Administration (which is part of the Department of Health, Education, and Welfare) is responsible for ensuring the quality of any drugs allowed on the market. The FDA is perennially in a double bind—it is vigorously and regularly criticized by both the industry it regulates and the consumers it protects. The pharmaceutical industry believes that the agency is overly conservative about allowing new drugs on the market: unnecessarily finicky about the testing it requires from would-be marketers. (It is generally accepted that the FDA is the most stringent government regulator of its sort in the world.) On the other hand, consumer groups criticize the agency for its long practice of allowing safety testing to be conducted by those who seek to benefit from its results, and for its slowness in removing harmful substances (such as the carcinogenic Red Dye 2) or useless ones (many over-the-counter preparations) from the market.

There was a major change in the FDA's role in 1962, when Congress required that the agency begin to review all over-the-counter drugs for effectiveness, as well as safety. In other words, it was no longer enough that Preparation ZYX wasn't likely to harm you, its manufacturers had also to demonstrate that it had a reasonable chance of actually helping you. This was theoretically an important new protection for consumers, because relying on a useless concoction can keep someone from finding an effective remedy. But the task given to the FDA was an enormous one, as there were between 100,000 and 500,000 over-the-counter preparations available then (although they contained only about 200 active ingredients).

In the years since then the FDA has been reviewing, slowly, different categories of over-the-counter drugs, not only for safety and effectiveness problems but for misleading advertising as well. The FTC also has been cracking down on what purveyors of cold remedies and sedatives can say about their products.

There is a movement afoot to thoroughly overhaul the federal drug law (passed in 1938). The amendments proposed in 1978 included such consumer reforms as:

- ◆ Requiring that a patient be given understandable written information about each prescription.
- ◆ Increasing consumer participation in decisions about marketing new drugs.
- ◆ Prohibiting drug companies from bombarding physicians with gifts and free samples.
- ◆ Requiring pharmacists to post drug prices.
- ◆ Beefing up FDA enforcement procedures.

It is too early to tell if such a bill can withstand the massive lobbying which will undoubtedly be mounted in opposition. To find out if an amendment has been passed, and what it provides, contact the FDA, the FTC, or your local consumer agency. If you are interested in voicing your views, contact your congressional representatives.

If you have a complaint about a medication (particularly about what

(Courtesy of The New York Historical Society, New York City)

seems to be a defective batch), the place to register it is with the FDA. Write to: FDA, 5600 Fishers Lane, Rockville, Md. 20852, or contact the regional office nearest you (there are 21 of them).

FOOD AND DRUG ADMINISTRATION OFFICES

FDA DISTRICT OFFICE	ADDRESS	AREA CODE & NO.
Atlanta, Ga. 30309	880 W. Peachtree St., N.W.	404-881-3162
Baltimore, Md. 21201	900 Madison Ave.	301-962-3731
Boston, Mass. 02109	585 Commercial St.	617-223-5857
Brooklyn, N.Y. 11232	850 Third Ave.	212-965-5043
Buffalo, N.Y. 14202	599 Delaware Ave.	716-432-4483
Chicago, Ill. 60607	433 W. Van Buren St., Rm. 1222 Main P.O. Building	312-353-7126
Cincinnati, O. 45202	1141 Central Parkway	513-684-3501
Dallas, Tex. 75201	500 S. Ervay, Suite 470-B	214-749-2383

FDA DISTRICT OFFICE	ADDRESS	AREA CODE & NO.
Denver, Colo. 80202	500 U. S. Customhouse	303-837-4915
Detroit, Mich. 48207	1560 Jefferson Ave.	313-226-6260
Kansas City, Mo. 64106	1009 Cherry St.	816-374-3817
Los Angeles, Calif. 90015	1521 W. Pico Blvd.	213-688-3771
Minneapolis, Minn. 55401	240 Hennepin Ave.	612-725-2121
Nashville, Tenn. 37217	297 Plus Park Blvd.	615-251-7127
Newark, N.J. 07018	20 Evergreen Place. East Orange, N.J.	201-645-6365
New Orleans, La. 70130	423 Canal St., Rm. 222, U. S. Customhouse Bldg.	504-589-2420
Orlando, Fla. 32802	P.O. Box 118	305-855-0900 305-855-5070
Philadelphia, Pa. 19106	2nd and Chestnut, Rm. 1204	215-597-0837
San Francisco, Calif. 94102	50 United Nations Plaza, Rm. 524	415-556-2682
San Juan, P.R. 00905	P.O. Box S4427, Old San Juan Station	809-753-6130
Seattle, Wash. 98174	Federal Office Bldg. 909 First Ave., Rm. 5003	206-442-5258

Be sure to save the container and any remaining contents.

It is worth remembering that the FDA's task has always been enormous (there are now 60,000 prescription drugs and 200,000 over-the-counter preparations on the market). It has been known to make major mistakes. So you can't rely on FDA approval as a complete guarantee of the safety or effectiveness of any drug.

WHAT TO EXPECT FROM YOUR PHARMACIST

Pharmacists often know a good deal more about the drugs they dispense than do physicians. They should be familiar with (or able to check on) probable interactions of drugs and the proper way of taking and storing medication. However, they rarely individually mix medicines any more; nowadays their role is often limited to measuring out a small quantity of medication from a larger container.

Some pharmacies maintain patient profiles or records on their customers. Notations about what other medications you are using can enable them to warn you if you are about to take contraindicated drugs. This only works, of course, if you buy all your medication from one pharmacy or remember to tell the druggist exactly what else you are taking.

There are two pharmaceutical services you can take advantage of. First, ask the pharmacist any questions you have about the medicine being dispensed, particularly about the optimum conditions for taking it and for storing it. And be certain that all the necessary information is put on the label: don't count on your memory. The label should state: the date, your name, the name of the medication, plus all instructions for taking it—the dosage, time, etc.

Pharmacists are licensed by the state, so any complaints about a pharmacy should be directed to your state board of pharmacy.

IN CONCLUSION

When you are ill it is comforting to think of your doctor as knowing exactly what medication you should take, when, and in what quantity, in order to get better. Comforting, but self-deluding. There are too many prescription drugs on the market and too many physicians relying solely on the drug company advertising for information about them. Some doctors prescribe medication when it would be better to let the illness run its natural course. They often do it because their patients *expect* a prescription as the fruit of every visit to the doctor. Finally, it is impossible for a physician to bear in mind every negative reaction to medication that you've ever had and a complete list of all substances you are currently ingesting (ranging from self-prescribed vitamins to substantial amounts of alcohol).

Being an effective consumer means being an aggressive one. Whenever medication is prescribed, tell the doctor—whether or not he or she asks about it:
    your history with medicines;
    all drugs, vitamins, alcohol that you ingest.
Remember to ask (don't wait to see if it's mentioned):
    what your diagnosis is;
    what the prescription is for;
    when you should take the drug (at what time of day, with or without food);
    whether you should avoid any other medication or foods or activities (like driving);
    whether you should expect any side effects.

The best way to be aware of what the drugs prescribed for you are and what they may do is to buy a consumer directory to the commonly prescribed drugs to use as a reference book. Two excellent ones are *The New Handbook of Prescription Drugs,* by Richard Burack, M.D., with Fred Fox, M.D. (gives drug-by-drug description and wholesale catalogue prices), and *The People's Pharmacy,* by Joe Graedon (treats nonprescription drugs and home remedies as well).

SELECTED BIBLIOGRAPHY

BURACK, RICHARD, M.D., *with* FRED J. FOX, M.D. *The New Handbook of Prescription Drugs.* New York: Ballantine Books, 1976.

GRAEDON, JOE. *The People's Pharmacy.* New York: St. Martin's Press, 1976.

The Medicine Show, by the editors of *Consumer Reports.* Mount Vernon, N.Y.: Consumers Union, revised periodically.

25

Hearing aids

> It is silent, painless and invisible, yet more people suffer from it than from heart disease, cancer, blindness, tuberculosis, venereal disease, multiple sclerosis and kidney disease put together. — "Deafness—The Silent Epidemic," quoted in *Hear Ye! Hear Ye!—A Study of Hearing Aid Sales Practices in Queens* (New York Public Interest Research Group, Inc., 1974)

In 1974 a 20-year-old Queens College student named Janet Lichten visited several hearing-aid dealers to have her hearing checked, complaining of trouble hearing in the classroom. Four out of the five dealers who "tested" her recommended a hearing aid. If she'd taken their advice, Ms. Lichten would have spent approximately $350 on a device that could not possibly have helped her. In fact, she was clinically deaf in her left ear (from birth), a condition which could not be corrected.

Ms. Lichten was performing a survey for a consumer research group and had previously had her true condition verified by a full battery of tests done by the college Speech and Hearing Clinic. The survey for which she and four other volunteers gathered data corroborated what earlier studies had found: that hearing-aid dealers are frequently wildly incorrect in their diagnoses and regularly suggest hearing aids when they are not needed or could not possibly help. Such dealers have a built-in conflict of interest, since their livelihood comes from selling hearing aids. In general, the tests they use to measure hearing loss are inadequate. Sometimes test environments are not soundproof—which is like taking an eye test outdoors on a foggy day. In the study in which Ms. Lichten participated (*Hear Ye! Hear Ye!—A Study of Hearing Aid Sales Practices in Queens,* New York Public Interest Research Group, Inc., 1974), not one of the nine dealers visited examined people in a soundproof room. At one place the phone rang repeatedly and the patient could hear several conversations while she was being "tested"!

Approximately 15 million people in this country have impaired hearing (one fifth of whom are school-age children). Most of them have not seen a doctor about their problem, although three million Americans do wear hearing aids. Many of those who have not sought medical help could have their hearing drastically improved (even restored to normal) by medical treat-

---

CAST OF CHARACTERS INVOLVED WITH
HEARING PROBLEMS

OTORHINOLARYNGOLOGIST — physician specializing in diseases of the ear, nose, and throat.

OTOLARYNGOLOGIST — physician dealing with ear and throat disease (but sometimes used as a short form for the ear, nose, and throat physician).

OTOLOGIST — physician who is exclusively an ear specialist.

Any one of the above professionals should be the first person contacted when a hearing impairment is suspected.

CERTIFIED AUDIOLOGIST — a health professional trained to diagnose and work with hearing impairments. Certification today requires a college degree; at least one year of graduate school; an internship; and passing a graduate examination. Audiologists often work at hospitals and clinics. They are well qualified to advise on and carry out hearing rehabilitation programs, and some dispense hearing aids.

HEARING-AID DEALER — a seller of hearing aids. They sometimes call themselves "hearing consultants" or "hearing-aid audiologists" or "hearing counselors." They may refer to their stores as "hearing centers" or "hearing clinics" or "speech and hearing centers." (The FTC is working to outlaw all of these representations.)

---

ment. Sometimes it's as simple as the removal of ear wax; at other times corrective surgery is required.

Hearing loss can be caused by a variety of illnesses and other factors, including the aging process. There are different kinds of hearing impairments, the major ones being "conductive" and "sensorineural." A conductive problem involves some failure in the tissue and bone system, which can frequently be corrected by surgery. A sensorineural problem means that there is damage to the nerve centers, with a hearing aid the usual, although imperfect, remedy.

Hearing impairment is a major disability because of the way it affects one's life. Happening slowly and often denied by those whom it affects, hearing loss can cause its sufferers to become withdrawn, to lose self-confidence, and even to become paranoid. The fear of being classified as "deaf" keeps many from seeking help.

Special problems are involved for children who are hard-of-hearing. Children born with hearing impairments or who develop them at an early age are sometimes misdiagnosed as retarded or disturbed. Even when the condition is correctly perceived and treated, a child born with a severe hearing loss often develops six to eight years slower than his or her peers. If these children are not given help as soon as the problem is discovered, they may also develop severe personality problems.

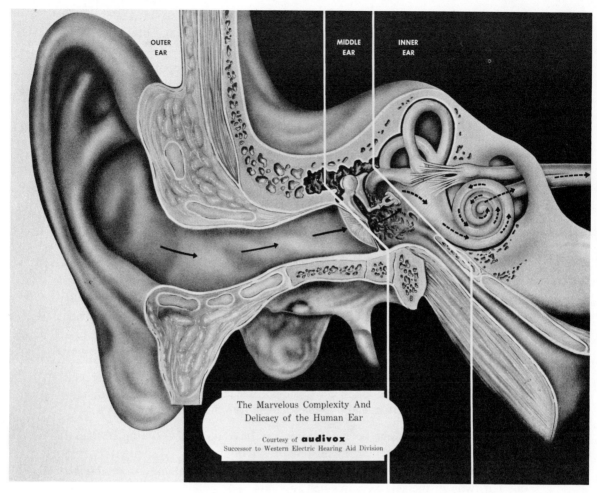

The Marvelous Complexity And
Delicacy of the Human Ear

Courtesy of **audivox**
Successor to Western Electric Hearing Aid Division

(Courtesy the American Museum of Natural History)

WHAT NOT TO DO ABOUT IT

Many people seeking treatment for a possible hearing problem go directly to a hearing-aid dealer. This is a serious mistake.

Hearing-aid dealers are salespeople, not medical professionals. You would never go straight to a medical supply store for crutches if you thought you'd broken your leg. Neither should you go directly to a hearing-aid dealer if you suspect that you have a hearing problem.

First, many common hearing problems are not correctable by a hearing aid. Second, some people who suspect that they have hearing problems simply don't. And finally, loss of hearing *can* be (although it usually isn't) a sign of a more serious medical problem, like a tumor, which requires immediate treatment by a physician.

Most dealers have only a high school degree and possibly some on-the-job training. Their trade association, the National Hearing Aid Society, has attempted to upgrade the occupation by offering certification to dealers who complete a course, pass an examination, and meet certain other requirements. About 15 percent of the country's 15,000 dealers—a small minority —have been certified. But even those dealers are usually poorly trained. The course, for example, consists of twenty weeks of correspondence school, with no practice in testing hearing or in fitting aids.

In fact, most of what these dealers know comes from two sources. They gain experience by practicing on their customers; and they are given selling lessons by the hearing-aid manufacturers.

THE BUSINESS OF SELLING HEARING AIDS

The manufacturers offer dealers all kinds of hard-sell advice. They include blatant lies and scare tactics about the consequences of not buying an aid immediately. Not surprisingly, the dealers are urged to push the more expensive models. (Two "training guides" put out by major manufacturers are called *How to Convert Objections into Sales* and *How to Get in the Door* [FTC Hearing Officer's Report, 1977].) One of the choice tidbits from another manual suggests a dialogue to be used on a reluctant potential customer.

> How many people don't come to visit you any more? Why? Because you act like a bump on the log in conversation. Because you don't answer right— you feel uncomfortable, and that makes them feel uncomfortable.*

For years, door-to-door hearing-aid sellers have done a booming business. They've offered a "free hearing test with no obligation." As might be expected, these "tests" almost always uncover a hearing problem, correctable by one (or two) of the salesperson's hearing aids.

The high-pressure techniques used are similar to those found in other door-to-door selling situations (see chapter 7 for more detail). What is different, though, is the tragic result. The people most vulnerable to door-to-door sellers are the elderly and the parents of hearing-impaired children. A recent FTC inquiry uncovered dozens of examples of people whose condition went uncorrected while they bought and wore (sometimes for years) hearing aids that were next to useless.

HEARING AIDS

A hearing aid is basically a miniature amplifying system—it makes existing sounds louder. It does not screen out "good" or welcome sounds, like conversation, from background noise. There are four basic types of aids, available in a myriad of models. They are worn either in the ear, over the ear, in eyeglasses, or on the body. The one worn entirely in the ear is most preferred by new users, because it is the least visible. But it is also the least

* Beltone Consultants Manual (Section IV-39), quoted on p. 87 of *FTC Hearing Officer's Report.*

powerful, and is probably appropriate for less than 20 percent of those who wear aids.

Various governmental hearings have shown the huge markups built into sales of hearing aids. (The average one costs between $350 and $400.) For example, if the cost of the parts, labor, *and* advertising for an aid costs $75, it will probably sell for $350—a markup of 367 percent. Interestingly, a small transistor radio, which is of equivalent complexity and made of comparable materials, can be bought for under $15. A number of elements create this kind of market, including the fact that most dealers sell relatively few hearing aids.

Regrettably, too, quality control is poor. Studies have shown that aids often do not meet the manufacturer's own specifications. Two identical brand and model instruments may differ substantially in performance.

Prescribing the appropriate hearing aid is a tricky business, even for a qualified professional. Many correctly prescribed hearing aids prove unwearable. An initial period of adjustment is always required, and the customer's motivation plays a large part in determining whether he or she will ever be comfortable wearing the aid.

The four kinds of hearing aids. Top left: eyeglass aid; top right: in the ear; bottom left: over the ear; bottom right: on the body. (Drawing by Jane Freeman)

To protect yourself from spending money on an aid which you will not wear, buy it on a trial basis. Many reputable dealers will permit a wearer to return the aid after the trial period (30 or 60 days, usually). The dealer will refund the price paid minus a rental charge, usually about $1 a day. Some states, like New York, require dealers to offer this option.

COMMON LIES—TURN A DEAF EAR TO THEM

♦ "If you don't get a hearing aid soon, your hearing will get worse. The nerves deteriorate unless they are exercised." (Nonsense! An aid will not affect the progress of a hearing disorder. And it's muscles which deteriorate through non-use.)

♦ "With this hearing aid, your hearing will be back to normal—it'll be like before you had a hearing problem." (Hearing aids cannot enable people to hear normally. There is always some distortion.)

♦ "If you are hard of hearing in both ears, two hearing aids will be better than one. Stands to reason, doesn't it?" (Wearing two aids is more troublesome than wearing one and rarely works well. Some experts believe it should never be prescribed; others say only for certain cases.)

♦ "This hearing aid will be invisible—really undetectable. No one will know." (Sorry, but hearing aids do show, even the in-the-ear variety usable by people with very mild hearing loss.)

♦ "This model is a great improvement, a real scientific breakthrough. It eliminates background noise so you hear conversation more clearly." (Background noise, which the hard-of-hearing are not accustomed to, is amplified by an aid, just like everything else. A period of adjustment is usually needed so the new wearer can learn to screen out noise, as everyone does normally.)

♦ "Of course, you get what you pay for. The more expensive models will work better for you." (Not so. There seems to be no correlation between cost and quality.)

THE LAW

Laws regarding the licensing of hearing-aid dealers have been passed by more than forty-one states since 1960. Unfortunately, they are largely ineffective, for a number of reasons. Many contain "grandfather" clauses which allow anyone who sold hearing aids before the law was passed to continue doing so without meeting the new legal requirements. Few provide any real protection against incompetent audiological testing, poor fitting of hearing aids, or gross misrepresentation of the hearing aids offered for sale. Enforcement of even the most minimal provisions rarely exists. Most licensing boards are dominated by hearing-aid dealers who are not anxious either to receive complaints or to prosecute them vigorously. In addition, their funding is usually totally insufficient.

In the mid-1970s, the federal government stepped in to protect the hearing-aid buyer. Following the lead of several states, the Food and Drug Administration issued an important regulation which took effect in August 1977. Its major provisions are:

◆   Hearing-aid dealers may sell an aid only if the buyer has a prescription for one from a physician, written within the last six months. *But* if the buyer is 18 or older, he or she can decide to give up this protection by signing a waiver statement. This is a potential loophole because some dealers will pressure potential buyers to avoid the "expense" of going to a doctor.

◆   Dealers must give every potential buyer, *before* he or she decides to buy an aid, a User Instructional Brochure. The brochure contains:

   1. information on the particular hearing aid's operation, maintenance, and repair;
   2. technical data on the aid;
   3. a warning about certain conditions which require consultation with a doctor;
   4. a statement that an aid will neither restore normal hearing nor improve a hearing impairment;
   5. a discussion of the need for a medical evaluation and, for children, an audiologist's evaluation as well.

The Federal Trade Commission has also become concerned with problems related to dealers' misrepresentations about hearing aids and with their selling techniques.

Where does this leave you? If you have been unjustly treated by a hearing-aid dealer, your best recourse is to complain in writing to the state licensing board, and send a copy of your letter to either the FDA or the FTC (depending on whose rule seems more applicable—send it to both if you're unsure). If a physician recommended the dealer, be sure to tell him or her too.

Quackery

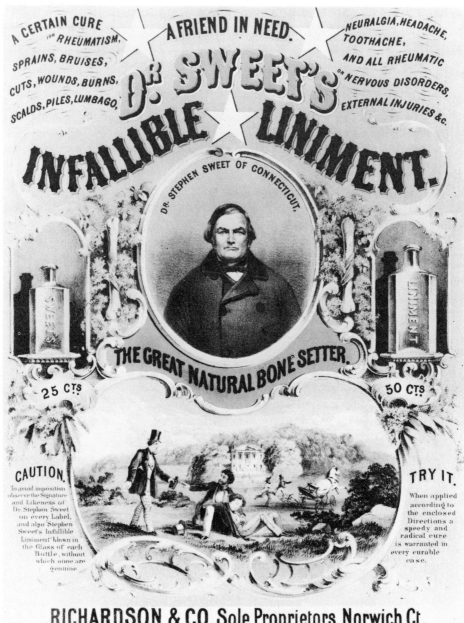

QUIZ

	TRUE	FALSE
1. More than fifteen times as much money is spent on arthritis quackery as on arthritis research.	——	——
2. The breasts are glands (not muscles). Therefore, their size is unaffected by exercise.	——	——
3. Ninety-five percent of all baldness can't be treated.	——	——
4. Large doses of "natural" vitamins can be harmful.	——	——
5. For a cancer patient, any "harmless" cure can be lethal.	——	——

The answer to all five questions is "true."

The number of victims affected and the almost unimaginable harm caused by medical quackery make it the worst consumer rip-off of all. The Arthritis Foundation estimates that arthritis patients alone spend $485 million each year on such frauds and rackets—more than fifteen times the amount spent on arthritis research.

The total annual cost of quackery to Americans has been estimated at $2 billion. This figure does not account for deaths caused, conditions worsened, or essential time lost by the victims. A district attorney in Los Angeles who prosecuted medical quacks said: "Quackery kills more people than those who die from all crimes of violence put together. It is public crime number one."*

People suffering from cancer or arthritis are particularly susceptible to fake schemes. They are often desperate for relief, but medical science has no complete and reliable cure for them. Arthritis (a group of separate ailments rather than a single disease) can be controlled, with varying degrees of success, by medical treatment, but not cured. Cancer (also a number of different illnesses) often *can* be cured, but only if detected early enough. The millions of arthritics and cancer patients who forgo legitimate medical treatment when they fall into the hands of quacks are risking their lives. Time is of the essence in treating most serious diseases. To delay medical treatment of cancer may render it untreatable. Letting arthritis progress unchecked makes it impossible to reverse its crippling effects, when they might have been avoided.

Unfortunately, there are so many sufferers of these two diseases alone (more than 675,000 Americans develop cancer each year and at least 20 million have some form of arthritis) that any worthless scheme has a large pool of potential takers. Even preposterous treatments, like sitting in a bath

* John Miner, quoted in Senator Warren G. Magnuson and Jean Carper, *The Dark Side of the Marketplace* (Englewood Cliffs, N.J.: Prentice-Hall, Inc., 1968), p. 159.

of colored light emanating from a miraculous machine, or eating huge quantities of grapes, attract some people.

Worthless remedies sometimes appear to be successful. Many physical ailments will respond positively to a "placebo" (a sugar pill or other non-medicinal substance given by a physician whom the patient trusts). It has been well documented, for example, that a substantial number of head-cold sufferers feel much better after being given *anything*. Some serious illnesses, including cancer and arthritis, have spontaneous remissions, during which the symptoms of the disease (but not the disease) disappear, leaving the patient feeling well and "cured." When a minor ailment runs its course, or a remission phase of a more serious one sets in, or a patient temporarily feels better, for any reason, phony "treatments" are quick to take credit for the improvement.

The number of people who try worthless potions and devices in order to shed a few pounds or enlarge their breasts or stop losing their hair is legion. Quacks have offered to cure or change just about everything that people are unhappy about relating to their bodies (and their psyches). Those people may only lose money. But others may not be so lucky—fad diets and offbeat remedies can endanger health.

Quacks, like their cures, come in all shapes and sizes. Some use the title "Dr." although they haven't progressed beyond high school. And some of them use unusual titles like "Philosopher of Naturopathy" or "Doctor of Metaphysics." A few are physicians who have rejected legitimate medicine. Many are ruthless entrepreneurs. Others believe they are true healers. (Not that it makes much difference if you are harmed by a sincere or an insincere quack.) Some act in a cool, professional manner, while others are flamboyant or evangelical. They do share some similarities, though. Here's how to identify them.

CHARACTERISTICS OF MEDICAL CHARLATANS

1. Promises of a quick or easy cure for all. (Sometimes a single cure is offered for a wide variety of illnesses.)

2. Use of "testimonials" from patients to support the claims. Legitimate physicians don't bolster their prescribed treatment by boasting of their "cure" record.

3. Accusations against the medical establishment for rejecting the cure. Medical associations and government officials have been justly criticized on a number of counts, but not of wanting to perpetuate suffering or cause death. Researchers, foundations, and physician groups are, correctly, skeptical of new "cures" and demand valid scientific proof before using them on patients.

4. Statements that surgery, X rays, and drugs used by "traditional" doctors are useless. Quacks generally refuse consultation with reputable physicians.

5. Secretiveness about their methods. A legitimate researcher who uncovers a useful treatment is eager to share it with the medical world, as it brings success, respect, even remuneration.

6. Isolation from legitimate associates, hospitals, and scientific facilities. Their chief supporters are usually laypeople (sometimes famous ones) who are not qualified to make medical judgments.

7. Manner of obtaining patients. Quacks advertise via the slick media, solicit door-to-door, and go on lecture tours. They do not receive recommendations from physicians or hospitals. Sometimes they appear at revivalist-type meetings or are associated with organizations devoted to spreading the word of the cure.

These illustrations are used as propaganda to scare people away from legitimate medical treatments.

WHY ISN'T SOMETHING BEING DONE ABOUT THIS?

The business of selling ineffective and/or harmful medical treatment, devices, and drugs to people is a highly profitable one. It is widespread and deeply rooted—efforts by the government and others concerned with preventing such profiteering on the sick have only limited success.

There are laws designed to stop phony healers and worthless treatments and to keep drugs from reaching their intended victims. Three federal agencies are involved—the Food and Drug Administration (for dangerous products or drugs which have not met the FDA's pre-marketing standards or for mislabeling), the Federal Trade Commission (for fraudulent advertising or unfair or deceptive acts), and the Postal Service (when the mail is used). State and local agencies are in the picture too, but are usually too understaffed and weak to do much, so the job is left to the federal government.

The agencies have been successful in getting rid of some quackery, but it is a long, difficult legal battle to go after a huckster, and almost impossible to keep a determined one out of business. It took the FTC sixteen years simply to get the meaningless word "liver" removed from "Carter's Little Liver Pills." The FDA spent ten years trying to halt the selling of the worthless

"Hoxsey cancer treatment." Often quacks who are caught make a minor change in their product or treatment or move elsewhere and stay in business. The laws are not forceful enough, it seems, and the phony healers are often amazingly tenacious.

A number of "clinics" run by quacks and catering to Americans have sprung up in Mexico, just over the border. They stay clear of our laws, while attracting hordes of American patients.

FOR MORE INFORMATION

If you want to check on the reliability of a proposed course of treatment, contact the nonprofit foundations set up to evaluate research and disseminate information about disease treatment. There are a number of foundations for the major diseases (many with local chapters). They include:

The Arthritis Foundation, Inc.
475 Riverside Drive
New York, N.Y. 10027

The American Cancer Society
777 Third Avenue
New York, N.Y. 10017

Also, the American Medical Association will send you material on any suspect method of treatment. Write to:

Division of Libraries and Archival Services
American Medical Association
535 N. Dearborn
Chicago, Ill. 60610

IF YOU'VE FOUND A QUACK

If you have been treated or offered treatment by someone you believe to be a quack, your warning can help others. Contact your state agency that licenses physicians (often the Health Department) *and* your local medical society. If a "drug" or device is involved, tell the U. S. Food and Drug Administration (contact a district office near you or the main office at 5600 Fishers Lane, Rockville, Md. 20852; 301-443-1240). If materials reached you through the mails, your nearest Postal Service Inspection Service headquarters should also be informed.

CHIROPRACTORS: A SPECIAL CASE

By even mentioning chiropractic in this chapter, we risk losing the confidence of some of the many people who believe that chiropractic has improved their health. But all reliable evidence convinces us that chiropractic and some overreaching practitioners of it have harmed many patients, either directly or indirectly, by preventing them from seeking timely medical treatment.

Basically, chiropractic is a form of healing based on a theory (developed by a layman in the nineteenth century) that misalignments of the vertebrae or "subluxations" are the principal cause of disease. Chiropractors are not physicians and have very limited training, almost none of it related to the diagnosis of disease (until 1942 one could obtain a Doctor of Chiropractic degree by mail order).

Physicians have opposed the acknowledgment of chiropractic as a healing art, but chiropractors have succeeded in gaining licensure in all the states. This gives them respectability, although the state licensing agencies do not allow them to prescribe drugs or perform surgery.

Undoubtedly, chiropractic has helped some people with back problems to feel better. Chiropractors themselves are often felt to be more accessible than medical doctors (this may result from their spending more time with "patients" or just from a general absence of the aloofness that is often associated with physicians). However, there is also a general absence of broad medical knowledge, with a resulting inability to warn patients of danger signs that call for immediate treatment by a physician. There are countless stories of people who died because symptoms of disease were ignored or grossly misdiagnosed by chiropractors.

Consumers Union, the most reputable and reliable private consumer testing organization, conducted a six-month study of chiropractic to try to weigh its claims of healing against the traditional hostility of the medical establishment. In no uncertain terms, CU concluded that the basic theory of chiropractic should have been totally discarded along with such other nineteenth-century "medical" ideas as bleeding and purging to cure disease. It found fairly widespread evidence of harmful consequences to patients from chiropractic manipulations. In summation, the organization found "that chiropractic is a significant hazard to many patients. Current [state] licensing laws, in our opinion, lend an aura of legitimacy to unscientific practices and serve to protect the chiropractor rather than the public."†

At the very least, see a chiropractor only after consulting a physician.

† Consumers Union, *Guide to Consumer Services* (Mount Vernon, N.Y., 1977), p. 265.

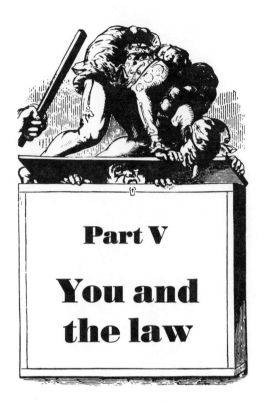

Part V

You and the law

27

Lawyers: devils or advocates

The Devil makes his Christmas pie of lawyers' tongues.   —English proverb

Go to law for a sheep—and lose your cow.   —German proverb

When God wanted to chastise mankind He invented lawyers.
                                                —Russian proverb

"Virtue in the middle," said the Devil, as he sat down between two lawyers.   —Danish proverb

Everyone's idea of a lawyer at work: the invincible Perry Mason.

Distrust of lawyers is widespread and time-honored. But whether they deserve such negative feelings is difficult to say. There are some 400,000 lawyers in the United States today. According to popular stereotype, some are shoddy, money-grubbing ambulance chasers; some are high-level influence peddlers entirely lacking in scruples or humility; and some are trial lawyers whose aggressive cross-examination leaves witnesses limp and gasping for air. Few lawyers, however, fall into one of these stereotypes. The large majority of lawyers render far more routine and undramatic services for their clients. They perform them with varying skill, at a wide range of cost to their clients.

There are three basic occasions when people usually consult a lawyer. The first is when they need advice: before starting a business, signing a contract, or buying a house; when considering separation or divorce; or after a serious accident. Obviously the magnitude of the undertaking will affect the need for legal advice.

You may also need a lawyer to effect specific legal changes or draw up legal documents. This is when most middle-class people use lawyers—to draw up wills, to arrange for a divorce, to buy or sell a piece of real estate. In most cases it will be better in the long run to let a carefully selected lawyer handle these matters or at least advise you on how to do so.

And finally, a lawyer is needed to bring or defend a lawsuit. Thanks to the popular media, lawyers are associated in most people's minds with

(Reprinted by permission of Charles Scribner's Sons from *The Confessions of Artemas Quibble* by Arthur Train, copyright 1911 by Charles Scribner's Sons)

courtrooms. But although trials are the most dramatic and visible evidence of legal work, the fact is that most of them rarely go to court—probably 90 percent of all legal work is unconnected with actual lawsuits. Since trials are unpredictable and expensive, lawyers work hard to keep their clients out of court. And of those cases which do go to court, the vast majority are settled without a trial. If you are sued, it is possible to defend yourself in some cases. But it is difficult at best, especially if the case is complex, the stakes high, or your opponent's lawyer either very skilled or very aggressive.

Bringing a lawsuit yourself is also difficult (except for small claims court cases; see the following chapter) and, unless you have some legal experience, definitely not advisable. Undoubtedly the judicial process could be simplified and made far more accessible to laypeople. However, right now it is unduly complicated, and judges and lawyers are in no hurry to simplify the system. So the odds are stacked heavily against you if you try to prosecute your own case.

Before hiring any lawyer, determine what you will be charged. Lawyers' fees are a topic of great interest and some misunderstanding. They are the greatest source of complaints filed against lawyers, often because the fees are never openly discussed by lawyers and their clients. One recent study demonstrated that most people greatly overestimate what lawyers will charge for particular services (and therefore don't go to them).

LEGAL FEES

There are four different ways of billing for legal services, and many lawyers use one or more for different situations. Usually court fees and other out-of-pocket expenses are added to the bill. The billing methods most commonly used are:

FLAT RATE—This method is practicable only for routine matters where the amount of legal work is easily determined. These include wills, uncontested divorces, name changes, incorporation of a small business, and other uncomplicated matters. This billing method makes comparison-shopping possible, particularly in areas where lawyers advertise.

BILLING BY THE HOUR—This method is particularly suitable when it is impossible to predict what the legal representation will involve—it is commonly used for corporate legal work, for contested divorces, and for other complex matters. The rate (which includes all attendant secretarial and paralegal services) covers telephone consultations, negotiations, and all other uses of the lawyer's time. It can run from $20 per hour to well over $100, depending on the geographic location and the age, experience, and skill of the lawyer. Lawyers often charge a higher rate for days spent in court.

PERCENTAGE OF THE AMOUNT INVOLVED—This system is used when the legal task involves handling a sum of money, as in purchasing a house or executing a will. It enables you to know be-

forehand what it will cost, but this method often bears no relationship to the amount of work involved.

CONTINGENCY FEE — Agreeing on a contingency fee means that the
client pays a substantial percentage (usually 25 to 40 percent) of
the amount recovered *if* the lawyer wins the case, and nothing if he
or she loses. The percentage usually varies according to the stage at
which the case is settled or won. This method is typically used for
clients who may win a sizable sum because of an accident or other
wrong suffered.

Lawyers sometimes ask for a *retainer*—a sum of money paid at the
beginning or on a regular basis by clients who have a good deal of
legal work done. Usually it is only an advance against the total fee,
which is determined by one of the other methods.

Whatever method is used, lawyers charge for their time (in preparing documents, on the phone, in the office or in court). So don't
expect legal advice for free.

As puzzling as legal fees may seem, even more boggling is the fact that
there often is no clear, correct answer to a legal question. The law (which
consists of legislation, court cases, and regulations promulgated by administrative agencies) is chock-full of ambiguities and unanswered questions. So a
good lawyer can often give you only a reading of the situation and some
educated advice—beware of one who is 100 percent positive of the answers
in complicated situations.

HOW TO FIND A GOOD LAWYER

A little background about the legal profession may help you in selecting a
lawyer. Most lawyers have completed four years of college, followed by
three years of law school. They must then pass a state bar exam. Lawyers
are trained as generalists, but most specialize as soon as they begin practicing law. (There are too many fields of law for any one person to become
proficient in more than a few.) Many lawyers *consider* themselves generalists, by which they mean they regularly handle the limited range of legal
issues which typically confront individuals or small businesses. Those lawyers, however, would be the wrong people to go to with major corporate
legal problems or complex tax questions.

The legal profession is organized into large law firms, which usually handle
the legal affairs of major corporations, and small firms or individual practitioners, who serve individuals and small businesses. Large firms have a
greater breadth of experience and knowledge to tap, although their lawyers
(partners, who own the firm, and associates, who work for it) specialize.
Offices are often plusher and more impressive (with higher overhead meaning
higher rates, of course), but the service is less personalized for all except the
largest clients. Individual lawyers or small firms, on the other hand, do give

more attention to individual cases and are better equipped to handle personal matters.

How can you best choose a lawyer? Here are some steps to take:

1. Analyze what you want—a one-time legal service (e.g., the drawing of a will); the establishment of a relationship with a lawyer whom you can turn to over the years; or the hiring of someone to handle your business' legal affairs. Try to determine (perhaps by talking with others) whether you have a particularly complicated problem or a relatively routine one.

2. Ask for referrals, *but* only from people who are able to judge well and who are likely to give you good advice. If you work for a business which has lawyers on staff they may be able to suggest someone. So may a bank officer you deal with or a stockbroker or a CPA. A friend or relative is a less reliable source, unless that person has had enough dealings with lawyers to have some sense of quality. If these sources fail, a university law school may work. Ask to speak to a professor who specializes in what you are interested in (family law, trusts and estates, real estate transactions, etc.—look at the law school catalogue if you are unsure), and ask for referrals. Many professors are helpful in this respect, as are law school librarians (often also lawyers).

Don't turn to strangers (such as ambulance drivers or court clerks) who may be receiving fees, payoffs, or additional business for making referrals, or to bar association "referral services." Local bar associations usually maintain lists of members who want more clients, but the associations rarely exercise any control over the quality or cost of those legal services, and make no attempt to refer the caller to a truly appropriate lawyer for his or her need.

Don't choose a lawyer on the basis of an advertisement—it is much safer to go on the personal recommendation of a trusted person. But do read the ads available in your community, to get an idea of prevailing rates, and don't hesitate to mention your findings to the lawyer you select.

Consumer directories to lawyers are available in a few places—they give such information as background, description of lawyer's practice, and fees charged. They can be helpful and give a good idea of comparative fees.

Until a couple of years ago lawyers (like doctors and other highly educated professionals) simply did not advertise. It wasn't "professional"; it was frowned upon if not totally forbidden by state bar associations; and, in many places, it was illegal. A landmark Supreme Court decision in 1977 changed that—states may no longer forbid advertising by lawyers, although they can restrict the kinds of advertising allowed.

Despite much furor on the part of many of the older, more established (and richer) bar associations and lawyers, advertising has now become commonplace in newspapers in some parts of the country. The advertising is usually for the small firms, individual practitioners, or clinics, and focuses on routine legal services, often at relatively low fees. Sometimes the ads state a specialty or an ability to handle foreign-language-speaking clients. As

(Wide World Photos)

might be expected, the rates of young, inexperienced lawyers are lower than those of older or large-firm lawyers.

3. Interview any seemingly good candidates—on the phone for an initial screening and in person if the lawyer seems right. (Many lawyers will give an initial consultation at no charge.) Use the interview to learn:

- how much of the lawyer's time is spent handling the kind of work you need done (the more, the better, as a general rule);
- how the lawyer bills;
- how comfortable he or she is discussing these matters and explaining things in comprehensible language;
- whether you are comfortable with the office and the way you are treated there.

Do trust your personal reaction to the person. You needn't be enormously fond of a lawyer, but you should respect and feel able to talk easily with him or her.

4. Tell any lawyer you are considering hiring exactly what you expect. You should seek:

- to know what's happening at all times on your matter (even though you'll pay for the phone calls and time involved, it's well worth it);
- to be told both sides of any complicated or problematic issue;

♦ to be involved in any key decisions, before they are made (the more routine the matter, the fewer of these there will be, of course);

♦ to have your affairs kept in confidence;

♦ to be given a full accounting of all charges.

Lawyers, like doctors, are often unused to dealing with people who seek both information and an active involvement in the professional services being rendered. If your lawyer isn't comfortable with that kind of arrangement, find another one.

5. Get any arrangement that you make, particularly about fees, in writing (in terms that you understand) and signed by both of you. *Consumer Reports* has even suggested that clients ask a new lawyer to sign a client-lawyer agreement (and had a sample one drawn up!). That seems to be overdoing it, but do embody your understanding in a letter.

IF YOU CAN'T AFFORD A LAWYER

Legal Aid (privately financed) and Legal Services (federally financed) offices give free legal services to some people who can't afford to hire a lawyer. But their clients must have a very low income, and the offices are often so understaffed that they can handle only certain types of cases (usually those of the most dire consequence). If you don't qualify for this free legal help, there are two other places to turn.

First, there are lawyers working for government agencies—federal, state, and local—paid for by your tax dollars, who may be able to help you with a legal problem. The U. S. Social Security Administration and the Internal Revenue Service, for example, are places to turn for legal advice. You run the chance of stumbling up against bureaucrats with narrow, parochial vision, but you may also get excellent, and free, advice from people who really know their subjects.

There is also a network of public interest lawyers who can give advice on the areas with which they are concerned: environmental, consumer, civil rights, etc. They even take selected cases to court, often at no charge to the client. For example, the American Civil Liberties Union (ACLU), the National Association for the Advancement of Colored People (NAACP), the Mexican American Legal Defense Fund (MALDEF), the National Organization for Women (NOW), may provide help, or at least referrals, if your problem involves an infringement of rights. Environmental organizations, like the Natural Resources Defense Council (NRDC) and the Environmental Defense Fund (EDF) handle cases of environmental concern.

If there is no lawyer who will handle your case for free, you might benefit from seeing a lawyer for a single consultation. One session might help you to handle the situation yourself—as in preparing you to defend a consumer case in a civil court. Many lawyers are not willing to give such self-help advice, but a growing number (particularly younger ones) are.

HOW TO GET THE MOST OUT OF YOUR LAWYER

Once you've selected a lawyer, you've got to remain vigilant if you want to be sure you're getting the best service possible.

Here are some dos and don'ts:

◆ *Do* give the lawyer all the facts. *Don't* try to make your side of a controversy appear more favorable by slanting it or by hiding facts.

◆ *Do* tell your lawyer of new developments as soon as they occur.

◆ *Do* make clear exactly what you want and *do* put your understanding in writing.

◆ *Don't* expect simple answers where they don't exist.

◆ *Don't* expect free advice.

◆ *Do* ask for and listen to an explanation of everything that is part of your case. Make notes if that will help you stay abreast.

◆ *Do* keep a timetable of key dates and call your lawyer to remind him or her of them.

◆ *Do* discuss fees at your initial appointment and whenever it seems relevant thereafter.

◆ *Do* ask for a fully itemized bill, one which you can understand.

◆ *Do* tell your lawyer any complaints you have about him or her or the staff as soon as they occur.

◆ *Do* remember that you've hired the lawyer and can fire him or her. (It is often difficult, however, to find another lawyer willing to step into a half-completed situation. So you might want to find the new lawyer first.)

DOING IT YOURSELF

General disenchantment with the legal profession, coupled with the do-it-yourself trend of the past few years, has led an increasing number of people to attempt to act as their own lawyers. They've been aided by the publication of how-to-get-a-divorce or write-a-will books and kits.

There is also a growing questioning of whether lawyers *should* be required for such routine transactions as drawing up wills, buying or selling real estate, changing names, or obtaining consensual divorces. If a couple can marry without the help of a lawyer, why shouldn't a couple without children be able to divorce by going through a similar simple administrative procedure? Why should a routine name change or adoption require an attorney's participation? In fact, a recent study of the legal profession concluded that "the bar should de-lawyer large numbers of problems for which an attorney's specialized training in legal analysis is not needed and which can be handled in a routine manner on a large volume basis."*

Unfortunately, the legal system is set up so that you generally do need a lawyer in order to take those legal steps with a reasonable degree of efficiency and certainty. The laws are more complex and finicky than they

* Sharon Tisher, Lynn Bernabei, and Mark Green, director, *Bringing the Bar to Justice—A Comparative Study of Six Bar Associations* (A Public Citizen Report, 1977).

need be. And the books which promise to help you obtain a divorce or write a will often do not enable even an intelligent, persistent layperson to do so. Doing it yourself can be risky in terms of the ultimate result. So, if you insist on handling a legal transaction by yourself, you'd be wise to find a lawyer who will give you an initial consultation and subsequent telephone or in-person advice if that becomes necessary. Such a lawyer should be able to spot potential problems and advise you if and why you need more help. Look for one who specializes in the procedure you want to undertake, and explain before making an appointment that you want only enough of the lawyer's time to allow you to act on your own behalf. (Naturally, this should cost you considerably less than if you turned the matter over to the lawyer.)

TWO NEW ALTERNATIVES

There are some 140 million Americans who have virtually no access to lawyers because of the expense involved and the difficulty of finding the right lawyer. Our legal system has not provided accessible, affordable, and dependable legal services for the vast majority of Americans, most of whom need a limited number of services performed. Two new ways of providing this basic legal help for middle-income people were developed in the early 1970s and hold out the potential of solving this problem: legal clinics and prepaid legal service plans.

Following the lead of some young lawyers in Los Angeles, a new kind of private legal office has sprung up in various parts of the country, usually in major cities. Calling themselves "clinics," these groups offer basic, standardized legal services at low cost—a sort of "no frills" legal alternative. By accepting only routine cases, systematizing their treatment of them, relying heavily on the support services of paralegals and secretaries, and cutting down on overhead, the clinic lawyers can sell their services at a price below the average.

The clinics often offer other convenience features—they tend to be located near where people live (many are in storefronts), to have bilingual staffs (where appropriate), and to maintain evening and Saturday hours. All in all, they can be an excellent way to cut down on the cost (and mystique) of legal services.

Some of the first clinics received favorable press and steady referrals from social and welfare agencies. Although they had to combat considerable flack from the bar associations, their business thrived. Unfortunately, since the use of the term "legal clinic" is not regulated in any way, a number of lawyers have tacked it on to their shingles in order to attract clients.

Here's how to tell if a so-called "clinic" is legitimate:

◆ Check its fees against those offered by other lawyers in ads—they should be at or near the lowest prices.
◆ Find out if they routinely use paralegals or assistants (who are paid much less than lawyers) to do initial interviewing, processing of forms, etc.
◆ Ask if the lawyers specialize. In most clinics they do. One does divorces and matrimonial work, another bankruptcies, etc.

◆ See if they refuse to handle long or complex cases or if they accept any and all clients (clinics do turn away nonroutine cases).

Prepaid legal service plans resemble health insurance. In return for small, regular payments, the members of such plans are assured free or low-cost legal help when they need it. The plans have been developed for groups of employees, union members, credit union shareholders, and others, sometimes as part of a comprehensive package of benefits. There are two basic types of plan: closed panel and open panel.

Closed panel plans hire a legal staff whose sole job is to serve members of the plan. The coverage is usually limited to certain common legal needs (avoiding very complex cases, which can be expensive). For example, the plan developed by the New York City Municipal Employees Union provides legal services for its members in the following areas:

credit rating problems
debt problems
defense in any civil (i.e., noncriminal) lawsuit
divorces, separations, and annulments (with an extra $300 charge for a
    contested divorce—still well below the prevailing rate)
evictions
government agency representation
purchases of goods or services (but not real estate)
public utility problems
review of contracts (*before* signing)
wills (for employee and spouse)

Open panel plans merely permit members to go to any lawyer of their choosing who agrees to cooperate with the plan (and accept its rates). The lawyer is then reimbursed by the plan.

The closed panel is favored by consumer groups for its advantages—it costs less (because of specialization, payment of reasonable salaries, and use of mass delivery techniques similar to those employed by legal clinics) and builds in accountability. Most closed panel plans have both grievance procedures and planning committees or boards composed of members and legal staff to resolve conflicts and to improve the service.

For more information about prepaid legal services contact:

National Resource Center for Consumers of Legal Services
1302 18th Street, N.W.
Washington, D.C. 20036

COMPLAINING

If you are dissatisfied with your lawyer you can make your feelings known in several ways. Complain first to the lawyer, even if you believe it to be fruitless, as it strengthens your case for later action. In each state there is one agency or committee given the power (by the highest court) to handle complaints about lawyers. It may be part of the court system or may be a bar association committee. The grievance committee may put out a booklet or fact sheet telling you how to complain—call to see.

Unfortunately, bar association grievance committees are usually made up entirely of lawyers and they are very cautious about taking even the mildest sort of disciplinary action. They frequently bend over backwards to justify lawyers' behavior. And grievance committees will rarely become involved in fee disputes, even though these are the greatest source of client dissatisfaction with lawyers. They do act sometimes, though, and the mere sending of such a complaint letter will be enough to make some lawyers think twice about repeating questionable behavior.

Finally, if you believe that a lawyer owes you money (for example, for services not rendered, but which you paid for), use small claims court to make your case. If you are right and can make a clear statement of why you're right, you'll probably win. And what a sweet victory that would be!

BASIC LEGAL VOCABULARY

attachment: the legal taking of a debtor's property, usually to be sold to satisfy the debt.

attorney: lawyer (there's no difference).

bar association: trade association of lawyers—all states (and many cities) have them.

civil case: any lawsuit that is not criminal.

class action: court procedure that allows an unlimited number of plaintiffs who have essentially the same claim against a defendant to bring a single court case. This makes it possible for people to seek justice even if individual harm is small.

complaint: the initial document in a lawsuit in which the plaintiff explains what the problem is; given to the defendant with the summons.

contract: a binding agreement between two or more people or businesses, each of whom is to do or pay something. It is usually, but not necessarily, written.

defendant: the person (or business) sued.

garnishment: deduction of a portion of a debtor's salary and paying it directly to the creditor, usually after a court judgment.

jurisdiction: the scope of a court's power to hear cases (for example, most small claims courts lack jurisdiction over lawsuits for more than $1,000).

litigation: suing.

paralegal: a lawyer's assistant, trained to do interviewing, researching, drafting of documents, etc. Recently recognized as a new profession (although there were always some secretaries or clerks who filled such roles), their increased use could cut the cost of legal services.

plaintiff: the person (or business) who begins a lawsuit.

subpoena: a court paper which orders a person to appear in court. It can also require the person to bring certain papers or records (*subpoena duces tecum*).

summons: a legal paper that tells a defendant that a lawsuit has been started; served with the complaint, which tells what the suit is about.

test case: a lawsuit brought to establish a key legal principle. Often brought by interested organizations or public interest groups.

tort: any noncriminal wrong which one person commits against another; everything from hitting someone with a car to slander.

SELECTED BIBLIOGRAPHY

DENENBERG, HERBERT S., Pennsylvania Insurance Commissioner. *A Shopper's Guide to Lawyers.* Insurance Department, Harrisburg, Pa. 1973.

"How to Choose a Lawyer (and what to do then)." *Consumer Reports,* May 1977, p. 284.

28

State your case: small claims court

Can you answer "yes" to one or more of the following? If so, you qualify as a small claims court plaintiff!

1. Has a landlord refused to return your security deposit on an apartment?

2. Did a dry cleaner ruin a garment and refuse to pay you for it?

3. Did an ex-roommate cop out on part of the rent or utilities money he or she owed?

4. Was your luggage lost by a bus company which would not give you what it was worth?

5. Did someone whom you paid to do a job do it poorly, forcing you to have further work done?

6. Did you do work for someone who failed to pay you?

7. Did you lose a refrigerator full of food in a power blackout?

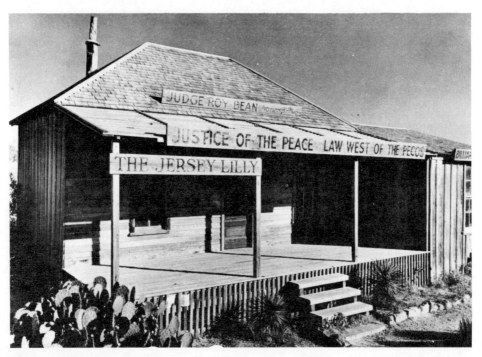

Small claims courts vary from state to state. (Andreas Feininger, *Life,* copyright 1944 Time Inc.)

In the early 1900s court reformers dreamed and schemed to set up "people's courts" where ordinary citizens could sue without suffering the crushing expense and delay of the regular court system. The speedy, low-cost justice which they envisioned is available today in most parts of the country, in "small claims courts" (also known as "justice of the peace" or "magistrate" courts).

SMALL CLAIMS IN A NUTSHELL

Small claims courts vary a great deal from state to state.* What they have in common is an informal, simplified court procedure set up to enable people to collect money in small cases without hiring an attorney.

When you sue in small claims court you've got several things going for you before you begin. The first is that the vast majority of plaintiffs win—often receiving less than they sued for, but recovering something. Second, the remedy is usually cheap; one 1973 nationwide study found that the majority of small claims court plaintiffs and defendants spent less than $25 for the filing fee and for all costs. Finally, as two recent studies of small claims court observed, the people suing derive a great deal of satisfaction from the very experience; they repeatedly say that the psychological benefits were at least as important as the money they recovered.

As the questionnaire at the beginning of this chapter indicates, you can use small claims court in an almost limitless number of situations. Basically, you can take your problem to small claims court if you have a complaint which you've tried to resolve in other ways; if you think you know who (individual, business, or both) is responsible; and if a dollar value, actual or estimated, can be put on your loss. Generally, small claims courts do not have the power to order someone to finish a job, to perform a service or to stop acting unlawfully. All they can do is order your adversary to pay you money, so you must be prepared to translate your gripe into a dollars-and-cents figure.

HOW TO BEGIN

Because small claims courts are usually part of larger courts, and are called by different names, it can be difficult to find the one in your area. Begin by looking in the phone book under "Courts" and calling the clerk of any of the lower noncriminal courts to ask.

Once you've located the court, you need to gather some basic information about how it operates. Many of the courts issue booklets which describe their workings: ask the clerk if one exists (local consumer agencies or groups

---

* As of 1976 eight states had no specialized, informal handling of small claims cases (Arizona, Delaware, Louisiana, Mississippi, South Carolina, Tennessee, Virginia, and West Virginia) and six had them available only in urban areas (Arkansas, Georgia, Kentucky, Montana, New Mexico, and Pennsylvania).

may also publish them). If there is a guide to the court, your task is easier; otherwise, find out from the court clerk:

- when the court is open for starting a case;
- how old you must be to sue (if you are underage, a parent or guardian must go with you);
- whether you or the defendant must live, work, or carry on business within the county (or other geographical area);
- how much you can sue for (a "small claim" in Texas is one for $150 or less; in Indiana it can go up to $3,000. If the amount owed to you is over the small claims limit, you may, if you wish, sue for less in order to bring the case in small claims court);
- how much the filing fee is (usually between $2 and $15);
- what the normal waiting time is between filing and trial;
- when trials take place (day or evening);
- how the notice of the case (summons and complaint) is served on the defendant;
- whether lawyers are allowed;
- whether the case will be heard by a judge or an arbitrator (referee)— you may have a choice.

Before you go to small claims court to file your claim, you must find the precise, legal name of the person or business you want to sue. If you skip this step and sue "Joe's Dry Cleaner," for example (which is the name on the sign outside or on your receipt), but the business is incorporated as "Joseph Hunter Dry Cleaners, Inc.," you are in trouble. You may win your case and then not be able to collect anything—because all the business' assets are in its proper name. There are ways of finding out the exact business name of your opponent. It may display a license or other official document which gives the company's legal name. Otherwise, you have to check with the county clerk or secretary of state. Procedures for doing this vary from place to place—ask the court clerk how to go about it.

PREPARING YOUR CASE

Because most small claims court plaintiffs win, you've got a superb chance of recovering money, if you have a reasonable case *and* if you prepare and present it properly. Here is how to do that.
- Sue for *all* expenses you've actually lost, as long as that doesn't put the total over the small claims court's limit. Think hard: include taxi fare to and from work because the car the defendant "repaired" wouldn't start; long-distance calls made to try to correct the matter which you're now suing about; wages lost; etc. The court can always cut down on the sum you've claimed, but it won't raise it. Usually, you will recover only the market value of an item (what it's worth now), not the cost of replacing it. And you'll have to pay for any benefit you received (such as a partial repair job).
- Put all the time you need into preparing for trial. Be sure all witnesses are there. A witness is anyone who saw the damaged goods or any part of the transaction which you're suing about. If necessary, you can get a *subpoena*

ordering them to appear (a subpoena may be useful for friendly witnesses too, if they have to explain taking time off from work).

◆   Arrange all documents in order, with a brief summary of any that are long or complex. Include: canceled checks or receipts, your own photographs (of broken furniture, a dented fender, etc.), and all complaint letters you wrote. (You can proceed even if you've lost some of the papers, though.)

◆   Organize and rehearse your story so you can tell it in a factual and concise manner. Make notes for yourself on the important points you wish to make. Don't be argumentative or theatrical—it will work against you.

◆   Remember that, at any time before the case is heard, both parties can reach a compromise or settlement. If you decide to settle, put your agreement in writing and have it signed by both parties. Keep one signed copy. Ask the clerk to look it over for you, if possible. The court may want you to file a copy of the settlement. If the amount involved is substantial or if your opponent has an attorney, you might be wise to get some legal advice before you sign a settlement.

It won't come up frequently, but you should be aware that a defendant can raise a *counterclaim*—a claim for money against you, based on the events which led to your case. If the counterclaim is for an amount higher than the small claims court's limit, the case may be transferred to a regular court. In any event, if the defendant puts in a counterclaim, be prepared to refute it. (This could be a problem for the plaintiff, but it rarely happens.)

An alternative to small claims court. (Copyright 1951
by Paramount Pictures Corporation. All rights reserved.)

AT THE TRIAL

Your opponent may try to delay the trial, hoping that you'll just go away. Courts will usually grant one postponement (or *adjournment*), especially if the defendant offers any justification for the request. If you are ready to proceed, object to any delay. Explain that you (and your witnesses) are losing valuable time (from work, if true), and that you can't afford the expense and inconvenience of repeated trips to the court. If the case is adjourned once because of defendant's non-appearance or at his or her request, ask the judge to "mark the case final" for the next time (meaning that no additional adjournments will be given).

When the defendant does not show up at all, ask the court to enter a *default judgment* in your favor. Some judges will do this on the spot; others may postpone the case to give the defendant one more chance. At this point, and at all others, be calm, reasonable, and non-dramatic. But be assertive.

Arrive on time for the trial, since the first step is usually a reading of the court calendar (i.e., the list of cases to be heard that day), and you may be penalized for not being there. Some courts grant adjournments by telephone, so you may want to call first to make sure your court date hasn't been changed. Bring your documents and any of your own notes which remind you of the details of your story.

Small claims court has been described as "high-volume, low-overhead, bargain basement (in the money sense) justice."† In other words, cases are moved through quickly and there is no time for frills or extra verbiage. The average case takes less than twenty minutes. So be especially careful to reduce your statement to a well-organized, bare-bones narrative (and caution any witnesses to do the same). As plaintiff, you go first: tell what happened, when, and what efforts you made to resolve the dispute before suing. Offer copies of all documents, photos, etc., and show the object itself if possible. Introduce any witnesses and let them make brief, factual statements.

The defendant is entitled to cross-examine you and your witnesses. When you are questioned, give truthful, precise, non-rambling answers (don't embroider), and if you don't know, can't remember, or aren't sure of an answer, say so.

After you've finished your presentation, the defendant is allowed to make a statement or bring in witnesses. If this procedure is unfamiliar to you or if you are particularly nervous about it, visit the court once as an observer before your case comes up.

Small claims court judges often help people to present their cases. They may ask witnesses questions; go to see, for example, the damaged car which is parked outside; and generally play an active and involved role, to see that justice is done. Some judges, however, are uncomfortable with such departures from tradition.

Your opponent may show up with an attorney, although most cases don't

---

† Douglas Matthews, *Sue the B*st*rds—The Victim's Handbook* (New York: Arbor House, 1973), p. 68.

warrant the expense. A few states absolutely prohibit lawyers in small claims cases. But where they are permitted, some businesses do use them. Don't worry if a lawyer appears for your adversary—studies have shown that in cases where only one side has a lawyer, the judge or arbitrator helps the unrepresented party with his or her case. If you have access to a lawyer who can spend a half hour or so helping you plan your case, that is a bonus, but it's not necessary.

Jury trials are not available in most small claims courts. A defendant who requests one (a rare occurrence) can usually get it but the case will be transferred to a higher court.

In some places, cases are heard by "arbitrators" or "referees," who are local lawyers volunteering their time. The general consensus is that arbitrators are somewhat more informal than judges, likely to interpret the law somewhat more broadly, and more inclined to make a compromise ruling or "split the difference."

The court's decision will be given to you at the end of the trial or by mail within a week or two. There is usually no right to appeal. This is no great loss, really, since a lawyer is usually needed for an appeal and most of the cases are too small to make hiring a lawyer feasible.

AFTER THE TRIAL

Winning plaintiffs in small claims court often face a problem in collecting their judgments. Some defendants will pay the money owed right away or after a letter reminding them to do so. (Such a letter should stress that you are writing in order to spare the defendant the time and expense of judgment collection procedures.) But some defendants won't pay voluntarily, and you will have to pursue them.

Collection procedures vary among the states, but they generally require you to take an aggressive role and, unfortunately, to advance additional fees (which are recoverable from your opponent). In most cases you will have to see that the judgment is formally "entered" (or registered on the court's books) and then enlist the services of a sheriff or marshal whose job it is to collect judgments. The two major collection tools available to the sheriff are seizure or *attachment* of a defendant's assets and *garnishment* of an individual's wages (i.e., automatic paycheck deductions).

A FINAL WORD

People have all sorts of experiences in small claims court. While most consumers do very well, there are complaints about long waits in overcrowded courtrooms, rude judges, and repeated case postponements.

With hundreds of thousands of cases heard every year, this could hardly be otherwise.

In a small claims court, much depends upon the temperament and fair-mindedness of the individual judge presiding. Don't avoid the court because a friend or acquaintance had a bad experience. The concept of a "people's court" designed to resolve problems quickly and inexpensively is a very valuable one for all consumers. But it can only work if ordinary citizens use it, and where problems exist, try to improve it. So if you feel you've been the victim of any scheme described in this book, and complaining gets you nowhere, put on your hat and coat and make the legal system work for you.

SELECTED BIBLIOGRAPHY

Little Injustices: A Preliminary Report to the Center for Auto Safety. The Small Claims Study Group, Cambridge, Mass., 1972.

MATTHEWS, DOUGLAS. *Sue the B*st*rds—The Victim's Handbook.* New York: Arbor House, 1973.

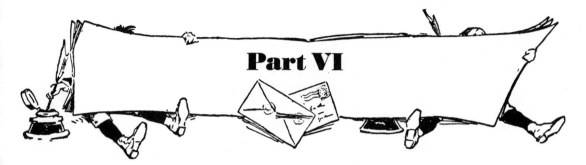

Part VI

Direct action

29

Organize: forming a consumer action group

A consumer will spend thousands of hours driving a new automobile or eating food from a supermarket, but can find no way to spend any time to correct the overpricing, fraud and hazards associated with these products! . . . It is no wonder that in the marketplace or in the halls of government, those who are organized and knowledgeable obtain their way. And those people who abdicate, delegate, or vegetate are taken. —RALPH NADER in Introduction to *A Public Citizen's Action Manual*

Participation is, in fact, the active expression of our faith in the dignity of the worth of the individual. —EDGAR S. CAHN and JEAN CAMPER CAHN, "Maximum Feasible Participation—A General Overview," in Edgar S. Cahn and Barry A. Passett, eds., *Citizen Participation: Effecting Community Change*

A visitor to the Albany, New York, office of the New York Public Interest Research Group, Inc. (NYPIRG), is left with the sense of having been in a cyclone. Phones ring, typewriters click, people rush around. A closer look shows interns running to and from committee meetings at the legislature; consumers placing orders for NYPIRG publications; legislators calling to ask for NYPIRG's support on their bills; a staff lawyer checking in after a court appearance; the director issuing public statements to the media; and staff members compiling research and writing reports in corners. Out of this chaos come concrete results. In NYPIRG's five-year history it has been instrumental in passing consumer protection bills on such matters as hearing-aid sales, generic drugs, and access to government records and meetings. It has distributed profiles on the 210 legislators and has educated the public via thousands of copies of dozens of publications.

Our visitor has had a glimpse of a large, multifaceted consumer issue group which uses education, publicity, litigation, and legislation to accomplish its ends. Volunteers, professional staff, door-to-door canvassers, and a vast body of student researchers working together comprise the most effective private consumer organization in New York.

In Philadelphia, in 1965, a group of frustrated consumers banded together to form a highly effective self-help group. One of their newsletters summarized recent accomplishments with these headlines:

> FOUR STATES BUILDERS REFUNDS $2,750 . . . ALLEN PONTIAC REFUNDS $1,100 . . . JOHN WANAMAKER REFUNDS $418 . . . DENTIST REFUNDS $400 . . . MCKAY CHEVROLET GIVES BACK $450 . . . ENGINE REPAIRS CUT FROM $800 TO $55 . . . 66,000 MILE MOTOR FIXED AT NO COST TO CONSUMER . . . $400 VIC SNYDER FRAUD CANCELLED.

The Consumers Education and Protective Association International, Inc. (CEPA), has been winning such victories steadily since it initiated what it calls its "grass-roots counter-attack upon widespread fraud, swindling, gouging, bait and switch and other unscrupulous and oppressive practices."*

CEPA's purpose is to resolve consumer complaints brought to it by community members, and it claims to succeed in about 95 percent of all the cases it accepts. Its method is ingenious and best summed up in three words: Investigate, Negotiate, and Demonstrate. A complaining consumer presents his or her problem to the weekly meeting of the neighborhood CEPA branch. The members ask questions about what happened, who was responsible, and what efforts have been made to resolve the complaint, prior to voting on whether to accept the complaint for action. If the complaint is accepted, a grievance committee conducts an "investigation" which includes examination of any relevant documents. If necessary, experts are consulted to give an assessment of the problem.

Next, the merchant is contacted, by letter, and asked to give his version of the story. The letter is followed up with a request for a meeting between the

---

* Max Weiner, "Consumer Alternative: Redress of Grievances," in *New Directions in Legal Services,* published by the Resource Center for Consumers of Legal Services, Vol. I, No. 7 (November 1976), p. 105.

merchant and the consumer, who is accompanied by a delegation of CEPA members. CEPA members try to negotiate a fair settlement of the case and in most cases succeed.

But if the consumer's case seems valid and the merchant refuses to make a reasonable adjustment, CEPA moves decisively into phase three and sets up a picket line outside the merchant's place of business. More than 90 percent of the complaints which move to this stage are settled shortly after the picketing begins. (See chapter 30 for more information about consumer picketing.)

A group of citizens in Virginia uses as its main tool a team of volunteers armed with clipboards who move rapidly from store to store taking notes. One of their most successful efforts involved a survey of prices charged by local pharmacies. The vast disparities that they uncovered was part of the data relied on by the U. S. Supreme Court in reaching its landmark decision that prohibited states from banning drug price advertising.

As these stories illustrate, the basic functions that consumer groups perform are complaint handling, market surveying, and bringing about governmental change on consumer issues. A consumer group may combine these functions once it is well established, but it's wise to focus on only one of them when beginning.

TYPES OF CONSUMER GROUPS

COMPLAINT HANDLERS

This type of group responds to people coming to it with specific grievances about sellers. It may actively intervene, like CEPA, or may limit itself to helping the consumer find out where to write, how to sue in small claims court, etc. (The broadcasting station and newspaper hot lines which have sprung up over the last ten years are examples of the latter type, although they are run by existing businesses rather than consumer groups. A consumer group might be able to convince a local station or newspaper to set up such a program, particularly if it could offer volunteer research help.)

MARKET SURVEYORS

A market survey compares a number of different sellers of goods or services. The most common example is a price survey. Recent consumer price surveys have looked at the cost of food, funerals, eyeglasses, gasoline, prescription drugs, and even surgery. The publication of the results of a survey can bring down prices and inform consumers as to what's available locally. Non-price surveys have reviewed compliance with consumer laws; the quality of various products; the cleanliness of stores and the freshness of the food sold; whether physicians prescribed drugs generically upon patient request to do so; and even the amount of violence on prime-time television shows sponsored by various advertisers. The end result of a market survey can be a local newspaper article, fliers, booklets, or broadcast media coverage.

A market survey is an excellent way to launch a new group or to involve people in an issue, since, if done properly, it results in a tangible
and impressive product. Instructions for conducting a market survey are
included at the end of this chapter.

SOCIAL CHANGERS

Attempting to change government is a challenging job, which becomes progressively more difficult as you move from the local to the
state to the federal level. Because new groups need concrete accomplishments to build on, keep short-term goals modest and specific. Among the
multitude of techniques available are the following:

◆ administrative agency petitioning and testifying (major decisions
  are made by agencies, an often overlooked point);
◆ legislative drafting and lobbying;
◆ litigation (bringing test cases can be very effective, although it is
  uncertain and often expensive);
◆ media campaigns (local radio and TV stations);
◆ publishing (fact sheets, fliers, booklets, comics, letters to the editor and columns in newspapers, newsletters, posters, books);
◆ researching (with the end product to be published, publicized, or
  used as a basis for litigation or teaching);
◆ teaching (classes, workshops, or lectures; consider also developing
  teaching materials for distribution);
◆ voter campaigns (evaluating candidates on past pronouncements
  and achievements, not promises).

MARKET SURVEY DONE BY INDIANA PUBLIC INTEREST RESEARCH GROUP.

___ LOW
(H) HIGH

Percentage cost difference relative to the lowest priced store for the model shopping basket

MODEL BASKET COMPOSITION (PERCENTAGE)	Overall	Dry groceries	Meats & poultry	Non-foods*	Fresh vegs and fruits	General** merchandise	Dairy	Baked goods
	100.0	32.7	22.0	11.9	10.5	9.7	6.9	6.3
Eisner Foods	0.0	2.0	2.1	2.7	22.2	3.3	0.4	0.0
Kroger Eastland	1.5	0.2	6.1	0.9	39.2	0.0	1.3	3.3
Kroger Sem. Squ.	1.7	0.0	7.3	0.7	39.2	0.3	1.5	4.2
Marsh West Hwy. 48	1.8	4.2	2.0	0.0	35.5	2.2	1.4	5.9
Marsh S. Walnut	2.0	4.0	4.0	0.0	33.8	2.2	1.5	6.0(H)
Highland V. IGA	2.8	3.9	1.5	3.9	27.6	18.7	2.0	3.8
Hays Market	3.1	9.1	0.5	9.5	0.0	20.6	4.4	4.7
Ralph's T-Mart	3.2	6.9	0.0	8.4	31.6	3.7	4.6	5.9
South IGA	4.7	3.4	8.8(H)	5.1	31.4	18.3	1.3	4.6
Ault's IGA	5.4	10.7(H)	2.2	9.3	22.2	17.9	5.7(H)	2.1
K-Mart Standard	6.1	6.7	2.1	10.7(H)	60.9(H)	6.0	0.0	4.2
Cascade IGA	6.5	7.9	3.1	8.4	41.4	21.2(H)	4.4	3.3
No. of items used	135	46	17	23	9	16	12	12

*Household, pet, and tobacco products/**Mostly health and beauty aids

Indiana Public Interest Research Group of Bloomington, (InPIRG), May 24, 1978 with funds provided in part by
the Family Student Council.

HOW TO START A CONSUMER ACTION GROUP

Before deciding to form a consumer group, see if there is an existing group which you might join or reactivate. It's easier to start with something (unless it's a group with a totally negative image) than to build from scratch. Furthermore, if people in your community are at all active on similar issues, it is better to enlist their help and tap their experience and good will than to evoke their jealousy.

If you are unaware of any such groups, check by reading local newspapers (especially back issues) and interviewing reporters who've specialized in covering consumer stories. Check with local government agencies and the larger church or social service organizations for leads. Also, look at the lists of state and local organizations contained in *HELP: The Useful Almanac* (a yearly publication of Consumer News, Inc., Washington, D.C. 20045); John Dorfman, *A Consumer's Arsenal* (New York: Praeger Publishers, 1976); and the Consumer Federation of America's *Directory of State and Local Consumer Groups* (available from CFA, 1012 14th Street, N.W., Washington, D.C. 20005).

Even if you decide not to ally yourself with an existing group, you could learn from its experiences.

But maybe you've thought it out, talked it over with some people you trust, and now want to form a new group. There's no sure-fire, clear-cut blueprint for success; the goals, background, and personalities of the founders will all determine the direction. With that caveat, here are a few general tips to follow:

1. Visit any remotely similar groups within, say, a 100-mile radius before starting. This will give you an idea of what works and what doesn't. Try to arrange to spend most of a day at each place and speak to the principal staff people and volunteers. It will also help set up a network of people to turn to for advice, to share information, and to cooperate on issues.

2. Hold an initial meeting as soon as you have several people who are really interested in participating (not just in joining). Set a specific agenda for the meeting and be businesslike in conducting it. (Otherwise busy people will become disinterested.) However, be careful not to dominate the meeting and to let others add agenda items and suggestions. There are many books and articles on running meetings.

3. Decide on the type of activity you want to do first. Don't dissipate your energies by tackling too many things too fast.

4. Assign specific tasks to people—in line with their experience, abilities, and willingness to work. Share the responsibility and any glory—it's a mistake to let the whole operation be dependent on one person. Be prepared for personality problems and ego clashes to evolve—they always do.

5. Set small, reachable goals. It's important to have some concrete achievements to show as soon as possible.

6. Don't worry about raising money at first; it can be time-consuming, and will be easier to do when you have one or two concrete accomplishments to point to. Meet in someone's home and chip in or share the costs of telephoning, supplies, and transportation. Such sharing can even bind the group together.

GETTING PRESS COVERAGE

Your success in getting good press coverage depends on several things, including the size of your community (the smaller, the better), the newsworthiness of what you have to say, and what else is going on that day. Rural or suburban newspapers are usually much more responsive to consumer group news than are large metropolitan ones; similarly big-city weeklies may cover news that the dailies won't. Small local TV and radio stations are much more receptive than large ones. You'll quickly get to know the best local press outlets. However, there are a number of things you can do to maximize press coverage of your activities:

1. Plan a press conference or press release. Call a conference if you've got an important statement or some good visual material to show (for television interest)—you'll soon learn what the media in your area will show up for. If you hold a conference, send out an invitation plus, usually, a copy of a press release for those who can't make it. Be sure that one well-informed person is designated as the spokesperson for the group. Hold the conference in an interesting and relevant place if possible—outside a government building, outside a merchant's store, etc. (But check first to see if you need a permit or permission.)

2. Time your press releases or press conferences carefully. Try to choose a quiet news day (Monday is a slow one in most communities) and give several days' notice. For press conferences, give four or five days' notice. Time press releases to reach reporters a couple of days before the release date (this allows them time to contact you for further information or to get reactions from others).

3. Write a good press release. The release should be clear; concise (one or two pages); typed double-space on one side of a sheet of paper (type "more-more-more" at the bottom if it goes on to a second sheet, and "-30-" at the end). Most important, it should be thoroughly accurate and reliable. Reporters often print them verbatim, and future press coverage will depend on how credible you are in the eyes of the press. A sample press release is shown on the following page. If the release pertains to a study or report, include a copy, or if it is lengthy, just summarize it.

4. Telephone any reporters you've dealt with or think will give good coverage to remind them of the conference or release and offer to answer any questions.

SAMPLE PRESS RELEASE

release date

FOR RELEASE: 9:00 A.M.
                          April 16, 1983

FOR FURTHER
INFORMATION
CONTACT:
Tabithia Tinear
313-123-4567
or
Edith Johnstanley
313-765-4321

who to contact

headline   VALLEYVIEW CONSUMERS FORM *ENOUGH!*

why press release is being issued   Today a group of Valleyview residents announced the formation of *ENOUGH!*, a consumer group dedicated to setting limits on rising car repair costs and inadequate repair service in the Town of Valleyview. The organization intends to "conduct market surveys of car repair establishments, determine who is giving the consumer a fair deal and who isn't, and act to improve the situation," according to chairwoman Tabithia Tinear.

quotable quote   "This essential consumer service has been a problem here for years," she continued, "and we've decided it's time to take action. We've had enough!"

other facts   *ENOUGH!* encourages residents who have had their cars repaired recently to share their experiences with the group. Members and volunteers are also greatly needed.

more-more-more

Contact Tabithia Tinear at 123-4567 from 6 P.M. to 9 P.M. or Edith Johnstanley at 765-4321 from 9 A.M. to 4 P.M. to learn more.

end of press release   -30-

ADVICE FROM EIGHT SEASONED LEADERS†

Eight seasoned consumer leaders were polled for answers to these questions:

Are there ways to help assure your organization of success?
What pitfalls should the new consumer organizer avoid?
The consumer leaders say you should:

1. Build a dues-paying membership. Enable your members to subscribe to a cause. "Your program should be worth people's making an investment."
2. Publish a newsletter (or some type of regular communication).

† Source: *A Guide to Consumer Action,* pp. 43–44.

3. Learn how others have succeeded. If this means finding an organization that is doing what your group wants to do and paying them to teach you, it's worth it.

4. Involve new members in projects and planning sessions right after they've joined, so that they aren't ignored when their enthusiasm is highest.

5. Give credit to people who do the work. "Share the goodies. The president should never miss the opportunity to take someone along to the TV station. It gets tiresome picketing and never getting any credit."

6. Disperse responsibility. "It is important that the organization continue to function even if a crucial person leaves the organization. You need multi-headed leadership."

7. Regard the business affairs of the organization in a businesslike manner. "Because you are volunteer and nonprofit doesn't mean you can ignore the nitty-gritty of operating efficiently. Budget a year at a time, including your projected income and its resources. Review and adjust your projected income and expenses quarterly."

8. Review your priorities periodically, with maximum membership participation.

On the other hand, the leaders had these caveats for new consumer groups. They warned:

1. Don't just service complaints. "It's depressing. There's nothing else for the members to do. It doesn't build a group feeling. Only a few members can share in a success. The public gets to thinking of you as a place to complain and that's all," said one leader. Another cautioned, "You need some broad issues that have meaning to lots of different people, members and non-members."

2. Don't insist on doing something yourself because you think you can do it better than anybody else. "You've got to delegate—challenge—grow new people."

3. Don't speak out on issues before you are completely prepared. "Just once lose your credibility and you have nothing," said one person.

4. Don't commit the organization to something the members are not committed to. "Keep activities of the group relevant to the members. Local groups respond to problems on the local level."

5. Don't let your energies be deflected into activities that are not building the movement. "Legislative action won't build membership," was one observation. Another: "You can't build an organization if you ignore pocketbook issues that speak to your members and get wrapped up in some arcane regulatory matter in Washington in which only you can participate."

6. Don't get most of your funding from a single source. "When we were first getting started, we got a grant. We lived on that for eleven months and forgot about building membership. It almost did us in," one leader recalled. Another said, "When too much of your income comes from one member group or one source, you get to counting on it too much. You get dependent. In making programs you are too responsive to the priorities of that member."

7. Don't underestimate the importance of a good board of directors. Said one leader, "Board members don't need to be prominent in the community. They need to care about the group's program, have the respect of the members, and be willing to give time and make hard decisions to help it succeed."

8. Don't be frightened away from ever considering hiring paid staff. "Sometimes there comes a point when it is more wasteful not to, so don't set your mind against it from the start," a leader cautioned from experience.

A GUIDE TO CONDUCTING MARKET SURVEYS‡

I. What is a Market Survey?

A. A market survey is simply a comparison of a number of different places selling the same goods or services. It can show whether stores are complying with the prescription drug price posting law or whether they carry certain dangerous toys. But, most often, a market survey compares prices that neighborhood stores are charging.

B. Price surveys compare prices for identical goods at a number of stores.

    1. They usually are limited to a particular community or neighborhood.

    2. The most common price surveys compare:

        a. supermarkets and/or grocery stores;

        b. drugstores;

        c. gasoline stations.

II. Why Do a Market Survey?

A. Market surveys can be used to steer people to the stores offering the lowest prices or the best compliance with a consumer law.

B. The ability to complete a market survey shows store owners that you have some clout. That can be a way of bringing pressure on store owners to lower their prices or change their hours or comply with an existing law.

C. They can serve, too, to establish a new community group or subgroup or to revitalize an existing one. Working on a common project with a definite final product that is useful to others can be a huge morale booster.

III. What Will It Look Like?

A. There are a number of good ways to use your results, and you can choose more than one form. The final product(s) can be:

    1. A mimeographed sheet for distribution to community members.

    2. An article in a local newspaper.

    3. A booklet put out by a local legislator.

    4. An announcement read over local radio station(s).

    5. A press release sent to newspapers and broadcast stations.

‡ Source: Consumer Law Training Center, a joint project of New York Law School, New York Public Interest Research Group, Inc., and Brooklyn Legal Services Corporation B.

B. Your choice should depend on what is likely to be of most value to your community and what resources you have available.

IV. How to Design One

You must take the time to carefully plan a market survey or it is guaranteed to flop. The following questions must be considered and decided before you can begin:

A. What do you basically want to learn or demonstrate?

It might be:

1. Which of the pharmacies in Bedford-Stuyvesant comply with the prescription drug price posting law?

2. How do thruway gas station prices compare with those of adjacent gas stations?

3. How do all the supermarkets in a particular neighborhood compare in prices?

B. How will you learn that *or* what specific information will you obtain? The answer could be:

1. By doing a compliance survey of all the pharmacies in Bedford-Stuyvesant.

2. By visiting 6 gas stations on a stretch of the thruway and 12 in adjacent neighborhoods and comparing their prices for all types of gas.

3. By comparing prices in 14 neighborhood supermarkets for 12 meat and produce and household goods items.

C. When will the information be gathered?

1. The information should all be collected on the same day (so that you are surveying the identical "market"—conditions change from day to day). This is essential for price surveys, since prices are constantly being changed and sometimes vary according to the day of the week.

2. For non-price surveys, you can do the surveying over several days, if need be.

D. How many places will be surveyed?

E. Which ones will they be?

You must have a complete master list of the places to be surveyed and their addresses.

F. Who will gather the information?

1. Obviously, the number of people needed depends on:

    a. the number of places to be surveyed;

    b. how geographically far apart they are; and

    c. how long the surveying of one store takes.

2. Once you know those facts and can estimate how many people you need, try to get at least one or two extra people. Someone almost always drops out at the last minute.

3. People whom you know and can rely on are preferable, of course. Whoever is involved should be impressed with the importance of letting the director know immediately if they are unable to do any part of their assignment.

    G. Who will direct the project?

      1. It is essential that *one* person be in charge.
The project director is needed to:

      a. give assignments and instructions to surveyors;

      b. answer questions;

      c. keep careful track of who is doing what;

      d. bear the responsibility of seeing that the survey is completed
and is accurate.

      2. The director should personally do a part of the surveying (a trial
run) before giving out assignments.

    H. What will it cost?

      1. Market surveys can be done quite inexpensively. But, even if the
surveyors are all volunteers, there are always some costs. They include:

      a. materials

        (i) paper for forms and final products

        (ii) pencils, pens, etc.;

      b. printing or mimeographing or photocopying of forms and
final products;

      c. postage;

      d. telephone costs;

      e. transportation.

      2. An organization which has office space can often absorb these
costs, particularly if you are not trying to print and distribute large numbers
of booklets.

      3. If your organization cannot, or if you want to conduct a survey
on your own, you might look for a *sponsor*.

      a. A sponsor can lend legitimacy to the survey and/or can lend
you office space and cover some of the other costs.

      b. A sponsor will usually want some credit for the survey results.
It can be called a "joint project" of both of you or a project carried out by
you "under sponsorship of" or "with the help of" the sponsor.

      c. Likely sponsors are local politicians, who can also help ensure
that you get coverage of the results.

    I. Where will the project be located?
You must have one central place to keep your materials and completed
forms; to meet with surveyors; and to put together the final product(s).

V. How To Get Started

    A. Answer all the questions raised in Section III.

    B. Decide what stores will be included.

      1. What kind of store.

2. Within what area(s). Logical ones include:

    a. neighborhood;

    b. town;

    c. borough;

    d. city.

3. All or some?

    a. Most surveys cover all stores (or stations) in a particular area.

    b. Some surveys take a sampling rather than a complete market survey to give an overall picture. If you don't survey all stores, you must be certain that the stores are selected in a fair and representative way. Otherwise your survey can be severely criticized. One fair way to do it is to start with a complete list of all stores and choose every other or every third or fourth one to survey. The Yellow Pages of the telephone book can sometimes be used for this purpose.

C. Decide what will be surveyed.

1. You must choose the exact quantity, forms, brand name (if relevant), and all other characteristics of the product in order to do a correct price survey.

    a. Unless you do this, you will wind up comparing oranges and apples. This is one of the easiest mistakes to make in designing a market survey.

    b. Pretesting your form will be a check on this.

2. Get as broad a range of products as possible. If you are looking to compare how expensive various stores are (the usual purpose of a price survey), choose several different types of items from different departments in the store. For example, a price survey of supermarkets could include items from the produce, meat, household products, prepared foods, frozen foods, dairy, and other departments.

3. Think about how many items you want to include. For a supermarket survey between 6 and 12 is a suggested quantity.

D. Design the survey form.

1. The purpose of the form is to ensure that every surveyor obtains the same information in a way that makes it simplest to compile the final product (report or press release or whatever).

2. It should be as simple as possible to use while containing all relevant information.

3. Designing a good survey form (that is, one which works for you) is much more involved than it looks. In fact, it is often the most difficult part of conducting a market survey, so be sure to take enough time and to have at least two people review it.

4. It should include:

    a. surveyor's name

        (i) this is essential for checking any questions when compiling the final product, and

(ii) to respond to questions or complaints after the final product is issued;

b. date surveying was done;

c. place to list price or other information you are seeking;

d. name and address of each store or station being surveyed (this information can be filled in before the forms are given to surveyors);

e. room for any additional notes and comments.

5. In order to be sure that the form will do what you want it to, and as a general check on the planned survey itself, it is important to *pretest*.

a. A pretest is simply a mini-version of the survey, best done by the project director. For example, if your survey will cover 40 drugstores, you would go to one or two first and fill out the form yourself.

b. It must be done *before* the survey forms are reproduced for the surveyors.

E. Talk with the surveyors.

1. A general meeting of everyone involved is preferable because it helps create a sense of togetherness and responsibility. If such a meeting is difficult to arrange, you can talk with the surveyors individually.

2. Be sure to explain the purpose of the survey.

3. Give very detailed instructions about what surveyors are to do. Be sure to also:

a. encourage them to ask questions; and

b. let them know how to reach you if they have questions while they are doing the surveying.

4. Stress the importance of being absolutely accurate and of completing the work on the assigned day(s).

5. Explain when and how you will collect the forms.

F. Collect the data—as soon as the survey is done, the surveyors must hand in all forms.

G. Compile the data.

1. There are usually several correct ways of compiling the data. Which ones are best for you depends on the kind and amount of information which you've gathered and what you plan to do with it.

2. Be sure that at least two people look over the proposed way of compiling the data and try to make it as clear and as easy to understand as possible.

3. Always double-check (by having two people do it separately) the figures when you transpose them from survey forms to the final compilation. It is very easy to make mistakes doing this kind of repetitive work.

H. Prepare the final product(s).

1. There are also a number of ways of doing this well.

2. Spend the extra time needed to make the final product(s) attractive and neat. It pays off in the greater amount of attention it will receive.

   I. Distribute the information. You can:

      1. Slip copies of the survey under doors of community residents.

      2. Send a copy of the survey to all local newspapers and radio stations.

      3. Distribute in community centers.

SELECTED BIBLIOGRAPHY

A Case Study or How to Form a Consumer Complaint Group, written by Cleveland's Consumer Action Movement. Pamphlet available from Consumer Federation of America, Suite 901, 1012 14th Street, N.W., Washington, D.C. 20005.

NADER, RALPH, and ROSS, DONALD K. *Action for a Change: A Student's Manual for Public Interest Organizing.* New York: Grossman Publishers, 1971.

NELSON, HELEN E., ALLEN, LIZ, and MCNALLY, KIT. *A Guide to Consumer Action.* Issued by the Office of Consumers' Education, U. S. Office of Education. Single copies available free from Consumer Information Center, Pueblo, Colo. 81009. An excellent booklet, and the source of the "Advice from Eight Seasoned Leaders."

ROSS, DONALD K. *A Public Citizen's Action Manual.* New York: Grossman Publishers, 1973.

30

Basic tools of social action: picketing, leafleting, and boycotting

The meat boycott of 1973 . . . was organized by women who are most often referred to by the press as "ordinary housewives," and are pictured in TV commercials, sniffing kitchen corners and putting daisies in their toilet tanks. These supposedly passive consumers were suddenly out in the streets picketing stores, organizing rallies, distributing leaflets, and demanding Butz' resignation. All across the country (a partial survey reported boycott organizations in at least 37 states), women were talking about farm policy, agribusiness, milk cooperatives, and payoffs by the Nixon Administration to generous campaign contributors.

Their tactics were effective: retail meat sales during the boycott week dropped an estimated 50 to 80 percent. — FRANCES CERRA, "After the Meat Boycott . . . What?" (*Ms.,* August 1974)

(Wide World Photos)

In the early 1970s a Wisconsin couple named Bloomberg took a sofa and two chairs to be reupholstered. The job, for which they were charged $431, was a mess—the pieces were so overstuffed that they lost their shape, the material had been badly pieced together, the sofa was lumpy, and the chair cushions were punctured with holes. The seller refused to discuss the matter with the Bloombergs, whom he claimed were "unreasonable." They went to a local group known as the Concerned Consumers League, which approached the upholsterer about the Bloombergs' complaints, but he wouldn't listen to them either. So the League began picketing the Park Furniture store and distributing to passers-by a leaflet that read as follows:

SATISFACTION NOT GUARANTEED AT PARK FURNITURE!!!

When Mr. & Mrs. Bloomberg, 5326 N. 63rd Street, took their furniture to be reupholstered at Park Furniture on June 18, they expected no less than an excellent job. The price charged for recovering their sofa and two chairs was a total of $431 of which $100 has been paid so far.

When Mr. & Mrs. Bloomberg went to pick up their newly (and expensively) reupholstered furniture, they found the following things were wrong:

1. Chairs and sofa had been overstuffed; furniture no longer had its original shape
2. Welting was sewn on unevenly on all pieces
3. Cushions overhang on chairs
4. The sofa padding has humps in the back
5. The cover trim doesn't cover
6. There are two small holes in the sofa cushion
7. Material in sofa and chair cushions was pieced as the result of sewing error (zippers were put in by mistake).

Is this a $431 job?

Mr. Johnson, owner of Park Furniture, says he doesn't want to talk to Mr. & Mrs. Bloomberg because he feels they are "unreasonable."

Concerned Consumers League feels that the upholstering should be done to Mr. & Mrs. Bloomberg's satisfaction or that their money and furniture should be returned.

What's *your* opinion?

If you have a consumer problem contact:

Concerned Consumers League
524 W. National Avenue
645-1808

We are a self-help group dedicated to ACTION on behalf of Milwaukee area consumers in which you will be involved in solving your own complaint and help others who helped you.

Park Furniture's owners perked up then and sued the Concerned Consumers League to stop its leafleting and picketing. But the League took the upholsterer into federal court and won, upholding the right of customers to picket and publicly voice their dissatisfactions. In fact, the court pointed out:

> The method of expression used by the plaintiffs in this case is probably the most effective way, if not the only way, to inform unsophisticated consumers, i.e., by direct contact at the particular place of business.*

A Philadelphia resident who had been receiving shots regularly from a hospital outpatient clinic would probably agree. He became permanently paralyzed in the left arm as a result of a medical error. The hospital began to pay him $500 a week in compensation, and then, without explanation, stopped. After a consumer group helped him to picket the hospital, he won a $75,000 settlement.

And finally, there was the used-car purchaser who was trying to get the dealer to listen to her side of the story. The hotheaded dealer locked the purchaser and the accompanying consumer group delegation in his office, where several mechanics threatened to beat them up. After a giant picket line was installed, the dealer offered a refund and a written apology.

Picketing, leafleting, and boycotting are effective means of social action long used by labor and activist political groups. The tools are old, but their utilization for the redress of consumer problems is fairly recent, and still relatively rare. All three methods are, in essence, ways of publicizing complaints, intended to pressure the seller to change. They try to persuade potential customers to stop patronizing a particular seller or to stop buying a particular product.

The courts have made it clear that consumers have the right, guaranteed by the First Amendment to the federal constitution, to use these methods. However, states or localities can impose certain limitations, including a requirement that demonstrators obtain a permit prior to picketing. If you decide to start or join a picket or boycott, it is advisable to talk with a sympathetic lawyer before beginning. If you don't have someone to advise you on local laws or regulations, contact the closest American Civil Liberties Union office or a law school teacher of constitutional law for advice.

PICKETING AND LEAFLETING

Consumer picketing is walking up and down in front of a store or place of business carrying signs describing a complaint. Leafleting is handing out to passers-by or shoppers handbills or booklets describing a problem with a seller. The two tactics are frequently used in conjunction with each other, although either method can be used effectively by itself. Picketing is more effective at attracting the attention of the public (and often the media), whereas leafleting can present a more detailed version of the complaint, one which can be taken home and read by any interested person.

The first consumer picketing case was reported in New York in 1934

* *Concerned Consumers League* v. *O'Neill,* 371 F. Supp. 644, 649 (E.D. Wisc. 1974).

(*Julie Baking Co., Inc.* v. *Graymond*†). It involved a neighborhood group angered by the high price of bread at the local bakery. The court upheld the right to picket (although limiting the number of people and the hours during which the group could protest), saying:

> to protest against what they regard as extortionate prices for necessities of life should be permissible to consumers.

This was an important precedent; the power of such actions has been evident to those consumer organizations which have utilized them, groups like the Consumers Education and Protective Association International, Inc. (CEPA), of Philadelphia, the Consumer Education and Protection Organization (CEPO) of Des Moines, and the Concerned Consumers League of Milwaukee.

Before setting up a picket or leafleting project, you should approach the seller with your complaint. If you receive no satisfaction and decide to go ahead, there are several basic legal requirements to observe (in addition to any local ones).

HOW TO PICKET OR LEAFLET LEGALLY

1. At least *one* picketer or person represented by the picketers must have a genuine dispute with the seller.

2. What the pickets seek must not be unlawful; nor can it be the closing of the business. It can be the resolution of a particular complaint or the changing of a specific bad practice.

3. The picket signs must not contain false claims or exaggerations.

   a. For example, it is permissible to state that the particular car you bought from a dealer is a lemon, but it is *not* O.K. to state that the dealer sells only lemons.

   b. The signs should state that a seller has or is violating the law *only* if you are positive that such is the case.

4. The picketers may not use violence or abusive language, or "breach the peace" (in other words, create a disturbance). Too many picketers or too much involvement with passers-by may be considered breaching the peace.

5. Picketers may not prevent people from walking on the sidewalk or entering and leaving the store.

6. The location (situs) of the picketing or leafleting should be related to its purpose. Demonstrating at the offending store is appropriate; at the seller's home usually is not.

The store being picketed may go to court to try to enjoin (stop) you. If the court agrees that the picketing exceeds permissible standards, it may issue an injunction stopping or limiting it. This is another good reason to have a local lawyer behind you and to alert the police beforehand.

† 152 Misc. 846, 274 N.Y.S. 250.

The mayor of Bridgeport, Connecticut, helps launch the national sugar boycott of 1974. (Wide World Photos)

BOYCOTTS

A boycott is an organized consumer refusal to buy a product or to buy from a particular seller. It can be backed up by a picket line or reinforced by leafleting. Boycotting has long been a means that labor unions have used to force producers to negotiate with them. The national boycott of iceberg lettuce and California grapes masterminded by the United Farmworkers is a prime example.

Recently, however, consumers have begun boycotting products or sellers to protest the price or quality of what they buy. The meat boycott of 1973 was a dramatic example; it was accompanied by demonstrations, vegetarian recipe teach-ins, and colorful press interviews. Another effective national boycott took place in 1977 when consumers refused to buy coffee at grossly inflated prices. And there are numerous local boycotts going on all the time, which are often more successful in achieving direct results than the wider ones.

A local boycott of a store or other provider is relatively simple to organize, particularly in a small community. It should usually be undertaken by groups which have first attempted to negotiate with the seller. In fact, the threat of a boycott can often make a seller willing to negotiate.

As with the other forms of direct action, the right to boycott carries with it the obligation to make only truthful statements about the seller and to avoid violence and any disturbance of the peace.

Picketing, leafleting, and boycotting, or any combination of the three, will be more effective if they receive media attention. (See chapter 29 for advice on how to deal with the press.)

SELECTED BIBLIOGRAPHY

HAIMAN, FRANKLYN S. *The First Freedoms: Speech, Press, Assembly*. American Civil Liberties Union, 156 Fifth Avenue, New York, N.Y. 10010.

NELSON, HELEN E., ALLEN, LIZ, and MCNALLY, KIT. *A Guide to Consumer Action*. Issued by the Office of Consumers' Education, U. S. Office of Education. Single copies available free from Consumer Information Center, Pueblo, Colo. 81009.

31

Cooperatives

All for one and one for all.　—ALEXANDRE DUMAS, *The Three Musketeers*

By uniting we stand, by dividing we fall. — JOHN DICKINSON, "Liberty Song," published in the Boston *Gazette,* July 18, 1768

A story is told about a mother who stormed out of a clinic in the Puget Sound area (Seattle), angry at the way a pediatrician had treated her child. A few hours later a car pulled up to her house and the doctor got out. She had come to apologize to the woman and explain why she had behaved as she had.

Atypical of doctors? Rather, but not atypical of the particular clinic for which the physician worked—the Group Health Cooperative of Puget Sound. The Cooperative is a marvelous example of what a group of determined consumers can do. In the mid-1940s, some people who were dis-

(Woodcut by Bob Marstall, from *The Food Co-op Handbook,* published by the Houghton Mifflin Company, Boston, 1975. Printed by permission)

satisfied with the medical care available banded together to form a health care cooperative. They began by buying a small medical clinic: the 400 families involved each contributed $100. Despite intense opposition by the medical establishment, the idea took hold and by 1972 the Group Health Cooperative was a major success. Today it serves 242,000 members and employs over 2,000 people (245 of them M.D.'s), working out of 10 health centers and three hospitals. The Cooperative offers two basic things to its members: comprehensive and personalized health coverage for a reasonable fee ($33.45 per month in 1978) and the chance to participate in the management of their health care organization. The entire membership convenes at an annual meeting, and elected representatives direct the project throughout the year.

This is but one modern permutation of the consumer co-op movement which began when a group of 28 weavers in Rochdale, England, banded together in 1844 to improve their lot as purchasers. Their efforts have had repercussions beyond their wildest dreams. Today cooperatives are commonplace in Europe, and an essential part of the economy in Scandinavia. Although less important in the United States, they are used in a wider variety of ways here than anywhere else. It's been estimated that over 50 million Americans are members of cooperatives of one sort or another. There are cooperatives which market butter for dairy farmers; cooperatives which enable city dwellers to buy better produce at cheaper prices; cooperatives which enable people to obtain health care or legal help which they might otherwise do without; and cooperatives which supply electricity or telephone service to rural households not served by the major utilities. Consumer co-ops now exist for a vast assortment of goods and services: hardware, furniture, gasoline and oil, credit, insurance, health care, and even funerals (see chapter 9).

Co-ops vary in their size and their function, but they all share certain characteristics:

- open membership; anyone in the geographic (or occupational) category can join.
- membership control; no outside investors.
- one vote per member (no matter what size share has been invested).
- money invested earns only interest; no profit.

Thus a co-op is run by and for its members.

WHY JOIN A CO-OP?

The reasons for joining a co-op are almost as disparate as the kinds of co-ops one can join. Some people join co-ops because it makes them eligible for the groups' charter flights. Newcomers to an area sometimes join co-ops to meet people and make friends. But most people turn to consumer co-ops because:

1. *The goods or services offered aren't available elsewhere,* either because there is no provider or because the price is too high. An example

of the first type is the rural electric co-ops. The newly emerging legal and health insurance cooperatives fall into the second type.

2. *Co-ops offer lower prices or better-quality goods.* **Co-ops generally save between 15 and 50 percent of the cost of goods—because of bulk buying, because the labor involved is volunteer or low-cost, and because no profits are involved. Furthermore, food co-ops are often able to get better-quality goods because they buy directly from the supplier.**

3. *Co-ops offer the consumer a sense of control or participation.* **This motivation was emphasized by the citizen activism and back-to-the-earth movements of the 1960s. People who have become disgusted with the impersonality and commercialism of the marketplace have found another way of buying goods, credit, and services.**

If you are interested in setting up a cooperative or finding one to join, a good starting point is the Cooperative League of the U.S.A., 1828 L Street, N.W., Washington, D.C. 20036 (202-872-0550), a national clearinghouse. In operation since 1916, the League has an extensive publication list of books, pamphlets, teaching guides, posters, etc., a number of which are free. It's the best place to begin learning about co-ops.

FOOD CO-OPS

Farmers' cooperatives flourished in the nineteenth century and were the first co-ops to succeed in America. Among other functions, they provided for the cooperative marketing of food. Consumer co-ops set up to buy food represent the other end of the process.

Some of the smallest, most transient co-ops are food-buying clubs. No legal transaction or investment is needed to set one up, nor is any capital equipment or inventory required. There must be merely a few people or families interested in pooling their shopping dollars in order to eat better for less money. If ten families in a neighborhood decide to buy wheels of cheese to share, they constitute a co-op. Food co-ops sometimes grow much larger and become the springboard for other cooperative ventures. The Consumers Cooperative of Berkeley, California, for example, owns several supermarkets and now controls 2½ percent of the retail food trade in the San Francisco Bay area. Its 75,000 member families also own a gas station and repair shop, a bookstore, a pharmacy, a hardware store, a natural food shop, and a taxi service, as well as operating a credit union and a travel agency.

In between these two extremes falls the bulk of the 2,000 U.S. and Canadian food co-ops. What they have in common is the desire to buy food (like produce, grains, and cheese) at reduced prices, for which they are willing to contribute some labor. The larger co-ops have paid staff, but even then, co-op members often volunteer time and keep labor costs down.

Weighing in at the West End Co-op: Judy DeCoster and Ellen Reiss. (Photo by Ron Hollander)

BUYING TIP

If you are interested in locating a food co-op near you, there's a Food Co-op Directory *with "listings of over 2,300 consumer co-op[s] . . . stores, warehouses, bakeries, restaurants, etc." available from* Food Co-op Directory, *106 Girard S.E., Albuquerque, N.M. 87106.*

Several veterans of food co-ops wrote *The Food Co-op Handbook,* a book which makes a strong case for the position that food co-ops provide a great deal more than food. It views the consumer co-op movement as providing "both an alternative to profit-making food distribution and a center of community activity and consumer awareness." The authors see the co-op movement itself as an instrument for social change, arguing that, if it keeps growing,

> we will create something new to contemporary America: humanized, democratically controlled, nonprofit, economic enterprises. We can build a food distribution system that carries safe nutritious food for reasonable prices based on the necessary costs of production. No one will make a profit or an exorbitant salary from our need to eat. (p. 326)

Whether that's your cup of tea or not, food co-ops do offer bargains on food and can be pleasant, if not fun, to participate in. They work best in urban or suburban areas, among people with similar tastes in food and life styles. There is a minimum number of people necessary in order to buy most food in bulk and share the work comfortably; 15 to 20 families (or more than double that number of single people). Access to a car, station wagon, or truck is necessary to bring food back from the market to its distribution point.

Small food co-ops generally require that all members (families or individuals) contribute to the workload. The basic tasks include ordering, buying, transporting, distributing, and paying for the food, as well as administering the co-op, especially keeping the books.

There are no legal requirements, in general, for small co-ops. They need not be incorporated, although some are. Sometimes local health regulations pertain, usually if the co-ops go beyond a certain size, or cut and sell meat. Check with your local department of health or consumer affairs agency.

If there is no food co-op to join and you are interested in starting one, an excellent how-to guide is Tony Vellela's *Food Co-ops for Small Groups,* published by Workman Publishing Company, 231 East 51st Street, New York, N.Y. 10022. It discusses all aspects of setting up and operating the co-op, and it contains a list of regional sources of information about co-ops and sources of supply. The co-op which Mr. Vellela helped found in New York City grew so large that it had to split up into chapters, so he speaks from happy experience.

SIDELIGHT
Co-ops tend to communicate with their members in a variety of ways when they grow too large to do it all by word of mouth. At first they rely on messages and recipes on the back of order sheets, overflowing bulletin boards, etc., and eventually a regular newsletter springs up as the co-op grows in size or vitality.

CREDIT UNIONS

Savings and loan cooperatives, called credit unions, are more widely used in this country than any other kind of co-op. In 1977, more than one out of every six Americans was a credit union member. Developed in nineteenth-century Germany to protect poor people against usury, credit unions today aim at bettering the lot of their members (usually middle-income people) by making loans available at lower interest rates, as well as offering more personalized and convenient services.

Credit unions, unlike banks, exist to serve their member/owners, not to make money from them. Their philosophy includes teaching prudent financial management and they "encourage thrift" by offering such plans as payroll savings deductions. They talk about trusting one's neighbor or co-worker—i.e., someone in a lasting relationship to the other members—and theoretically, loans are made to people because they know each other, not solely because of their earning ability. This difference in purpose is reflected in the very style of the credit unions (usually less elegant and less formal than banks) and in the type of financial advice they give members.

Members invest their savings, on which they receive interest, and the credit union makes loans for such personal needs as bills, taxes, medical expenses, education, home improvements, and for the purchase of cars, mobile homes, vacations. The officers and board of directors who run the credit union serve without pay (except for the treasurer, who may be paid), backed up by volunteers or paid staff. Volunteers are the key to the credit union's low interest rates—without donated services (and often space) they would not be possible.

Unlike food cooperatives, which can be informal, credit unions must be chartered by the government and are held legally accountable for their actions. The members who deposit their savings become shareholders, and are usually the only ones who can borrow from the credit union. They elect a board of directors to serve as the governing body and set up committees which pass on applications for credit, oversee the books, and ensure compliance with the charter and bylaws. This self-regulation has worked amazingly well—credit unions have a very low rate of loss due to officer negligence or embezzlement.

Credit unions can be set up under federal law (the Federal Credit Union Act) or under the laws of all but five states (Alaska, Delaware, South Dakota, Wisconsin, and Wyoming) and the District of Columbia. Of the $45.1 billion invested in them in 1977, $24.4 billion was held in federal and $20.7 billion in state credit unions. The laws are all similar, and a decision to seek a federal or state charter may depend on which agency offers more assistance or can act more rapidly at a given time. The chartering agencies (in most states, the Banking Department) require periodic reports and examinations, with varying degrees of stringency.

In order to form a credit union you must have a group of people who share one of three types of "common bonds" (the purpose of which is to make members feel a sense of responsibility toward one another). A minimum group consists of at least 100 to 300 members.

COMMON BONDS

1. *OCCUPATIONAL:*   **people who work together, as in a labor union, a manufacturing company, or a teacher's union. Eighty percent of all credit unions are based on this bond, the easiest one to establish. Companies often give physical space and employee time to set up and operate the credit unions. (They have an interest in their employees being financially stable.) They will frequently make automatic payroll deductions for savings or loan payments when asked by individual employees to do so. Federal credit unions need a minimum of 200 such members for chartering.**

2. *ASSOCIATIONAL:*   **people who have some similar quality or membership. Traditional examples are religious groups or ongoing co-ops, but more imaginative approaches have succeeded: the New York Feminist Federal Credit Union was chartered to serve women living in New York City, and a group of Bronx welfare recipients succeeded in setting up a credit union. Federal credit unions require 300 such members.**

3. *RESIDENTIAL:*   **people who live within a well-defined neighborhood or community. This is the least frequently used bond. Federal credit unions require 300 such families as members.**

Credit unions vary greatly in size: about one half of them have fewer than 400 members, and the largest, the Navy Federal Credit Union, has more than 400,000 members. Their size determines whether they can manage without full-time paid staff and sets their lending limitations. None of them are geared for large-scale lending: federal credit unions can make unsecured loans (i.e., no co-signer or collateral) of only $2,500 and secured loans of up to $10,000.

The National Credit Union Administration furnishes extensive information about setting up a federal credit union and will send an organizer out to meet with a group that is seriously interested. Contact the main office (2025 M Street, N.W., Washington, D.C. 20456) or your regional office.* The Credit Union National Association (CUNA), 1730 Rhode Island Avenue, N.W., Washington, D.C. 20036, is also a good source of information about state and federal credit unions.

* There are six regional offices: Region I in Boston serves Connecticut, Maine, Massachusetts, New Hampshire, New York, Puerto Rico, Rhode Island, Vermont, and the Virgin Islands; Region II in Harrisburg serves Delaware, the District of Columbia, Maryland, New Jersey, and Pennsylvania; Region III in Atlanta serves Alabama, the Canal Zone, Florida, Georgia, Kentucky, Mississippi, North Carolina, South Carolina, Tennessee, Virginia, and West Virginia; Region IV in Toledo serves Illinois, Indiana, Iowa, Michigan, Minnesota, North Dakota, Ohio, South Dakota, and Wisconsin; Region V in Austin serves Arkansas, Colorado, Kansas, Louisiana, Missouri, Nebraska, New Mexico, Oklahoma, Texas, Utah, and Wyoming; and Region VI in San Francisco serves Alaska, Arizona, California, Guam, Hawaii, Idaho, Montana, Nevada, Oregon, and Washington.

SELECTED BIBLIOGRAPHY

THE CO-OP HANDBOOK COLLECTIVE. *The Food Co-op Handbook*. Boston: Houghton Mifflin Company, 1975.

Materials available from the National Credit Union Administration, 2025 M Street, N.W., Washington, D.C. 20456, including:
Federal Credit Unions
Organizing a Federal Credit Union
The Federal Credit Union Act

Materials are available from the Cooperative League of the U.S.A., 1828 L Street, N.W., Washington, D.C. 20036. There is a wide range of papers, pamphlets, and books, so write for a publication list. For starting a food co-op or buying club, *Moving Ahead with Group Action* provides an easy-to-understand skeletal introduction.

VELLELA, TONY. *Food Co-ops for Small Groups*. New York: Workman Publishing Company, 1975.

Appendix

Directory of federal consumer offices

ADVERTISING
  Director, Bureau of Consumer Protection, Federal Trade Commission, Washington, D.C. 20580; phone 202-523-3727.

AIR TRAVEL / ROUTES AND SERVICE
  Director, Office of Consumer Protection, Civil Aeronautics Board, Washington, D.C. 20423; phone 202-673-5937.

AIR TRAVEL / SAFETY
  For general information contact the Community and Consumer Liaison Division, Federal Aviation Administration, APA-430, Washington, D.C. 20591; phone 202-426-8058. For specific safety problems contact the above office, marking correspondence: APA-100; phone 202-426-1960.

ALCOHOL
  Chief, Trade and Consumer Affairs Division, Bureau of Alcohol, Tobacco, and Firearms, Department of the Treasury, Washington, D.C. 20226; phone 202-566-7581.

ALCOHOLISM, DRUG ABUSE, AND MENTAL ILLNESS
  Office of Public Affairs, Alcohol, Drug Abuse, and Mental Health Service, 5600 Fishers Lane, Rockville, Md. 20857; phone 301-443-3783

ANTITRUST
  Bureau of Competition, Federal Trade Commission, Washington, D.C. 20580; phone 202-523-3601.
  Consumer Affairs Section, Antitrust Division, Justice Department, Washington, D.C. 20530; phone 202-739-4173.

AUTO SAFETY AND HIGHWAYS
  Director, Office of Public and Consumer Affairs, Transportation Department, Washington, D.C. 20590; phone 202-426-4518.
  National Highway Traffic Safety Administration; toll-free hot line *800-422-9393*. In Washington, D.C., call 426-0123.
  Associate Administrator for Planning, Federal Highway Administration, Washington, D.C. 20590; phone 202-426-0585.

BANKS
  Federal Credit Unions
  National Credit Union Administration, Washington, D.C. 20456; phone 202-254-8760.

  Federally Insured Savings and Loans
  Consumer Division, Office of Community Investment, Federal Home Loan Bank Board, Washington, D.C. 20552; phone 202-377-6237.

Federal Reserve Banks
Office of Saver and Consumer Affairs, Federal Reserve System, Washington, D.C. 20551; phone 202-452-3000.

National Banks
Consumer Affairs, Office of the Comptroller of the Currency, Washington, D.C. 20219; phone 202-447-1600.

State-Chartered Banks
Office of Bank Customer Affairs, Federal Deposit Insurance Corporation, Washington, D.C. 20429; phone 202-389-4427.

BOATING
Chief, Information and Administrative Staff, U. S. Coast Guard, Washington, D.C. 20590; phone 202-426-1080.

BUS TRAVEL
Consumer Affairs Office, Interstate Commerce Commission, Washington, D.C. 20423; phone 202-275-7252.

BUSINESS
Office of the Ombudsman, Department of Commerce, Washington, D.C. 20230; phone 202-377-3176.
Director, Women-in-Business and Consumer Affairs, Small Business Administration, 1441 L Street, N.W., Washington, D.C. 20416; phone 202-653-6074.

CHILD ABUSE
National Center on Child Abuse and Neglect, P.O. Box 1182, Washington, D.C. 20013; phone 202-755-0593.

CHILDHOOD IMMUNIZATION
Office of the Assistant Secretary for Health, Office of Public Affairs, Washington, D.C. 20201; phone 202-472-5663.

CHILDREN AND YOUTH
Director of Public Affairs, Office of Human Development Services, Department of Health, Education, and Welfare, Washington, D.C. 20201; phone 202-472-7257.

COMMODITY TRADING
Consumer Hotline, Commodity Futures Trading Commission, 2033 K Street, N.W., Washington, D.C. 20581; toll-free hot line in California and states east of the Mississippi, *800-424-9838;* states west of the Mississippi except California, *800-227-4428.* In Washington, D.C., call 254-8630.

CONSUMER INFORMATION
For a copy of the free *Consumer Information Catalog,* a listing of more than 200 selected federal consumer publications on such topics as child care, automobiles, health, employment, housing, energy, etc., send a postcard to the Consumer Information Center, Pueblo, Colo. 81009.

COPYRIGHTS
Copyright Office, Crystal Mall, 1921 Jefferson Davis Highway, Arlington, Va. 20559; phone 703-557-8700.

CREDIT
Director, Bureau of Consumer Protection, Federal Trade Commission, Washington, D.C. 20580; phone 202-523-3727.

CRIME INSURANCE

Federal Crime Insurance, Department of Housing and Urban Development, P.O. Box 41033, Washington, D.C. 20014; toll-free hot line *800-638-8780*. In Washington, D.C., call 652-2637.

CUSTOMS

Public Information Division, U. S. Customs, Washington, D.C. 20229; phone 202-566-8195.

DISCRIMINATION

U. S. Commission on Civil Rights, 1121 Vermont Avenue, Washington, D.C. 20425; phone 202-254-6697.

Equal Employment Opportunity Commission, 2401 E Street, N.W., Washington, D.C. 20506; phone 202-634-6930.

For complaints about discrimination in lending practices by financial and retail institutions based on race, color, religion, national origin, sex, marital status, age, or receipt of public assistance, contact the Housing and Credit Section, Civil Rights Division, Justice Department, Washington, D.C. 20530; phone 202-739-4123. (See also HOUSING.)

DRUGS AND COSMETICS

Consumer Inquiry Section, Food and Drug Administration, 5600 Fishers Lane, Rockville, Md. 20852; phone 301-443-3170.

EDUCATION GRANTS AND LOANS

Office of Public Affairs, Office of Education, Washington, D.C. 20202; phone 202-245-7949. Toll-free hot line for Basic Education Opportunity Grants, *800-638-6700*. In Maryland, call 800-492-6602.

ELDERLY

Administration on Aging, Washington, D.C. 20201; phone 202-245-2158.

EMPLOYMENT AND JOB TRAINING

Since nearly all employment and training programs are handled at the state or local levels, check your phone directory under your state government for the Employment Service or under your local government for the mayor's office. If you cannot reach these sources, you can obtain general information by writing to the Employment and Training Administration, Department of Labor, Washington, D.C. 20213; phone 202-376-6905.

ENERGY

Director, Office of Consumer Affairs, Department of Energy, Washington, D.C. 20585; phone 202-252-5141.

ENERGY EFFICIENCY

Information Office, National Bureau of Standards, Washington, D.C. 20234; phone 301-921-3181.

ENVIRONMENT

Office of Public Awareness, Environmental Protection Agency, Washington, D.C. 20460; phone 202-755-0700.

FEDERAL JOB INFORMATION

Check for the Federal Job Information Center under the U. S. Government in your phone directory. If there is no listing, call toll-free directory assistance at *800-555-1212,* and ask for the number of the Federal Job Information Center in your state. In the Washington, D.C., metropolitan area contact the Civil Service Commission, 1900 E Street, N.W., Washington, D.C. 20415; phone 202-737-9616.

FEDERAL REGULATIONS

For information on federal regulations and proposals, the Office of the Federal Register (OFR) is offering, among other services, recorded "Dial-a-Reg" phone messages. Dial-a-Reg gives advance information on significant documents to be published in the Federal Register the following workday. The service is currently available in three cities: Washington, D.C., telephone 202-523-5022; Chicago telephone 312-663-0884; and Los Angeles telephone 213-688-6694.

FIREARMS

See ALCOHOL.

FISH GRADING

National Marine Fisheries Service, Department of Commerce, Washington, D.C. 20235; phone 202-634-7458.

FISH AND WILDLIFE

Fish and Wildlife Service, Office of Public Affairs, Washington, D.C. 20240; phone 202-343-5634.

FLOOD INSURANCE

National Flood Insurance, Department of Housing and Urban Development, Washington, D.C. 20410; toll-free hot line *800-424-8872*. In Washington, D.C., call 755-9096.

FOOD

Assistant Secretary for Food and Consumer Services, U. S. Department of Agriculture, Washington, D.C. 20250; phone 202-447-4623.

Consumer Inquiry Section, Food and Drug Administration, 5600 Fishers Lane, Rockville, Md. 20852; phone 301-443-3170.

FRAUD

Director, Bureau of Consumer Protection, Federal Trade Commission, Washington, D.C. 20580; phone 202-523-3727.

HANDICAPPED

Director, Division of Public Information, Office of Human Development Services, Department of Health, Education, and Welfare, Washington, D.C. 20201; phone 202-472-7257.

HOUSING

Division of Consumer Complaints, Department of Housing and Urban Development, Washington, D.C. 20410; phone 202-755-5353.

For complaints about housing discrimination call the housing discrimination hot line *800-424-8590*. In Washington, D.C., call 755-5490.

IMMIGRATION AND NATURALIZATION

Information Services, Immigration and Naturalization Service, 425 I St., N.W., Washington, D.C. 20536; phone 202-376-8449.

INDIAN ARTS AND CRAFTS

Indian Arts and Crafts Board, Washington, D.C., 20240; phone 202-343-2773.

JOB SAFETY

Office of Information, Occupational Safety and Health Administration, Department of Labor, Washington, D.C. 20210; phone 202-523-8151.

MAIL

Fraud

Check with your local postal inspector about problems relating to mail fraud and undelivered merchandise or contact the Chief Postal Inspector, U. S. Postal Inspection Service, Washington, D.C. 20260; phone 202-245-5445. (For a listing of regional postal inspectors see *Consumer News,* July 15, 1977.)

Service

Check with your local postmaster or contact the Consumer Advocate, U. S. Postal Service, Room 5920, Washington, D.C. 20260; phone 202-245-4514.

MAPS

Public Inquiries Office, Geological Survey, National Center, Reston, Va. 22092; phone 703-860-6167.

MEDICAID / MEDICARE

Health Care Financing Administration, Department of Health, Education, and Welfare, Washington, D.C. 20201; phone 202-245-0312.

MEDICAL RESEARCH

Division of Public Information, National Institutes of Health, 9000 Rockville Pike, Bethesda, Md. 20014; phone 301-496-5787.

Center for Disease Control, Attention: Public Inquiries, Atlanta, Ga. 30333; phone 404-653-3311, ext. 3534.

MENTAL ILLNESS

See ALCOHOLISM, DRUG ABUSE, AND MENTAL ILLNESS.

METRIC INFORMATION

See ENERGY EFFICIENCY, National Bureau of Standards.

MOVING

Interstate Commerce Commission, Washington, D.C. 20423; toll-free moving hot line *800-424-9312.* In Florida call *800-432-4537.* In Washington, D.C., call 275-7852.

PARKS AND RECREATIONAL AREAS

National Forests

Forest Service, U. S. Department of Agriculture, Washington, D.C. 20250; phone 202-447-3760.

National Parks and Historic Sites

National Park Service, Washington, D.C. 20240; phone 202-343-7394.

Recreation Areas on Army Corps of Engineers Project Sites

Recreation Resource Management Branch (CWO-R), Army Corps of Engineers, Washington, D.C. 20314; phone 202-693-7177.

Other Recreation Areas

Office of Public Affairs, Department of the Interior, Washington, D.C. 20240; phone 202-343-3171.

PASSPORTS

For passport information check with your local post office or contact the Passport Office, Department of State, 1425 K Street, N.W., Washington, D.C. 20524; phone 202-783-8200.

PATENTS AND TRADEMARKS

Patents
Commissioner, Patent Office, Department of Commerce, Washington, D.C. 20231;
phone 703-557-3080.

Trademarks
Commissioner, Trademark Office, Department of Commerce, Washington, D.C.
20231; phone 703-557-3268.

PENSIONS

Office of Communications, Pension Benefit Guaranty Corporation, 2020 K Street,
N.W., Washington, D.C. 20006; phone 202-254-4817.
Labor Management Standards Administration, Department of Labor, Wash-
ington, D.C. 20210; phone 202-523-8776.

PHYSICAL FITNESS / SPORTS

President's Council on Physical Fitness and Sports, 400 6th Street, S.W., Washington, D.C. 20201; phone 202-755-8131.

PRODUCT SAFETY

Consumer Product Safety Commission, Consumer Services Branch, Washington,
D.C. 20207; toll-free hot line *800-638-2666*. In Maryland call *800-492-2937*.

RADIO AND TELEVISION BROADCASTING/INTERFERENCE

Consumer Assistance Office, Federal Communications Commission, Washington,
D.C. 20554; phone 202-632-7000.

RUNAWAY CHILDREN

The National Runaway Hotline, toll-free *800-621-4000*. In Illinois call *800-972-6004*.

SMOKING

Office on Smoking and Health, 12420 Parklawn Drive, Room 158, Park Building,
Rockville, Md. 20852; phone 301-443-1575.

SOCIAL SECURITY

Check your local phone directory under U. S. Government. If there is no listing,
check at your local post office for the schedule of visits by Social Security representatives, or write Division of Public Inquiries, Social Security Administration,
6401 Security Boulevard, Baltimore, Md. 21235; phone 301-594-7705.

SOLAR HEATING

National Solar Heating and Cooling Information Center, P.O. Box 1607, Rockville, Md. 20850; toll-free hot line is *800-523-2929*. In Pennsylvania call
800-462-4983.

STOCKS AND BONDS

Consumer Liaison Office, Securities and Exchange Commission, Washington, D.C.
20549; phone 202-523-5516.

TAXES

The Internal Revenue Service (IRS) toll-free tax information number is listed in
your tax package and is generally listed in your local telephone directory. If you
cannot locate the number, call your Information operator for the number for
your area. If you wish to write, send the letter to your IRS District Director,
Problem Resolution Program (PRP). Offices have been established in each district to solve unique problems and complaints which have not been satisfied
through normal channels. Taxpayers may call the toll-free number and ask for
the PRP office.

TRAIN TRAVEL

Amtrak (National Railroad Passenger Corporation). For consumer problems first try to contact a local Amtrak consumer relations office listed in your phone directory. If there is not an office near you, contact Amtrak, Office of Consumer Relations, P.O. Box 2709, Washington, D.C. 20013; phone 202-383-2121.

TRAVEL INFORMATION

U. S. Travel Service, Department of Commerce, Washington, D.C. 20230; phone 202-377-4553.

VENEREAL DISEASE

VD toll-free hot line *800-523-1885*. In Pennsylvania call *800-462-4966*.

VETERANS' INFORMATION

The Veterans Administration has toll-free numbers in all fifty states. Check your local phone directory, or call *800-555-1212* for toll-free directory assistance. For problems that can't be handled through a local office, write Veterans Administration (271), 810 Vermont Avenue, N.W., Washington, D.C. 20420.

WAGES AND WORKING CONDITIONS

Employment Standards Administration, Department of Labor, Washington, D.C. 20210; phone 202-523-8743.

WARRANTIES

For a problem involving the failure of a seller to honor a warranty, contact the Division of Special Statutes, Federal Trade Commission, Washington, D.C. 20580; phone 202-724-1100. Or you may contact the FTC regional office nearest you. They are listed in your telephone directory under U. S. Government.

FOR MORE INFORMATION

If you have questions about any program or agency in the federal government, you may want to call the Federal Information Center (FIC) nearest you. FIC staffs are prepared to help consumers find needed information or locate the right agency—usually federal, but sometimes state or local—for help with problems. Each city listed below has an FIC or a tie line—a toll-free local number connecting to an FIC elsewhere. Local listings printed in *italics* are tie lines to the nearest FIC.

ALABAMA	
Birmingham	*205-322-8591*
Mobile	*205-438-1421*
ARIZONA	
Phoenix	602-261-3313
Tucson	*602-622-1511*
ARKANSAS	
Little Rock	*501-379-6177*
CALIFORNIA	
Los Angeles	213-688-3800
Sacramento	916-440-3344
San Diego	714-293-6030
San Francisco	415-556-6600
San Jose	*408-275-7422*
Santa Ana	*714-836-2386*

COLORADO
    Colorado Springs   303-471-9491
    Denver   303-837-3602
    Pueblo   *303-544-9523*

CONNECTICUT
    Hartford   *203-527-2617*
    New Haven   *203-624-4720*

DISTRICT OF COLUMBIA
    Washington   202-755-8660

FLORIDA
    Fort Lauderdale   *305-522-8531*
    Jacksonville   *904-354-4756*
    Miami   305-350-4155
    Orlando   *305-422-1800*
    St. Petersburg   813-893-3495
    Tampa   *813-229-7911*
    West Palm Beach   *305-833-7566*

GEORGIA
    Atlanta   404-221-6891

HAWAII
    Honolulu   808-546-8620

ILLINOIS
    Chicago   312-353-4242

INDIANA
    Gary / Hammond   *219-883-4110*
    Indianapolis   317-269-7373

IOWA
    Des Moines   *515-284-4448*

KANSAS
    Topeka   *913-295-2866*
    Wichita   *316-263-6931*

KENTUCKY
    Louisville   502-582-6261

LOUISIANA
    New Orleans   504-589-6696

MARYLAND
    Baltimore   301-962-4980

MASSACHUSETTS
    Boston   617-223-7121

MICHIGAN
    Detroit   313-226-7016
    Grand Rapids   *616-451-2628*

MINNESOTA
    Minneapolis   612-725-2073

MISSOURI
Kansas City	816-374-2466
St. Joseph	*816-233-8206*
St. Louis	314-425-4106

NEBRASKA
Omaha	402-221-3353

NEW JERSEY
Newark	201-645-3600
Paterson / Passaic	*201-523-0717*
Trenton	*609-396-4400*

NEW MEXICO
Albuquerque	505-766-3091
Santa Fe	*505-983-7743*

NEW YORK
Albany	*518-463-4421*
Buffalo	716-846-4010
New York	212-264-4464
Rochester	*716-546-5075*
Syracuse	*315-476-8545*

NORTH CAROLINA
Charlotte	*704-376-3600*

OHIO
Akron	*216-375-5638*
Cincinnati	513-684-2801
Cleveland	216-522-4040
Columbus	*614-221-1014*
Dayton	*513-223-7377*
Toledo	*419-241-3223*

OKLAHOMA
Oklahoma City	405-231-4868
Tulsa	*918-584-4193*

OREGON
Portland	503-221-2222

PENNSYLVANIA
Allentown / Bethlehem	*215-821-7785*
Philadelphia	215-597-7042
Pittsburgh	412-644-3456
Scranton	*717-346-7081*

RHODE ISLAND
Providence	401-331-5565

TENNESSEE
Chattanooga	*615-265-8231*
Memphis	901-521-3285
Nashville	*615-242-5056*

TEXAS
    Austin   *512-472-5494*
    Dallas   *214-749-2131*
    Fort Worth   817-334-3624
    Houston   713-226-5711
    San Antonio   *512-224-4471*

UTAH
    Ogden   *801-399-1347*
    Salt Lake City   801-524-5353

VIRGINIA
    Newport News   *804-244-0480*
    Norfolk   804-441-6723
    Richmond   *804-643-4928*
    Roanoke   *703-982-8591*

WASHINGTON
    Seattle   206-442-0570
    Tacoma   *206-383-5230*

WISCONSIN
    Milwaukee   *414-271-2273*

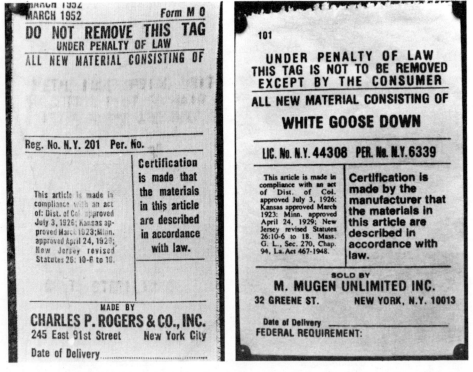

Consumers have long been terrorized by their mattress tags. Nothing at all will happen if you rip them off.